A HISTORICAL GUIDE TO

F. Scott Fitzgerald

HISTORICAL GUIDES TO AMERICAN AUTHORS

The Historical Guides to American Authors is an interdisciplinary, historically sensitive series that combines close attention to the United States' most widely read and studied authors with a strong sense of time, place, and history. Placing each writer in the context of the vibrant relationship between literature and society, volumes in this series contain historical essays written on subjects of contemporary social, political, and cultural relevance. Each volume also includes a capsule biography and illustrated chronology detailing important cultural events as they coincided with the author's life and works, while photographs and illustrations dating from the period capture the flavor of the author's time and social milieu. Equally accessible to students of literature and of life, the volumes offer a complete and rounded picture of each author in his or her America.

A Historical Guide to Henry David Thoreau
Edited by William E. Cain

A Historical Guide to Edgar Allan Poe
Edited by J. Gerald Kennedy

A Historical Guide to Nathaniel Hawthorne
Edited by Larry Reynolds

A Historical Guide to Mark Twain
Edited by Shelley Fisher Fishkin

A Historical Guide to Edith Wharton
Edited by Carol J. Singley

A Historical Guide to Langston Hughes
Edited by Steven C. Tracy

A Historical Guide to Emily Dickinson
Edited by Vivian R. Pollak

A Historical Guide to Ralph Ellison
Edited by Steven C. Tracy

A Historical Guide to F. Scott Fitzgerald
Edited by Kirk Curnutt

A Historical Guide to F. Scott Fitzgerald

EDITED BY
KIRK CURNUTT

OXFORD
UNIVERSITY PRESS

2004

OXFORD
UNIVERSITY PRESS

Oxford New York
Auckland Bangkok Buenos Aires Cape Town Chennai
Dar es Salaam Delhi Hong Kong Istanbul Karachi Kolkata
Kuala Lumpur Madrid Melbourne Mexico City Mumbai Nairobi
São Paulo Shanghai Taipei Tokyo Toronto

Published by Oxford University Press, Inc.
198 Madison Avenue, New York, New York 10016

www.oup.com

Library of Congress Cataloging-in-Publication Data
A historical guide to F. Scott Fitzgerald / edited by Kirk Curnutt.
p. cm.— (Historical guides to American authors)
Includes bibliographical references and index.
ISBN 0-19-515302-2; 0-19-515303-0 (pbk.)
1. Fitzgerald, F. Scott (Francis Scott), 1896–1940—Criticism and interpretation.
2. Fitzgerald, F. Scott (Francis Scott), 1896–1940—Knowledge—History.
3. Historical fiction, American—History and criticism. 4. Literaature and history—United States. 5. History in literature. I. Curnutt, Kirk, 1964– II. Series.
PS3511.I9 Z6623 2004
813′.52—dc22 2003022931

1 3 5 7 9 8 6 4 2
Printed in the United States of America
on acid-free paper

For
Ruth, Jack, and Alan,
founders of the Fitzgerald Society,
for the many fêtes

Contents

A HISTORICAL GUIDE TO

F. Scott Fitzgerald

Introduction

Kirk Curnutt

F. Scott Fitzgerald (1896–1940) belongs to that handful of American writers whose life stories threaten to overshadow their art. As is also the case with Mark Twain, Ernest Hemingway, and Jack Kerouac, popular culture remembers the author of *The Great Gatsby* as much for his exploits and tragedies as for the influential and enduring literature he produced during his brief career. When pressed to name one of Fitzgerald's literary accomplishments, few readers are capable of citing more than the title of his aforementioned 1925 classic or that of his second best-known work, *Tender Is the Night* (1934). Yet many who remain unfamiliar with his actual writing can recount at least a fragment of his personal history: *He was young and famous in the 1920s; he invented the flapper and coined the term "Jazz Age"; he served as spokesman for the "Lost Generation"; he drank a lot; he died young after falling out of fashion*. And, oh yes—*his wife went crazy*.

More informed aficionados argue that the sustained fascination with the Fitzgerald story arises from its irresistible blend of glamour and dissolution. As a personality, Fitzgerald possesses the kind of complexity necessary for an artist to excite audience interest long after the passing of his or her initial vogue. At once gifted, handsome, and charming, he epitomizes the youthful vim and vigor of the decade known as the Roaring Twenties. At the same time, the debilitating tendency toward self-destruction that made him, as he admitted, "a mediocre caretaker of most of the things left in my hands, including my own talent" (*Crack-Up* 71), places him in that pantheon of distinctly American icons—one thinks of Jackson Pollock, James Dean, and Elvis Presley, among others—who embody the "live fast, die young" credo. Fitzgerald's leading lady and chief foil, his wife, Zelda Sayre (1900–1948), is every bit as arresting a personality, a dynamic, often outrageous southern belle whose beauty and impulsiveness are the very qualities that her husband strove to incarnate in his art. The couple's love affair makes for a roller-coaster ride of a plot, its highs and lows wrought vivid through scenes of passion, jealousy, betrayal, and decline. Mix in a heartbreaking conclusion (he dies in obscurity from a heart attack, she in a sanitarium fire), exotic settings (Paris, the French Riviera, Hollywood), and a stellar supporting cast (Hemingway and Gertrude Stein, among others), and it is little wonder that the Scott and Zelda story has been told so many times in so many forms. Versions include everything from memoirs, biographies, and collections of correspondence to films, documentaries, and theatrical dramas. Even as recently as the summer of 2003, a musical called *Beautiful and Damned* premiered in London.[1] Simply stated, Fitzgerald's life was the stuff of high drama.

One question not asked often enough, however, is whether that fact has anything to do with why we value his writing.

Of course, to a large extent Fitzgerald was responsible for his own predicament. From the moment that he burst upon the literary scene in 1920 with his debut novel, *This Side of Paradise*, the precocious twenty-three-year-old encouraged audiences to acknowledge the umbilical connection between his life and art. As one critic complained in 1925, the vast majority of Fitzgerald's fiction belongs to the tradition of the roman à clef, the thinly veiled memoir:

> He cannot create beyond himself nor imagine experience[s] very different from his own. He is continuously autobiographic. His heroine is his wife, and his hero himself. He grad-

> uates from college; he writes a novel of college life [*Paradise*]. He marries; he writes a novel of young married life [*The Beautiful and Damned*, 1922]. He has a little girl, and she appears in *The Great Gatsby*. (Eagleton 438)[2]

Fitzgerald countered such judgments by insisting that the autobiographical elements in his work were not exclusively personal. Rather, his tales of idealistic young "jelly-beans" and the flirtatious flappers who symbolize their aspirations for a heightened appreciation of life reflected the experience of peers who like him came of age amid the welter of cultural change that marked the first two decades of the twentieth century. In this way, Fitzgerald was not writing about private concerns but about the historical transformations that shaped the character of his generation. Whether describing the emerging culture of consumption and leisure that promoted a heady attitude of frivolity and indulgence, the permissive social mores that encouraged more liberal and public expressions of sexuality, or the cynical disregard for authority that became fashionable in the aftermath of World War I, he cast himself as a social historian.[3] It just so happened that his own life was his prima facie evidence.

Despite Fitzgerald's claims that he was chronicling generational uncertainties, it remains inarguable that he capitalized upon his early success to fashion a personal mythology that the media eagerly promulgated. Not unlike Walt Whitman, he composed flattering puff pieces about himself that appeared in major metropolitan newspapers. Fitzgerald also coveted the free publicity provided by the era's gossip columns. Clippings gathered in the scrapbooks he meticulously maintained (portions of which were published as *The Romantic Egoists* in 1974) testify to his notoriety: "Fitzgerald Knocks Officer This Side of Paradise" reads one headline after he was embroiled in a police fracas (*Crack-Up* 28; LeVot 85). More important, when Fitzgerald's expenses outpaced his income (which was often), he could spin humorous episodes from his marriage into remunerative essays for popular magazines such as the *Saturday Evening Post*. As titles like "The Cruise of the Rolling Junk" and "How to Live on $36,000 a Year" imply, these pieces satirize the media image of him and Zelda as prodigal globe-trotters. So pervasive was the couple's celebrity that Fitzgerald made the hard work of living up to the public's perception of him a central theme of his nonfiction.

Even as he reveled in his fame, however, Fitzgerald understood that his popular reputation undermined the literary credibility he also craved. While critics commended his witty repartee and acute social observations, they also insisted he had best concentrate on his craft instead of his celebrity if he were to realize his artistic potential. Whatever charm *This Side of Paradise* and its follow-up, *The Beautiful and Damned*, might possess, reviewers found them both hastily constructed, rife with plot digressions and lapses in characterization. Reaction to the two short-story collections Fitzgerald published before 1925, *Flappers and Philosophers* (1920) and *Tales of the Jazz Age* (1922), was equally lukewarm. At their best ("Bernice Bobs Her Hair," "The Ice Palace," "The Diamond as Big as the Ritz"), the stories were hailed as deft comedies of manners whose ambiguous attitude toward their "baby vamp" heroines recalled the moral ambivalence of Henry James's *Daisy Miller*. At their worst ("Head and Shoulders," "The Jelly-Bean," "The Camel's Back"), they seemed formulaic, commercial confections that pandered to their author's post-adolescent fan base. Edmund Wilson's 1922 assessment of Fitzgerald, although stinging, is by no means atypical of how critics regarded him at the height of his popularity: "He has been given imagination without intellectual control of it; he has been given the desire for beauty without an aesthetic ideal; and he has been given a gift for expression without many ideas to express." The reason Fitzgerald suffered these flaws, Wilson opined, was his unapologetic longing for the limelight: "F. Scott Fitzgerald is a rather childlike fellow, very much wrapped up in his dream of himself and his projection of it on paper" (404, 407).

Had Fitzgerald not challenged himself to more substantive accomplishments, literary history might remember him alongside Anita Loos (*Gentlemen Prefer Blondes*), Elinor Glyn (*It*), Warner Fabian (*Flaming Youth*), and other minor writers whose racy flapper novels rode the cusp of the twentieth century's first youth-culture fad. Yet Fitzgerald knew he was capable of greater things.

In 1924, at the age of twenty-seven, he traded the media whirl of New York for the expatriate isolation of the French Riviera, where he set out to fulfill the immodest intention of writing "a novel better than any novel ever written in America" (*Life in Letters* 141). If *The Great Gatsby* did not accomplish this feat, it certainly came close. Initial readers might be forgiven for assuming Fitzgerald was again reworking familiar material, for the story of a young middle-class man striving to prove himself worthy of a beautiful socialite had already provided the plot for *This Side of Paradise* and several short stories ("Winter Dreams" in particular). Yet in composing *Gatsby* Fitzgerald at once broadened and deepened his trademark theme to make a more substantial statement about the inefficacy of idealism in the modern age. For starters, the novel's lovers/protagonists are no longer the young and glib revelers of such entertaining diversions as "The Offshore Pirate" (1920) or "Diamond Dick and the First Law of Woman" (1924). As a result, their desire to live a life less ordinary is complicated by a palpable sense of desperation and self-delusion. As Fitzgerald informed a friend, he was no longer interested in the vagaries of young love but in "the loss of those illusions that give such color to the world so that you don't care whether things are true or false as long as they partake of the magical glory" (*Life in Letters* 78).

Foremost among the illusions to which *Gatsby*'s titular hero clings is the American dream of self-making, the belief that one can slip the constraints of social class and family background simply by inventing an ideal identity. In narrating Jay Gatsby's failure to win Daisy Fay Buchanan from her old-money husband, Fitzgerald dramatizes the ephemeral nature of this dream. Despite his mysteriously obtained millions and the mystique they afford him, Gatsby will always be "Mr. Nobody from Nowhere," as the vacuous villain Tom Buchanan labels him (137). In the novel's closing paragraphs, Fitzgerald's narrator, Nick Carraway, specifically associates Gatsby's unwillingness to relinquish his pursuit of Daisy with the American spirit of inviolable optimism. As Nick suggests, such unquestioning faith in one's desires requires equal parts idealism and willful naïveté:

> As the moon rose higher the inessential houses began to melt away until gradually I became aware of the old island here that flowered once for Dutch sailors' eyes—a fresh, green breast of a new world. Its vanished trees, the trees that had made way for Gatsby's house had once pandered in whispers to the last and greatest of all human dreams; for a transitory enchanted moment man must have held his breath in the presence of this continent, compelled into an aesthetic contemplation he neither understood nor desired, face to face for the last time in history with something commensurate with his capacity for wonder.
>
> And as I sat there brooding on the old, unknown world, I thought of Gatsby's wonder when he picked out the green light at the end of Daisy's dock. He had come a long way to this blue lawn, and his dream must have seemed so close that he could hardly fail to grasp it. He did not know that it was already behind him, somewhere back in the vast obscurity beyond the city, where the dark fields of the republic rolled on under the night.
>
> Gatsby believed in the green light, the orgastic future that year by year recedes before us. It eluded us then, but that's no matter—tomorrow we will run faster, stretch out our arms farther. . . . And one fine morning—
>
> So we beat on, boats against the current, borne back ceaselessly into the past. (189)

As this passage (certainly Fitzgerald's most famous) suggests, another reason that *Gatsby* remains an American classic is the bejeweled opalescence of its style. In earlier fiction Fitzgerald had proved that his expressive strength lay in evoking a lachrymose mood of loss through intense bursts of elegiac rhetoric. In more commercially minded short stories such as "The Popular Girl" (1922), this tendency could seem overheated to sentimental extremes. With *Gatsby*, however, Fitzgerald tempered his excesses with the imagism and sensory disassociation typical of modernist poets such as T. S. Eliot and William Carlos Williams. *Gatsby* takes place in a world in which gardens are blue, and the cocktail music of summer parties sounds yellow. It is, moreover, a world in which observed abstractions are always supercharged with a hallucinatory luminosity to create an aura of magisterial unreality. One might cite any number of lines that capture the surreal dreaminess that results: a random breeze ripples Daisy's curtains like "pale flags, twisting them up toward the frosted wedding-cake of the ceiling" (12); the "white wings" of a sailboat gliding across the Long Island Sound beat against "the blue cool limit of the sky," framed by "the scalloped ocean and the abounding blessed isles" (94); faced with the truth of Daisy's inconstancy, Gatsby, wearing a "gorgeous pink rag of a suit that made a bright spot of color against the white steps," offers Nick a "radiant and understanding smile" that knowingly suggests the pair have worked in "ecstatic cahoots" to gain entry to a moneyed world indifferent to men of their caliber of imagination (162). Such examples abound. As Fitzgerald wrote, with justifiable pride, he now knew how to swaddle rather than suffocate his plots in "blankets of excellent prose" (*Life in Letters* 109).

With some exception, critics recognized that *The Great Gatsby* represented a breakthrough for Fitzgerald. The recurring word in reviews was "maturity." The *Saturday Review of Literature* hailed the novel for its "thoroughly matured craftsmanship" (Benét 353), while the *Dial* declared, "Fitzgerald has more than matured; he has mastered his talents and gone soaring in a beautiful flight, leaving behind him everything dubious and tricky in his earlier work" (Seldes 360). Fitzgerald was poised to enjoy what should have been the prolonged apogee of a career, à la William Faulkner a few years later when, between 1929 and 1936, *The Sound and the Fury* led to *As I Lay Dying* and *Light in August* to *Absalom, Absalom!*

Unfortunately, events proved otherwise. *Gatsby* was a commercial disappointment, selling far fewer copies than either *This Side of Paradise* or *The Beautiful and Damned*. Relinquishing his (perhaps unrealistic) expectation of attracting a literary audience as large as his popular readership—for Fitzgerald a succès d'estime was no success at all—he returned out of financial necessity to writing stories of young love toward which he harbored increasing contempt. Although he went on to author several top-notch short stories (his Basil and Josephine series, "Babylon Revisited," "The Swimmers"), nine years would pass before he could complete *Tender Is the Night*. If *The Great Gatsby* is, in the words of one recent essayist, "a book so tightly crafted that much of it seems as inevitable as unrhymed writing gets," *Tender Is the Night* remains a rare example of a work whose flaws make it all the more compelling (Pierpont 79). With a nonchronological plot structure and shifting points of view, the novel bears the scars of its prolonged incubation, which included multiple drafts begun and abandoned as its author struggled to stave off the twin distractions of his alcoholism and of Zelda's deteriorating mental condition (which began to require extended stays in various sanitariums).

Given the high expectations fostered by *Gatsby*, it is not surprising that reviewers proved oblivious to *Tender*'s ragged glory. The reaction of the *New York Times Book Review* was typical:

> Because *The Great Gasby* seemed a manifesto of growth and because its author is now approaching middle age, the appearance of his new book is an interesting event of the Spring season. But bad news is best blurted out at once: *Tender Is the Night* is a disappointment. . . . [It is] clever and brilliantly surfaced, but it is not the work of a wise and mature novelist." (Chamberlain 372)

Fitzgerald's commercial prospects fared no better. With three press runs and some 15,000 copies in print, *Tender Is the Night* was a middling success for a Depression-era fiction. Yet its modest sales confirmed what the literary establishment had long surmised: its author was no longer a bankable star.

The central pathos of the Fitzgerald story is that he was thus forced to live the last years of his life with the ignominy of being regarded as a has-been. On the rare occasions he made news, the news was not good. In 1936, shortly after his fortieth birthday, the *New York Post* published an interview with the formerly famous writer. Entitled "The Other Side of Paradise," the article depicted Jay Gatsby's creator as a self-pitying drunkard. (Although Fitzgerald had previously confessed his woes in a series of *Esquire* magazine articles known collectively as *The Crack-Up*, he claimed that the *Post*'s portrait had so slandered him that he was driven to attempt suicide.) Such was the anachronistic stigma Fitzgerald perceived attached to his name that just nine months before his death on December 21, 1940, he considered resuscitating his career by adopting a pseudonym. As he told one of the few remaining magazine editors still willing to publish his work, "I'm awfully tired of being F. Scott Fitzgerald. . . . I'd like to find out if people read me just because I am Scott Fitzgerald or what is more likely, don't read me for the same reason. In other words it would fascinate me to have one of my stories stand on its own merits completely and see if there is a response" (*Life in Letters* 433).

In the end, it may be too much to ask that popular culture honor this request and judge Fitzgerald's fiction solely on its aesthetic merits. The story of his meteoric rise and equally precipitous decline (not to mention his posthumous rediscovery) has by now become so imposingly familiar that general readers may be forgiven for perusing his work out of biographical curiosity. Fortunately, academia has demonstrated a persistent determination to spirit the Fitzgerald oeuvre out of its author's shadow. Since the mid-1940s, with the advent of what has become referred to as the "Fitzgerald revival," critics have sought to identify the central themes and literary techniques that make his writing worth studying.

Two broad tendencies divide this six-decade effort roughly in half. Up through the early 1970s, critics strove to validate Fitzgerald's artistry by demonstrating its universal import. If his fiction once struck detractors as too faddish to resonate beyond its Roaring Twenties backdrops, this first wave of analysis broadened its perceived relevance by arguing that it addressed certain "timeless truths" about the human condition. From this perspective, Fitzgerald was no longer a lightweight chronicler of social mores but a figure of gravitas whose work offered serious philosophical reflections on such abstract concerns as morality, tragedy, and desire.

Among the "timeless" topics critics explored, none proved as vital to confirming Fitzgerald's stature as the question of his attitude toward the American Dream. According to Marius Bewley, whose oft-republished essay "Scott Fitzgerald's Criticism of America" (1954) set the agenda for a scholarly generation, Fitzgerald could be judged a major writer because his fiction addresses "the problem that has always confronted American artists dealing with American experience—the problem of determining the hidden boundary in the American vision of life at which the reality ends and the illusion begins" (223). This and similar assertions, it should be remembered, were voiced amid the heightened nationalism of the early Cold War era when it was inevitable that the "Americanness" of writers would prove a key criterion of their literary value. Nevertheless, the fact that so many of Fitzgerald's protagonists must reconcile idealism with reality allowed such influential arbiters as Bewley and Lionel Trilling to place Fitzgerald at the literary forefront alongside other writers limning the "American vision of life."

In addition to his theme, critics also rehabilitated Fitzgerald's reputation by examining his style and technique. Not coincidentally, the Fitzgerald revival started as the practice of New Criticism was fast becoming the dominant mode of interpretation in American universities. By studying how a narrative's aesthetic design expedites the expression of its theme, New Critics (or "formalists," as they were also called) lavished scrupulous attention upon images, symbols, motifs, and other internal textual patterns. Because New Criticism valued such Aristotelian principles as unity and proportion, practitioners not surprisingly focused on *The Great Gatsby* at the expense of the more ramshackle *This Side of Paradise* and *Tender Is the Night*. Indeed, *Gatsby* provided such abundant opportunities for formalist analysis that between the 1950s and 1960s the Fitzgerald revival turned into a veritable industry, with every literary detail significant enough to merit explication. In essay after essay, New Critics dissected the book with forensic intensity, analyzing everything from its musical references to its color schemes to its ocular imagery. These efforts in turn provided interpretive models for secondary and postsecondary students reading *The Great Gatsby* in introductory literature courses. Even today, a good three decades after New Criticism lost its scholarly currency to more historically minded approaches, formalist analysis remains the preferred method by which students first learn to interpret Fitzgerald's fiction.

The second stage of Fitzgerald's posthumous reputation began in the late 1960s as the academy turned its attention back to the historical context of literary works. Led by Matthew J. Bruccoli, the *éminence grise* of Fitzgerald studies, scholars made public the correspondence, manuscript drafts, and personal notebooks necessary for documenting not only when and where but, more important, *how* Fitzgerald wrote. These primary materials facilitated the clarification of several misperceptions that had previously plagued the author. Whereas Fitzgerald was once presumed to be more concerned with his lifestyle than his literary style, composition histories of *Gatsby* and *Tender Is the Night* revealed a craftsman attuned to the problems of fictional presentation. And whereas his early flapper tales had once earned him censure for pandering to the popular marketplace, studies of his short fiction demonstrated instead that he was a writer with uncanny commercial savvy.[4] More broadly, historical criticism allowed for more informed analyses of how his characteristic themes reflect the temper of his times. No longer dismissed as debutante valentines, for instance, the jazzier of his Jazz Age tales could be read as evidence of the moral confusion that arose from the postwar sexual revolution. Similarly, works inspired by the Fitzgeralds' life abroad (*Tender*, "Babylon Revisited") no longer bespoke the couple's personal rootlessness but the felt exile of an entire literary generation for whom expatriation was synonymous with artistic freedom. Finally, Fitzgerald's recurring inquiry into the effect of easy money on individual morality reflects 1920s anxieties over American culture's sudden glorification of fiscal and emotional irresponsibility. Thanks to the many useful inquiries into these concerns published over the past thirty years, critics can now discuss Fitzgerald as a representative voice of the 1920s without fear of slighting his literary standing.

As this book's title suggests, *A Historical Guide to F. Scott Fitzgerald* belongs to this second wave of Fitzgerald scholarship. The essays that follow have been commissioned to call attention to the cultural and intellectual crosscurrents of the 1920s and 1930s that circulate below the surface of his prose. That the collection begins with a biographical overview may seem contradictory given the argument in this introduction that Fitzgerald's work is too often read as a mere adjunct of his life. Yet Jackson R. Bryer's compact account eschews sensationalism in favor of a measured assessment of Fitzgerald's career, showing how his dominant themes—aspiration and failure—were products of his inveterate class consciousness, while his fixation with character and moral resilience reflects his disappointment with his own weaknesses and insecurities. As Bryer insists, while personal experience was always the primary inspiration for Fitzgerald's fiction, his best work eludes the solipsism that writing about oneself can occasion through a combination of empathy and historical observation.

Following this overview, James L. W. West III assesses Fitzgerald's output according to the professional opportunities offered by the literary marketplace of the era. With the exception of Sinclair Lewis, Fitzgerald was the only major figure in the 1920s to make his living exclusively through fiction.[5] West thus examines how financial necessity forced Fitzgerald to maximize his profit potential by recycling his writing through various secondary outlets, including not only the commercial short-story market but film and stage adaptations and serialization in mass-circulation magazines (for his novels). Because subsidiary opportunities were in their infancy, their rewards constituted a mere pittance compared to the sums writers today routinely reap. Yet while Fitzgerald considered himself a failure, his career earnings suggest otherwise: over his two decades as a professional author, his income totaled just under $300,000, an estimable sum hardly indicative of the "deliberate loafing" for which he chastised himself (*Crack-Up* 70).

West's essay sets out to counter the notion that Fitzgerald lacked professional know-how when it came to career development. In a similar vein, Ronald Berman challenges the idea (again promoted by Edmund Wilson) that Fitzgerald's work lacks intellectual substance. Instead, as Berman demonstrates, Fitzgerald's fiction explores concerns over American morality and resolve more overtly discussed by such influential "public philosophers" as H. L. Mencken, William James, and Walter

Lippmann. Like Mencken, whose favor he curried, Fitzgerald drew from Nietzschean ideas of superior will to explain the failings of the American patrician class. And like James, he insisted that character was essential to forging individual morality. (Not for nothing, Berman insists, is Gatsby "great".) Finally, like Lippmann, Fitzgerald was troubled by the sense of drift and indirection then creeping into discussions of America's manifest destiny. That these issues are less overt in *The Great Gatsby* or the short stories than in essays by these public philosophers does not mean, as Wilson claimed, that Fitzgerald's style swamped his subject matter. As Berman concludes, it was, rather, because Fitzgerald was first and foremost an artist who understood that ideas are more satisfyingly articulated through aesthetic rather than argumentative means.

The next two essays switch the focus to the popular culture (as opposed to strictly literary) contexts of Fitzgerald's work. My own contribution to the volume, "Fitzgerald's Consumer World," discusses the ways his writing reflects the effects of the consumer revolution of the 1920s. The Jazz Age was a period of unprecedented prosperity during which the rising standard of living enjoyed by many Americans fueled an expanding marketplace of purchasable goods, from automobiles to fashion to cosmetics. Fitzgerald—born just two years before Thorstein Veblen coined the phrases "conspicuous consumption" and "pecuniary emulation" to characterize the new American obsession with leisure and lifestyle—both valorized and criticized this phenomenon. His work acknowledges how advertising promoted new, more flexible models of selfhood that excited concerns about authenticity and choice. It also reflects the shift in values that suddenly denigrated preservation and thrift in favor of obsolescence and squandering. Indeed, one of the more remarkable (and overlooked) aspects of his fiction is its cautionary take on the emerging ethic of wastage, which celebrated disposability as not only an earmark but a privilege of abundance.

Ruth Prigozy's essay, meanwhile, explores how the film industry of the 1920s appropriated the flapper, the character type that Fitzgerald's early fiction brought to cultural prominence. For Fitzgerald, the flapper was an icon not just of liberated femininity but of moral uncertainty. Although he celebrated the impudent antitraditionalism of modern young women, he also recognized that the freedoms they assumed were only transitory and that their vitality would fade with their youth. Yet Hollywood proved wholly obtuse to this predicament, depicting flappers instead as shallow whirligigs whose lasting legacy was not their dramatic quandary but the innovations in the medium they inspired. As Prigozy demonstrates, capturing the flamboyant ebullience of such memorable starlets as Clara Bow, Colleen Moore, and Joan Crawford required lavish backdrops and decor, energetic staging, and novel camera techniques. The result was an arresting visual spectacle that proved far more stimulating than the plots themselves. Nowhere is the discrepancy between literary and cinematic flappers more apparent, Prigozy insists, than in Fitzgerald's own unproduced screenplay, *Lipstick* (1927). Never proficient at screenwriting, Fitzgerald labored to insert his complex heroine into what he thought were the conventions of Hollywood farce, only to be shocked to discover that studio moguls found his slapstick too frivolous to film.

The final historical essay, James H. Meredith's "Fitzgerald and War," offers an exhaustive assessment of the impact of war on Fitzgerald's work. Unlike Hemingway, John Dos Passos, and E. E. Cummings, Fitzgerald did not witness the carnage of World War I, even though he was a commissioned officer in the U.S. Army. (The war ended before the date of his scheduled embarkation.) Nevertheless, throughout his writing, Fitzgerald did address the consequences of various armed conflicts, including not only the Great War but also the American Civil War and the fascist incursions of the 1930s that led to World War II. As Meredith argues, Fitzgerald was not interested in debunking military ideals or condemning governments. Instead, war provided a prism through which he could articulate his vision of the past, present, and future. The aftereffects of World War I forced him to temper his instinctual Romanticism with the reality of devastation, while the Civil War provided an opportunity to assess the individual's ability to comprehend the significance of war through the genre of historical fiction. Perhaps most interestingly, fascism inspired him to reach centuries back to the medieval age to allegorize the looming Dark Age of totalitarianism. That Fitzgerald's stories about the ninth-century nobleman Philippe are universally regarded as artistic debacles in no way impugns their significance. Indeed, Fitzgerald's attempt to impose an antiquated literary form on the upheavals of the 1930s was perfectly congruent with modernist peers who could only envision a global future by looking to the distant past.

Finally, Albert J. DeFazio III's bibliography provides readers with a valuable reference tool by canvassing several decades of criticism. His opening note further offers a concise overview of the various stages of the critical response to Fitzgerald. As DeFazio's numerous bibliographical entries confirm, Fitzgerald continues to inspire abundant scholarly interest. Despite popular culture's prurient interest in his private life, his literary legacy is clear: Fitzgerald stands among the twentieth century's greatest elegists, his writing a testament to the always intertwining emotions of longing and loss.[6] In the end, the most insightful summation of his contribution to American literature may come—appropriately enough—from Zelda Fitzgerald, who lovingly if somewhat verbosely memorialized her husband for a proposed magazine tribute shortly after his death:

> His tragedies were hearts at bay to the inexorable exigence of a day whose formulas no longer worked and whose ritual had dwindled. . . . His poignancy was the perishing of lovely things and people on the jagged edges of truncate[d] spiritual purpose. . . . Such Fitzgerald made into many tragic tales; sagas of people compelling life into some more commensurate and compassionate measure. His meter was bitter, and ironic and spectacular and inviting: so was life. (709-10)

NOTES

1. Among the many retellings of the Fitzgeralds' story are at least two cable TV docudramas: *Zelda* (1993, TNT), loosely based on Nancy Milford's 1970 biography, and *Last Call* (2002, Showtime), a sensitive adaptation of Frances Kroll Ring's *Against the Current* (1985), a memoir of her life as Fitzgerald's secretary in 1939–1940. Several

other cable networks also produced Fitzgerald documentaries in the 1990s, most notably Arts & Entertainment (for its "Biography" series, 1997), E! Entertainment Television (*Mysteries and Scandals*, 1999), and PBS (the Peabody Award–winning *Winter Dreams*, 2001). The musical *Beautiful and Damned* features music by London-based songwriters Roger Cook and Les Reed. For more on the project's development, see its official Web site, www.beautifuland damned.com.

2. In fact, Fitzgerald never graduated from Princeton. He dropped out in the winter of 1915–1916, ostensibly because of poor health, although poor grades were the real cause. The university allowed him to return the following fall, but his academic performance remained lackluster, and he never completed a degree.

3. Fass's *The Damned and the Beautiful* (its title an obvious homage to Fitzgerald's second novel) offers an informative overview of these social changes.

4. Two studies of Fitzgerald's short fiction are essential to appreciating the finesse with which he appeased the popular marketplace: Mangum and Petry.

5. As West reminds us, even Hemingway in his artistic heyday remained dependent on the financial largesse of his first two wives' families.

6. Fitzgerald's talents as an elegist proved appropriate even in the aftermath of September 11, 2001, when terrorists killed more than 2,000 people in New York and Washington, D.C. by crashing hijacked planes into the World Trade Center and the Pentagon. Several commentators quoted his *Crack-Up* era essay "My Lost City," a tribute to Manhattan, to convey the immense sense of grief felt throughout America.

WORKS CITED

Benét, William Rose. "*The Great Gatsby*: An Admirable Novel." In Bruccoli and Bryer 352–54.

Bewley, Marius. "Scott Fitzgerald's Criticism of America." *Sewanee Review* 62 (Spring 1954): 223–46.

Bruccoli, Matthew J. *Some Sort of Epic Grandeur: The Life of F. Scott Fitzgerald*. 1981. Rev. ed. New York: Carroll and Graf, 1991.

Bruccoli, Matthew J., and Jackson R. Bryer. Eds. *F. Scott Fitzgerald in*

His Own Time: A Miscellany. Kent, Ohio: Kent State University Press, 1971.

Bruccoli, Matthew J., Scottie Fitzgerald Smith, and Joan P. Kerr. Eds. *The Romantic Egoists: A Pictorial Autobiography from the Scrapbooks and Albums of Sean and Zelda Fitzgerald*. New York: Scribner's 1974, rpt. Columbia: University of South Carolina Press, 2003.

Chamberlain, John. Review of *Tender Is the Night*. In Bruccoli and Bryer 372–75.

Eagleton, Harvey. "Prophets of the New Age: F. Scott Fitzgerald and *The Great Gatsby*." In Bruccoli and Bryer 436–39.

Fass, Paula S. *The Damned and the Beautiful*. Princeton, N.J.: Princeton University Press, 1977.

Fitzgerald, F. Scott. *The Crack-Up*. Ed. Edmund Wilson. New York: New Directions, 1945.

———. *F. Scott Fitzgerald: A Life in Letters*. Ed. Matthew J. Bruccoli and Judith S. Baughman. New York: Scribner's, 1994.

———. *The Great Gatsby*. 1925. Ed. Matthew J. Bruccoli. New York: Cambridge University Press, 1991.

Fitzgerald, Zelda. "Tribute to F. Scott Fitzgerald." In Bruccoli 707–10.

LeVot, André. *F. Scott Fitzgerald: A Biography*. 1979. Trans. William Byron. Garden City, N.Y.: Doubleday, 1983.

Mangum, Bryant. *A Fortune Yet: Money in the Art of F. Scott Fitzgerald's Short Stories*. New York: Garland, 1991.

Petry, Alice Hall. *Fitzgerald's Craft of Short Fiction: The Collected Stories 1920–1935*. Tuscaloosa: University of Alabama Press, 1989.

Pierpont, Claudia Roth. "For Love and Money." *New Yorker* 75 (July 3, 2000): 77–83.

Seldes, Gilbert. "*The Great Gatsby*: Spring Flight." In Bruccoli and Bryer 360–62.

Wilson, Edmund. "F. Scott Fitzgerald." In Bruccoli and Bryer 404–9.

F. Scott Fitzgerald 1896–1940

A Brief Biography

Jackson R. Bryer

There never was a good biography of a good novelist. There couldn't be. He is too many people if he's any good.
—F. Scott Fitzgerald

Perhaps the silliest but nonetheless most persistent question asked of fiction writers is whether their work is autobiographical. It is a foolish query because, on the one hand, no novelist or short-story author writes directly about his life, but just as surely no author fails to incorporate his own experiences into his work. Knowledge of a writer's biography, then, can be very useful in analyzing his writing, although seeking one-to-one connections between real-life persons and events and fictional characters and situations is often less fruitful than finding the bases for themes and emphases in an author's life story. So it is that, in the case of F. Scott Fitzgerald, many of his fictional concerns and motifs can be illuminated by a knowledge of his biography.

The Early Years: 1896–1912

Fitzgerald was born on September 24, 1896, in St. Paul, Minnesota, the first surviving child of Mollie McQuillan Fitzgerald and Edward Fitzgerald, whose two young daughters had died earlier that year. Fitzgerald's mother was the daughter of an Irish immigrant who had been extremely successful in the wholesale grocery business, leaving an estate of more than a quarter of a million dollars at his death at age forty-three in 1877. The McQuillans were a respected family, but in the strict St. Paul social hierarchy later described by Fitzgerald their position was clearly defined:

> There were the two or three enormously rich, nationally known families—outside of them rather than below them the hierarchy began. At the top came those whose grandparents had brought something with them from the East, a vestige of money and culture; then came the families of the big self-made merchants, the "old settlers" of the sixties and seventies, American-English-Scotch, or German or Irish, looking down somewhat in the order named—upon the Irish less from religious difference—French Catholics were considered rather distinguished—than from their taint of political corruption in the East. After this came certain well-to-do "new people"—mysterious, out of a cloudy past, possibly unsound. (*Crack-Up* 233)

This description is telling, not only because of its location of the McQuillans—and, by extension, the Fitzgeralds—in this rigidly stratified social structure, but also because it demonstrates Fitzgerald's acute understanding of that structure. He acquired this understanding at a very early age, for he was born in a rather shabby apartment on the edge of St. Paul's most fashionable neighborhood—in "a house below the average / Of a street above the average," as he once described it (*Life in Letters* 33)—and his childhood playmates were the offspring of the city's most prominent families, who lived in the huge mansions along Summit Avenue.

While Fitzgerald's mother's family had money but little social standing, his father was descended from the Scotts and Keys of Maryland: Francis Scott Key, the composer of "The Star-Spangled Banner," for whom he was named, was Scott's second cousin three times removed. Although Edward Fitzgerald could trace his American lineage back to the seventeenth century, he was a shy, ineffectual man with impeccable southern manners but little energy and less financial acumen. His successive business failures took his family to Buffalo, New York, in 1898, to nearby Syracuse in 1901, back to Buffalo in 1903, and finally in 1908 back to St. Paul, where thereafter they were essentially supported by the McQuillans. Fitzgerald never forgot the day in March 1908 when his father lost his job at Proctor & Gamble: "That morning he had gone out a comparatively young man, a man full of strength, full of confidence. He came home that evening, an old man, a completely broken man. . . . He was a failure the rest of his days" (*In His Own Time* 296). Nonetheless, "I loved my father," Fitzgerald admitted in 1931 on the occasion of Edward Fitzgerald's death. "Always deep in my subconscious I have referred judgements [*sic*] back to him, what he would have thought or done" (*Apprentice Fiction* 178). Despite this valedictory, in Fitzgerald's fiction, the protagonists' fathers are often deceased or absent.

In contrast to Edward Fitzgerald, Scott's mother was a determined, forceful figure who saw to it that her son was raised in the Catholic faith of both his parents and that he went to the best private and parochial schools that her family's money could provide. If his father's love of poetry and history gave impetus to Fitzgerald's literary interests, his mother's encouragement and belief in his uniqueness and the McQuillans' financial assistance inspired his social aspirations. In a 1933 letter to fellow novelist John O'Hara, whose background was also Catholic, Fitzgerald succinctly analyzed the complicated family background that so influenced his fiction:

> I am half black Irish and half old American stock with the usual exaggerated ancestral pretensions. The black Irish half of the family had the money and looked down upon the Maryland side of the family who had, and really had, that cer-

tain series of reticences and obligations that go under the poor old shattered word "breeding." (*Life in Letters* 233)

As this suggests, throughout his life, Fitzgerald would aspire to a social position that he fervently sought but was painfully aware he could never reach. His friend, critic Malcolm Cowley, perfectly caught this ambivalence, which would permeate Fitzgerald's fiction and give it tension and complexity: "It was as if all his novels described a big dance to which he had taken . . . the prettiest girl . . . and as if at the same time he stood outside the ballroom, a little Midwestern boy with his nose to the glass, wondering how much the tickets cost and who paid for the music" (149).

When the Fitzgeralds came back to St. Paul in 1908, Scott and his sister, Annabel (born 1901), lived for a time with grandmother McQuillan. After the family was reunited, they moved frequently, always to a modest rented house or apartment in the Summit Avenue neighborhood. Scott was enrolled at St. Paul Academy, a private school where his classmates included the children of the city's leading families. Although he distinguished himself playing football and baseball and by publishing his first story, "The Mystery of the Raymond Mortgage," in the academy's literary magazine, *Now and Then*, he also strove so hard for recognition that he was labeled the boy who knew exactly "How to Run the School" (Cross 6). During his three years at St. Paul Academy, he published four stories in *Now and Then* and also began writing plays, the first of which, "The Girl from Lazy J," was performed in August 1911 in the backyard of a neighbor—with the playwright acting the lead role.

Because Scott's academic performance at St. Paul Academy did not match his extracurricular prowess, he was sent east to boarding school at the Newman School in Hackensack, New Jersey, in the fall of 1911. Newman was a parochial school that drew its student body from wealthy Catholic families across the country. There Fitzgerald replicated his experience at St. Paul Academy by publishing poetry and fiction in the *Newman News* and by displaying occasional stardom on the football field. He also earned poor grades and quickly became the most unpopular boy in the school because of his bossiness and ego. During his second year at Newman, he met Father Cyril Sigourney Webster Fay, a prominent and worldly Catholic priest who became a mentor and father figure. Fay further encouraged Scott's belief that he was destined for greatness and introduced him to luminaries such as American man of letters Henry Adams and Anglo-Irish writer Shane Leslie.

While he was at Newman, Scott's frequent trips to the theater in New York fueled his ambition to write musical comedies. Each summer, he returned to St. Paul and wrote another play in which he and his friends performed. When he learned that one of the most socially prestigious student organizations at Princeton University, the Triangle Club, wrote and produced an annual musical, "that," he later wrote, "was enough for me. From then on the university question was settled" (*Afternoon of an Author* 84). His grandmother McQuillan's death during the summer of 1913 settled the tuition problem. Although he did poorly on the entrance exams, he was admitted to Princeton on the basis of a personal interview.

Princeton and the Army: 1913–1919

The Princeton University Fitzgerald entered in September 1913 fed perfectly his need for social distinction; in his first novel, *This Side of Paradise* (1920), he described it as "the pleasantest country club in America" (41). While his dream of glory on the football field was quickly dashed when he was unceremoniously cut from the freshman team within a week, he found compensatory recognition elsewhere. Almost immediately, he began to contribute to the *Princeton Tiger*, the campus humor magazine, and to work on the libretto for the Triangle Club show, *Fie! Fie! Fi-Fi!*—both impressive feats for a freshman. He also met and formed lifetime friendships with two members of the staff of the *Nassau Literary Magazine*, his classmate John Peale Bishop and Edmund Wilson, who was a year ahead of Fitzgerald and Bishop. Bishop, later a leading poet and novelist of his generation, and Wilson, destined to be America's preeminent literary critic and essayist, became, respectively, the person who educated Fitzgerald about poetry and his "intellectual conscience" (*Crack-Up* 79). While at Princeton, Fitzgerald published a play, seven stories, ten poems, two humor pieces, and five book reviews in the *Nassau Literary Magazine*, many humorous verses, parodies, and anecdotes in the *Princeton Tiger*, and the book and lyrics for three Triangle Club shows. In 1915, he was elected secretary of the Triangle Club, a certain indication that he would eventually become its president; that same year, he was elected to the editorial board of the *Tiger* and invited to join the University Cottage Club, which he regarded as the most socially prestigious of the school's eighteen eating clubs.

Early in 1915, while he was home for Christmas vacation, he met and fell in love with Ginevra King, the attractive sixteen-year-old daughter of a wealthy and prominent family in Lake Forest, Illinois. She was his romantic ideal—beautiful, rich, and popular, a combination that he would give to many of his fictional heroines—and he pursued her avidly. He wrote her daily letters (none of which survive; she apparently failed to save them), invited her to the Princeton prom, and visited her in Lake Forest. According to biographer Arthur Mizener, Scott kept the letters Ginevra wrote him to the end of his life; he had them typed and bound, and they ran to 227 pages (48).

As his junior year at Princeton began, Fitzgerald's success started to crumble. Two years of poor grades caught up with him, and he was declared "ineligible for extra-curricular activities" (Cross 9). His dreams of social prominence at Princeton were effectively dashed, and his recollection twenty years later testifies to what Matthew J. Bruccoli calls "the intensity of his commitment to the prizes of life" (57): "To me college would never be the same. There were to be no badges of pride, no medals, after all. It seemed . . . that I had lost every single thing I wanted" (*Crack-Up* 76). When his grades slipped further and he became ill in November 1915, he dropped out of Princeton for the remainder of the school year, returning in September 1916 to repeat his junior term. His relationship with Ginevra King, which had cooled gradually during 1915 and 1916, ended in January 1917. In his *Ledger*, a year-by-year account of his life from birth to age thirty-eight, he wrote, "poor boys shouldn't think of marrying rich girls" (170), a phrase which would come to describe many of the failed romances in his fiction.

By the spring of 1917, Princeton was preoccupied with America's imminent entry into World War I, which occurred on April 6; in the summer, Fitzgerald applied for an appointment as a second lieutenant in the army and received his commission on October 26 in Princeton, where he had returned for his senior year. He was assigned to Fort Leavenworth, Kansas, and, after ordering his uniforms at Brooks Brothers' fashionable haberdashery in New York, he left the university in November, informing his mother that he had enlisted "perfectly cold bloodedly" and "purely for *social reasons*" (*Life in Letters* 14). With his departure from Princeton, to which he never returned to finish his studies, he felt, as Mizener has asserted, "the end of youth, the end of experiments with life and fresh starts undertaken with easy confidence that there was plenty of time, the end of the period when one is irretrievably committed to nothing" (68).

During his time at Fort Leavenworth, where his training platoon was commanded by a young captain named Dwight D. Eisenhower, Fitzgerald, sure that he would be killed when he went overseas, began writing a novel. "Every evening," he would recall, "concealing my pad behind Small Problems for Infantry, I wrote paragraph after paragraph on a somewhat edited history of me and my imagination" (*Afternoon of an Author* 84). He finished the 120,000-word manuscript in three months, called it "The Romantic Egotist," and, with the assistance of Shane Leslie, sent it to Leslie's publisher, Charles Scribner's Sons, in May 1918. By then, Fitzgerald had been transferred, first to Camp Zachary Taylor near Louisville, Kentucky, then, briefly, to Camp Gordon in Georgia, and, finally, to Camp Sheridan on the outskirts of Montgomery, Alabama. It was in Montgomery in July, probably at a country club dance, that the handsome first lieutenant (he had been promoted a month earlier) met Zelda Sayre, the eighteen-year-old daughter of Judge Anthony D. Sayre of the Alabama Supreme Court. As Bruccoli has observed, "Even more dramatically than Ginevra [King], Zelda possessed the qualities that Fitzgerald required in a girl. She was beautiful, independent, socially secure (although not wealthy), and responsive to his ambitions. . . . She and Fitzgerald wanted the same things—metropolitan glamour, success, fame" (87).

Within a month or two, Scott became Zelda's primary suitor, although she continued to see other men, a circumstance that, for Scott, simultaneously aroused his jealousy and increased her desirability. In August, Scribner's turned down "The Romantic Egotist," although the rejection letter, which began, "no ms. novel has come to us for a long time that seemed to display so much originality" (qtd. in Bruccoli et al. 34), urged Fitzgerald to revise and resubmit it. He did so, very rapidly, only to have it rejected again in October. This occurred just before his infantry division was shipped north for embarkation to the European front, although the war ended before the scheduled departure. Because he saw the war as yet another in a series of great romantic adventures that he had been denied, the refrain "I didn't get over" became one of the phrases of disillusioned regret that remained important in Fitzgerald's memories.

Fortunately, however, while he was awaiting his discharge from the service, Scott was reassigned to Camp Sheridan and was able to continue his courtship of Zelda. Although she accepted the engagement ring he sent her in April 1919, she came to see that marriage to a dashing army lieutenant was far more romantic than an alliance with an impoverished writer with no foreseeable income. She made it clear that he would have to show evidence of some clear prospects before she would consent to marry him. Accordingly, after his discharge in early 1919, he went to New York, took a job with an advertising agency, and spent his evenings trying to write salable fiction, verse, and humor. At one point, he later claimed, he accumulated "one hundred and twenty-two rejection slips pinned in a frieze about my room" (*Afternoon of an Author* 85). In June 1919, after several trips to Montgomery in which he tried unsuccessfully to persuade Zelda to marry him, she broke off their engagement. Scott went to St. Paul to rewrite his novel, to become successful and famous, and to win her back.

Early Success: 1920–1924

After working for two hot summer months in his old room on the third floor of his parents' house, he completely revised *The Romantic Egotist*, retitled it *This Side of Paradise*, and resubmitted it to Scribner's early in September. Within two weeks, he received a special delivery letter from editor Maxwell Perkins informing him, "The book is so different that it is hard to prophesy how it will sell but we are all for taking a chance and supporting it with vigor" (*Dear Scott/Dear Max* 21). The risk taken by Scribner's and Perkins, who became Fitzgerald's editor and friend, proved to be a profitable one; published on March 26, 1920, *This Side of Paradise* sold out its first printing of 3,000 copies in three days. By the end of 1921, it had sold nearly 50,000 copies and had gone through twelve printings (Bruccoli 133). Fitzgerald's earnings, which totaled $879 in 1919, rose to $18,850 in 1920 and $19,065 in 1921 (*Ledger* 51, 52, 53). Virtually overnight, he became a celebrity, an acclaimed literary talent, and financially successful enough to afford the lifestyle of which he and Zelda dreamed. On April 3, 1920, they were married in the rectory of New York's St. Patrick's Cathedral. In 1936, Fitzgerald would recall:

> The man with the jingle of money in his pocket who married the girl . . . would always cherish an abiding distrust, an animosity toward the leisure class—not the conviction of a revolutionist but the smouldering hatred of a peasant. In the years since then I have never been able to stop wondering where my friends' money came from, nor to stop thinking that at one time a sort of *droit de seigneur* might have been exercised to give one of them my girl. (*Crack-Up* 77)

This Side of Paradise, a quite autobiographical account of young Amory Blaine's initiation into life through a series of romances and experiences at prep school and college, both shocked and excited reviewers. Typically, the anonymous critic of *The Independent* observed that the book's picture of youth "is so obviously founded on solid facts that Victorian mamas are likely to be quite upset by it," and the *Springfield Union* complained, "In the search for the 'unusual,' Mr. Fitzgerald has . . . produced a story in which the leading persons are of a nature disgusting to the average taste." H. L. Mencken hailed it as "a truly amazing first novel—original in structure, extremely sophisticated in manner, and adorned with a brilliancy that is . . . rare in American writing," and Burton Rascoe proclaimed that it gave its author "a fair claim to membership in that small squad of contemporary American fictionists who are producing literature" (qtd. in Bryer 7, 9, 10, 11).

The newlyweds became New York's most celebrated couple, as much for their eccentric behavior (riding on top of taxicabs, diving into fountains, undressing at a performance of *George White's Scandals*, and fighting with policemen) as for their photogenic good looks. As Fitzgerald remembered in "My Lost City" (1932), he, "who knew less of New York than any reporter of six months standing and less of its society than any hall-room boy in a Ritz stag line, was pushed into the position not only of spokesman for the time but of the typical product of that same moment." "We felt," he said, "like small children in a great bright unexplored barn." At the same time, he also recalled "riding in a taxi one afternoon between very tall buildings under a mauve and rosy sky; I began to bawl because I had everything I wanted and knew I would never be so happy again" (*Crack-Up* 27, 28, 29). After living in several Manhattan hotels, they moved to a rented house in Westport, Connecticut, where Scott began to work intensively on a second novel.

In September 1920, Fitzgerald and his publisher began a practice they were to continue throughout his career, publishing a volume of his short stories shortly after the appearance of each of his novels. *Flappers and Philosophers*, capitalizing, as its title suggests, on the popularity of *This Side of Paradise*, sold extremely well. By November 1922, it had gone through six printings and sold more than 15,000 copies (Bruccoli 145). The reviews were mixed, however, with many finding it a disappointment after the novel, and it contains only two of Fitzgerald's best stories, "The Ice Palace" and "Bernice Bobs Her Hair."

Early in 1921, Scott finished his second novel. When the Fitzgeralds found that Zelda was pregnant, they decided to go to

Europe before her condition would prevent them from traveling. In England, they had tea with John Galsworthy and lunch with Lady Randolph Churchill and her son Winston, and they also visited Paris, Florence, Rome, and Venice. Scott's first impression of Europe was surprisingly negative given the amount of time he was to spend living there later in his life. He wrote to Edmund Wilson: "God damn the continent of Europe. It is of merely antiquarian interest. Rome is only a few years behind Tyre + Babylon. . . . France made me sick. It's silly to pose as the thing the world has to save. I think it's a shame that England and America didn't let Germany conquor [*sic*] Europe. It's the only thing that would have saved the fleet of tottering old wrecks" (*Life in Letters* 46–47).

Upon their return from Europe, the Fitzgeralds went to St. Paul to await the birth of their child; while they were there, Zelda met Scott's parents for the first time, and Scott completed the final revisions on his novel. Frances Scott Fitzgerald, nicknamed "Scottie," was born on October 26, 1921. At her birth, her mother, according to Scott, exclaimed, "I hope it[']s beautiful and a fool—a beautiful little fool" (*Ledger* 176), words he later gave to Daisy Buchanan in *The Great Gatsby* (1925).

In March 1922, the Fitzgeralds were back in New York for the publication of *The Beautiful and Damned*, and, according to Bruccoli, "for Zelda to have an abortion because she did not want a second child so soon" (159). Reviews of *The Beautiful and Damned*, which tells the story of the deteriorating marriage of Anthony and Gloria Patch, a young couple whose drinking and extravagant spending habits more than slightly resemble Scott and Zelda's, were decidedly mixed. Several critics were surprised by the novel's pessimism; the *Columbus Dispatch* observed that "the superior cynicism and the fine irony of Mr. Fitzgerald are poorly adapted to the serious things he is recording" (qtd. in Bryer 32). Sales were quite good—there were three printings totaling 50,000 copies by the end of 1922 (Bruccoli 162)—but not sufficient to support the Fitzgeralds' spending habits. From early in his career until the end of his life, Fitzgerald found himself constantly needing to borrow against his future earnings from his publisher and from his agent, Harold Ober.

The Fitzgeralds spent the summer of 1922 at the White Bear Yacht Club just outside St. Paul, where Scott worked on a play, *The Vegetable*, and conceived a third novel. ("I want to write something *new*—something extraordinary and beautiful and simple + intricately patterned," he wrote Perkins in July [*Life in Letters* iv].) He also selected stories for a second collection. The eleven he chose appeared as *Tales of the Jazz Age* in September and included two of his best, "May Day" and "The Diamond as Big as the Ritz." In that same month, the Fitzgeralds came back east and rented a house in Great Neck, Long Island, where they became part of a social circle that included entertainers Ed Wynn and Eddie Cantor, socialite Herbert Bayard Swope, playwright Sidney Howard, and writers Ring Lardner and John Dos Passos, among others. Lardner became an especially close friend and frequent drinking companion, and Fitzgerald persuaded Scribner's to begin publishing collections of Lardner's stories. When he could not find a producer willing to put on his play, Fitzgerald decided to have Scribner's bring it out in book form—which the publisher did in April 1923. A satire on the notion that any American, no matter how humble his origins, can become president, *The Vegetable; or, From President to Postman*, while it received some positive reviews, was largely dismissed. Finally produced onstage by Sam H. Harris, it opened on November 19, 1923, at the Apollo Theatre in Atlantic City, New Jersey, for a disastrous one-week run. "After the second act," Fitzgerald recalled in a 1924 essay, "I wanted to stop the show and say it was all a mistake but the actors struggled heroically on" (*Afternoon of an Author* 93–94). It was his last attempt to write a play.

Although the Fitzgeralds drank and socialized steadily in Great Neck—"it became a habit with many world-weary New Yorkers to pass their week-ends at the Fitzgerald house in the country," Scott later noted (*Afternoon of an Author* 93)—he still managed to make considerable progress on his novel, as well as write ten short stories between the end of 1923 and March 1924. The latter were necessary to pay off his debts to Scribner's and Ober and to finance an uninterrupted summer of work on the novel. Although Fitzgerald earned $25,135 in 1922 and $28,759 in 1923 (*Ledger* 54, 55), it was never enough. In April 1924, to get away from the distractions of Long Island and to take advantage of a favorable exchange rate of nineteen francs to the dollar, the Fitzgeralds decided to relocate to France.

They settled on the Riviera, where Scott worked intensively on his novel, but in July, Zelda met and became infatuated with a young French aviator, Edouard Jozan. While Jozan apparently later maintained that it was nothing more than a flirtation (Mayfield 97), both Scott and Zelda came to embellish their accounts of it in fiction—he in several short stories and in his novel *Tender Is the Night* (1934) and she in hers, *Save Me the Waltz* (1932). The Fitzgeralds also told the story to their friends, and it clearly affected Scott deeply. He wrote, "I knew something had happened that could never be repaired" (*Notebooks* 113). For Fitzgerald, the Zelda-Jozan relationship represented yet another loss of a romantic dream, and the emotions he felt as a result of it lay behind the central love triangles in *The Great Gatsby*, the novel he was completing during the summer of 1924. (The feelings are present as well in *Tender Is the Night*.) He admitted in an August 1924 letter that "the whole burden" of *Gatsby* was "the loss of those illusions that give such color to the world so that you don't care whether things are true or false as long as they partake of the magical glory" (*Life in Letters* 78).

The Great Gatsby, Expatriation, and Dissolution: 1925–1930

On the Riviera that summer, the Fitzgeralds became part of a group of writers, artists, actors, and musicians affiliated with an attractive, independently wealthy American couple, Gerald and Sara Murphy. The circle included Pablo Picasso, Cole Porter, Philip Barry, Rudolph Valentino, Dorothy Parker, Robert Benchley, Fernand Léger, Donald Ogden Stewart, Archibald MacLeish, John Dos Passos, and others. The Murphys, whom the Fitzgeralds may have originally met in May 1923 in Paris, had adopted as their motto an old Spanish proverb, "Living well is the best revenge," a sentiment with which Scott and Zelda obviously agreed. During that summer, Fitzgerald read Ernest Hemingway's book of short fiction *in our time*, recently published by a small press in Paris, and in October recommended the young writer, whom he had yet to meet, to Maxwell Perkins and Scribner's.

After Fitzgerald sent a final draft of *Gatsby* to Scribner's, he and Zelda decided to spend the winter in Rome and Capri, where the exchange rate was even more favorable than in France. While the Fitzgeralds drank and quarreled a good deal, Scott was able to make substantial and important revisions in the galley proofs of the novel, some at Perkins's urging, which greatly improved it. By April 1925, when *Gatsby* was published, the Fitzgeralds were back in Paris. Although the reviews were primarily positive, in light of its later status as one of the twentieth century's most highly regarded works of fiction, *The Great Gatsby* received some quite negative notices. "An inferior novel, considered from any angle whatsoever," commented *America*; it "probably will not be counted among those novels which will make up a small list of the distinguished fiction of the season," asserted the *Boston Transcript*. "It is only as permanent as a newspaper story, and as on the surface," observed the *Milwaukee Journal* (qtd. in Bryer 61, 60). A first printing of 20,870 copies apparently sold out within four months, but Bruccoli reports that copies of the second printing of 3,000 were still in the Scribner's warehouse in 1940 (217).

Shortly after *Gatsby* was published, Scott met Hemingway in Paris, probably at the Dingo bar, a meeting described in detail in Hemingway's posthumously published and not always reliable memoir, *A Moveable Feast* (1964). There he describes Fitzgerald as "a man . . . who looked like a boy with a face between handsome and pretty" (149), and reports that, after asking Hemingway whether he had slept with his wife before they were married, Fitzgerald got drunk on champagne and had to be sent home in a taxi. Some time later, Hemingway tells us, he and Scott went to Lyon to pick up a car the Fitzgeralds had left there, a trip during which Scott was almost always drunk, ill, or hung over. Fitzgerald also supposedly told Hemingway about Zelda's affair with Jozan. Subsequently, back in Paris, Hemingway met Zelda, whom he describes as "jealous of Scott's work" (180) and a major impediment to her husband's writing career. He quotes

Scott as telling him that "Zelda said that the way I was built I could never make any woman happy" (190), an accusation that Hemingway, after a trip to the men's room with Fitzgerald, assured him was unfounded. Fitzgerald's friendship with Hemingway, which was to have many vicissitudes, was a complicated one, characterized by a mix of admiration for and envy of one another's talents. Hemingway introduced Fitzgerald to Gertrude Stein and to Sylvia Beach, the proprietor of Paris's Shakespeare & Company bookstore, a gathering place for the city's literary elite. In July 1925, Scott paid a visit to Edith Wharton at her villa outside Paris. For the most part, however, the Fitzgeralds tended to patronize the city's bars and nightclubs rather than its literary salons: "1000 parties and no work" was how Scott described the period in his *Ledger* (179).

After spending part of the summer of 1925 with the Murphys and their circle on the Riviera, the Fitzgeralds returned to Paris, where Scott began work on a new novel while Zelda, who had not danced since she was a teenager, began a ballet regime with former Russian ballerina Lubov Egorova. Fitzgerald also devoted a good deal of time trying to further Hemingway's career, eventually helping to arrange for Scribner's to become Hemingway's publisher and later helping him revise *The Sun Also Rises*, assistance that Hemingway was later to deny he had received. In February 1926, *All the Sad Young Men*, Fitzgerald's third short-story volume, was published. Generally considered the strongest of the collections issued during his lifetime, it included such major stories as "The Rich Boy," "Winter Dreams," "Absolution," "'The Sensible Thing,'" and "The Baby Party" and sold quite well.

The Fitzgeralds spent most of the remainder of 1926 at Juan-les-Pins, on the Riviera, and their increasingly erratic drunken behavior began seriously to alienate them from the Murphys and other friends. On one occasion when they met Isadora Duncan at a party where the famed dancer began to flirt with Scott, Zelda threw herself head first down a flight of stone stairs; on another, at the Murphys, Scott drunkenly punched Gerald and began smashing the Venetian stemware. As an essentially wasted year drew to a close, Fitzgerald plaintively wrote to Perkins, "I wish I were twenty-two again with only my dramatic and feverishly enjoyed miseries. You remember I used to say I wanted to die at thirty—well, I'm now twenty-nine and the prospect is still welcome" (*Life in Letters* 131).

With Fitzgerald unable to make any progress on his novel, the couple returned to America in December and spent Christmas in Montgomery with Zelda's family. In January 1927, Scott, who was, as usual, without funds, was offered $16,000 by United Artists to come to Hollywood and write a screenplay about a flapper for starlet Constance Talmadge. Zelda went with him, but the trip was a professional and personal disaster: Scott's script, *Lipstick*, was rejected, and he received only $3,500. His infatuation with seventeen-year-old actress Lois Moran led Zelda to burn her own clothes in a hotel bathtub and to throw from the train window on the trip back east a platinum watch Scott had given her in 1920.

Back in the East, the Fitzgeralds rented "Ellerslie," a nineteenth-century Greek Revival mansion outside of Wilmington, Delaware. There Zelda resumed her dance studies—now with the Philadelphia Ballet—and also began to publish humorous magazine essays. (These pieces usually appeared under the byline "by F. Scott and Zelda Fitzgerald" and occasionally as "by F. Scott Fitzgerald" because editors wanted to capitalize on Scott's reputation.) Because Scott was not making much progress on his novel, tensions between him and Zelda increased during this period, despite the fact that he earned almost $30,000 for the year, a new high for him.

When they returned to France for the summer, they settled in Paris so that Zelda could continue her obsessive ballet studies with Egorova. In late June 1928, Scott met James Joyce at a party given by Sylvia Beach; but he was feeling increasingly isolated and abandoned by his wife, and he was twice thrown in jail for public drunkenness. Back at Ellerslie for the fall and winter of 1928–1929, Zelda's ballet work continued. Gerald Murphy later commented, "There are limits to what a woman of Zelda's age can do and it was obvious that she had taken up the dance too late" (qtd. in Milford 141).

Fitzgerald's inability to make significant progress on his novel continued through that winter and into the spring of 1929, when he, Zelda, and Scottie returned to Paris where Zelda resumed her studies with Egorova and published some short fiction pieces. Although Hemingway was also in Paris, he resisted Fitzgerald's attempts to contact him because he and his second wife, Pauline, were unwilling to deal with the Fitzgeralds' drinking. Hemingway also ridiculed Scott's advice about revising his new novel, *A Farewell to Arms*: he wrote "kiss my ass" on the nine-page memo Fitzgerald wrote him after reading the typescript, although he adopted some of the suggestions (Bruccoli 271). It was about this time that Zelda, who had impugned Fitzgerald's masculinity in the past, began to accuse him of a homosexual relationship with Hemingway; she also became concerned that she might be a latent lesbian. The toll this conflict was taking on Fitzgerald can be gauged from a letter he wrote to Hemingway in September 1929:

> My latest tendency is to collapse about 11:00 and, with the tears flowing from my eyes or the gin rising to their level and leaking over, + tell interested friends or acquaintances that I havn't [*sic*] a friend in the world and likewise care for nobody, generally including Zelda, and often implying current company—after which the current company tend to become less current and I wake up in strange rooms in strange palaces. The rest of the time I stay alone working or trying to work or brooding or reading detective stories—and realizing that anyone in my state of mind who has in addition never been able to hold his tongue, is pretty poor company. But when drunk I make them all pay and pay and pay. (*Life in Letters* 169)

On the Riviera for the summer and fall of 1929, Scott completed two chapters of his novel, but his *Ledger* entry for September read, "Zelda dancing + sweating. Rows + indifference" (183). As America began to enter its Great Depression, Scott and Zelda's lives, which had already frequently paralleled the national fortunes and moods, went further into decline. Although Zelda danced professionally for the first and only time in Nice and Cannes during the summer of 1929 and inexplicably turned down an invitation to perform a solo in *Aida* with the San Carlo

Ballet Company in Naples in September, she also began to suffer hallucinations. On April 23, 1930, almost exactly ten years after her marriage, she was admitted to Malmaison Clinic outside Paris. Her admittance report indicated that she was "exhausted from work in an environment of professional dancers" and suffered from a "fear of becoming a homosexual" (Bruccoli 289). A month later, against her doctor's advice, she discharged herself and tried to resume her ballet studies, but she had more hallucinations, attempted suicide, and in late May entered Val-Mont Clinic in Glion, Switzerland. In early June she transferred to Dr. Oscar Forel's Les Rives de Prangins Clinic at Nyon, Switzerland, where she remained for the next fifteen months.

Tender Is the Night, Schizophrenia, and the Great Depression: 1931–1934

For most of that time, Scott shuttled back and forth between Paris, where Scottie had been left in school and in the care of a governess, and Switzerland, where his relationship with Zelda alternated between periods of bitter recrimination and optimism about a future together. Although he wrote numerous short stories during 1930 and 1931, paying for Zelda's treatment out of their sales and earning his pre-Hollywood peak of $37,599 in 1931 (*Ledger* 67), Scott did virtually no work on his novel. In June 1930, he met Thomas Wolfe, whose *Look Homeward, Angel* had been a big success for Scribner's and Perkins the previous year, and the two saw each other in Paris and in Switzerland. Fitzgerald's father died in January 1931, and when he went to the United States for the funeral, he also visited Zelda's family in Montgomery to fill them in on her illness. Upon his return, he wrote a valedictory essay about the 1920s, "Echoes of the Jazz Age," for *Scribner's Magazine*, in which he expressed nostalgia for and regret over the passing of "the most expensive orgy in history," a time when "it seemed only a question of a few years before the older people would step aside and let the world be run by those who saw things as they were." Now, he added, "it all seems rosy and romantic to us who were young then, because we will never feel quite so intensely about our surroundings any more" (*Crack-Up* 21, 22).

During the spring and summer of 1931, Zelda's condition improved, and she was permitted to spend extended periods of time away from the hospital with her family. In September, she was discharged from Prangins and the Fitzgeralds returned to America, settling in Montgomery so that Zelda could be in relatively quiet and familiar surroundings and near her father, whose health was failing. In November, Scott was offered $1,200 a week by Metro-Goldwyn-Mayer to work on the screenplay of a Jean Harlow movie being produced by the young Hollywood genius Irving Thalberg. Because, as always, he desperately needed the money, he accepted, spending almost two months in California while Zelda and Scottie remained in Montgomery; but his script was not used for the film. During his absence, Zelda's father died, and although she dealt with his passing quite well, she suffered a major relapse shortly after Scott's return. In February 1932, she was admitted to the Henry Phipps Psychiatric Clinic of Johns Hopkins University in Baltimore.

Despite the return of her illness, Zelda was able while at the Phipps Clinic to complete a novel she had started a few months earlier. When she sent it to Perkins before showing it to her husband, Scott, who was still, seven years after the publication of *The Great Gatsby*, struggling with his own novel, was furious. He accused his wife of using material from his work-in-progress, but eventually he was mollified when she agreed to revise her novel under his supervision. She sent the reworked version to Perkins in April 1932 with Scott's blessing: "Zelda's novel is now good, improved in every way. It is new. . . . You'll like it. . . . I am too close to it to judge it but it may be even better than I think" (*Life in Letters* 217).

By the time Zelda's *Save Me the Waltz*, an extremely autobiographical novel about the Fitzgeralds' courtship and marriage, was published in October 1932, Scott had rented a large Victorian house, "La Paix," on the Turnbull estate in the Baltimore suburb of Towson, Maryland. In late June 1932, Zelda had been discharged from the Phipps Clinic and, encouraged by Scott, began to paint, something she had done in a desultory way on and off for several years. She also resumed dancing, although at a much less frenetic pace than previously, and continued to write. During this period, the Fitzgeralds also saw a good deal of H. L. Mencken and his wife, Sara Haardt, who was a friend of Zelda's from Montgomery.

Comfortably settled at La Paix, Scott, after several abortive drafts, began to bring *Tender Is the Night* into its final shape as the story of a young and promising psychiatrist who makes the fatal mistake of falling in love with and marrying one of his patients, only to have her leave him for another man when she is cured. Tensions in the Fitzgerald household mounted as Scott worked on his novel and drank heavily while Zelda pursued her artistic interests (her play, *Scandalabra*, was produced by an amateur theater group in Baltimore in June 1933), and they briefly considered divorce. As 1933 drew to a close, Scott finished his novel but also spent short periods of time in the hospital recuperating from alcoholic binges, and Zelda's mental health continued to be uncertain. In his *Ledger*, he summarized 1933 as "*A strange year of Work + Drink. Increasingly unhappy. —Zelda up + down. 1st draft of novel complete Ominous!*" (187).

Fitzgerald's fourth novel, *Tender Is the Night*, was published in April 1934. In February, Zelda had reentered the Phipps Clinic and had been transferred in March to Craig House, an expensive, resortlike hospital on 350 acres in Beacon, New York. At about the same time as his novel appeared, Scott arranged a showing of Zelda's artwork at a small New York gallery, and she was well enough to attend the opening. Although *Tender Is the Night* sold reasonably well—about 15,000 copies in the first couple of months (Bruccoli 363)—its portraits of wealthy expatriates on the Riviera did not sit entirely well with readers and reviewers in Depression-era America. The most extreme example of this response was Philip Rahv's notice in the communist *Daily Worker*, which was headlined "You Can't Duck Hurricane Under a Beach Umbrella" (qtd. in Bryer 85). Some reviewers found the book a disappointment after the long wait since *Gatsby*, while others found the decline of its central character, Dr. Dick Diver, insufficiently explained. Yet most reactions were positive. Rowena Wilson of the *Savannah Morning News* spoke for many when she observed that Fitzgerald's "consummate artistry succeeds in transforming a fantastic, at times repellent, tale into a thing of delicacy" (qtd. in Bryer 87).

To the end of his life, Fitzgerald was apparently troubled by the mixed reception accorded *Tender Is the Night*. In 1938, he suggested to Perkins, "It's [sic] great fault is that the *true* beginning—the young psychiatrist in Switzerland—is tucked away in the middle of the book. If pages 151–212 were taken from their present place and put at the start the improvement in appeal would be enormous" (*Dear Scott/Dear Max* 251). In 1951, acting on this assertion and on the presence among Fitzgerald's books at the time of his death of a rearranged copy of the novel labeled "This is the *final version* of the book as I would like it" (qtd. in Bruccoli 368), Malcolm Cowley edited for Scribner's an edition that reversed books 1 and 2 of the original. It was never reprinted, however, and all current editions retain the 1934 structure.

In May 1934, Zelda was moved again, to Sheppard and Enoch Pratt Hospital, which was literally next door to La Paix, but in December 1933, Scott had moved into an apartment in downtown Baltimore. Nevertheless, he was still only a few miles away and visited her frequently, although he was drinking heavily, during the spring and summer of 1934. His summary of his thirty-seventh year, September 1933–September 1934 (the last recorded in his *Ledger*), was "*Zelda breaks, the novel finished. Hard times begin for me, slow but sure. Ill Health throughout*" (188). Zelda remained at Sheppard-Pratt for nearly two years. In April 1934, Scott began work on a historical novel, set in ninth-century France, about Philippe, the count of Villefranche. (Ultimately, only four sections were completed, and they were published as separate stories.) He also continued to sell stories, primarily to the *Saturday Evening Post*, which in 1933–1934 was paying him $3,000 per story. In March 1935, Scribner's published *Taps at Reveille*, a collection of eighteen Fitzgerald stories including "Babylon Revisited" (generally thought to be his best story), but the book sold poorly. At about the same time, the *Post* began to reject his stories—they had published thirteen between 1932 and 1934, but only published four more in the next six years—and he was forced to accept $250 apiece for contributions to a new men's magazine, *Esquire*, which thereafter became his principal market.

The Crack-Up, Hollywood, and Premature Death: 1935–1940

In early 1935, concerned about his health—doctors had diagnosed tuberculosis—Fitzgerald took Scottie out of school and went to Tryon, in the mountains of North Carolina, for two weeks. He returned to the region for the summer, staying at Asheville's fashionable Grove Park Inn, where he had a brief affair with another guest, a married woman named Beatrice Dance. Convinced that he and Zelda would never again live together as husband and wife, Fitzgerald needed female companionship. Yet he never contemplated abandoning Zelda, whom he referred to as "my invalid" (qtd. in Bruccoli 394). Returning to Baltimore that fall, Fitzgerald continued drinking, his health worsening until he was hospitalized. In November 1935, he went back to North Carolina and settled in much cheaper accommodations in nearby Hendersonville, an indication of the financial difficulties caused by his inability to get top dollar for his stories combined with the necessity of paying for Zelda's hospitalization and Scottie's upkeep.

In Hendersonville he wrote a three-part series of confessional essays for *Esquire*. "The Crack-Up" (February 1936), "Pasting It Together" (March 1936), and "Handle with Care" (April 1936), while remarkably candid and articulate in their admissions that "for two years my life has been a drawing on resources that I did not possess" and that he saw himself as "a cracked plate, the kind that one wonders whether it is worth preserving" (*Crack-Up* 72, 75), dismayed his fellow writers and further discouraged magazine editors from buying his fiction. "Inside the House," published on June 6, 1936, was his last story to appear in the *Saturday Evening Post*.

Zelda's condition did not improve, and in April 1936, Scott moved her to Highland Hospital in Asheville, where she seemed to respond well to Dr. Robert Carroll's regimen of exercise and a controlled diet. After returning briefly to Baltimore to be near his ailing mother, who was in a suburban Washington, D.C., nursing home where she died in September, Fitzgerald spent the remainder of the year in North Carolina at the Grove Park Inn. In September, Scottie entered the Ethel Walker School in Simsbury, Connecticut; thereafter, she spent her vacations with Harold Ober's family and saw her parents less frequently. On Fitzgerald's fortieth birthday, September 24, 1936, he was interviewed by a reporter for the *New York Post*, whose front-page article the next day was headlined "The Other Side of Paradise / Scott Fitzgerald, 40 / Engulfed in Despair / Broken in Health He Spends Birthday Re- / gretting That He Has Lost Faith in His Star" (qtd. in Bruccoli 410). Fitzgerald's earnings fell to a little over $10,000 in 1936 (*Ledger* 76), although he did inherit some additional money from his mother's estate.

Early in 1937, Fitzgerald moved back to Tryon. He was unable to sell any stories, and his earnings for the first six months of the year fell to less than $3,500. He was also more than $22,000 in debt. When in June MGM offered him $1,000 a week to come to Hollywood as a screenwriter, he accepted gratefully. He settled at the Garden of Allah Apartments on Sunset Boulevard, and in July he met Sheilah Graham, an attractive twenty-eight-year-old Englishwoman who was a gossip columnist. Though she was engaged to a British marquess when they met, Sheilah soon became Scott's lover. Their relationship had many rocky moments, most due to Fitzgerald's behavior when drunk, but it lasted for the rest of his life. Again, as with his earlier romance with Beatrice Dance, Fitzgerald never contemplated abandoning Zelda, and neither she nor Scottie ever knew anything of his relationship with Sheilah Graham.

Fitzgerald remained in California for the rest of his life, aside from three visits east to see Zelda in September 1937, March 1938, and April 1939, and an ill-fated trip in February 1939 to Hanover, New Hampshire, with young writer Budd Schulberg to work on a film about Dartmouth College's Winter Carnival. Although he worked on scripts for many films, including *Gone with the Wind* for a brief time in January 1939, he received screen credit for only one, *Three Comrades* (1938). In 1937, MGM raised his salary to $1,250 a week, but a year later, the studio did not renew his contract, and subsequently he was forced to do freelance work. Scottie entered Vassar College in September 1938. In April 1940, Zelda was released from Highland Hospital and returned to Montgomery to live with her mother.

For the first year and a half after he went to California, Fitzgerald focused on screenwriting and wrote no fiction. But sometime in 1938, he began working on a novel about Hollywood, centering it on a character to some extent modeled on the late boy-wonder producer Irving Thalberg. He also started a series of short stories about Pat Hobby, a hack Hollywood writer. Beginning in January 1940, *Esquire* published a Hobby story in each monthly issue until May 1941—seventeen in all. Throughout this time, despite brief periods of going on the wagon, Fitzgerald drank heavily and his health, already precarious, deteriorated further. In November 1940, he suffered what Bruccoli calls "a coronary episode" (485) and moved into Sheilah Graham's ground-floor apartment to avoid the exertion of climbing stairs. There, on December 21, he was reading the *Princeton Alumni Weekly* when he fell to the floor, dead of a heart attack at age forty-four. At Zelda's suggestion, Scott was buried in Rockville, Maryland, near his parents' graves. (He was denied burial with them in St. Mary's Church cemetery "because he had not been a practicing Catholic at his death" [Bruccoli 488]. Only in November 1975 would the diocese relent and allow his remains to be reinterred at St. Mary's.) Zelda, who did not attend Scott's funeral, continued living with her mother, returning occasionally to Highland Hospital when her illness recurred. On March 10, 1948, she died in a fire at Highland and was buried alongside her husband.

In 1941, Scribner's, with the assistance of Fitzgerald's college friend Edmund Wilson, published the unfinished text of Scott's Hollywood novel under the title *The Last Tycoon*, in a volume with *The Great Gatsby* and five of his best stories. Most reviewers took the opportunity to reassess Fitzgerald's career, and many agreed with Stephen Vincent Benét's pronouncement: "This is not a legend, this is a reputation—and, seen in perspective, it may well be one of the most secure reputations of our time" (qtd. in Bryer 100). More than sixty years later, with *Gatsby* selling some 300,000 copies annually and with academic and popular interest in Fitzgerald's life and writings seemingly inexhaustible, Benét's prediction has proven to be remarkably prescient and beyond dispute.

WORKS CITED

Bruccoli, Matthew J. *Some Sort of Epic Grandeur.* 1981. 2d rev. ed. Columbia: University of South Carolina Press, 2002.

Bruccoli, Matthew J., Scottie Fitzgerald Smith, and Joan P. Kerr. Eds. *The Romantic Egoists.* New York: Scribner's, 1974; rpt. Columbia: University of South Carolina Press, 2004.

Bryer, Jackson R. *The Critical Reputation of F. Scott Fitzgerald: A Bibliographical Study.* Hamden, Conn.: Archon, 1967.

Cowley, Malcolm. "Third Act and Epilogue." In *F. Scott Fitzgerald: The Man and His Work.* Ed. Alfred Kazin. Cleveland, Ohio: World, 1951. 147–54.

Cross, K. G. W. *F. Scott Fitzgerald.* New York: Grove, 1964.

Fitzgerald, F. Scott. *Afternoon of an Author: A Selection of Uncollected Stories and Essays.* New York: Scribner's, 1958.

———. *The Apprentice Fiction of F. Scott Fitzgerald 1909–1917.* Ed. John Kuehl. New Brunswick, N.J.: Rutgers University Press, 1965.

———. *The Crack-Up.* Ed. Edmund Wilson. New York: New Directions, 1945.

———. *Dear Scott/Dear Max: The Fitzgerald-Perkins Correspondence.* Ed. John Kuehl and Jackson R. Bryer. New York: Scribner's, 1971.

———. *F. Scott Fitzgerald in His Own Time: A Miscellany.* Ed. Matthew J. Bruccoli and Jackson R. Bryer. Kent, Ohio: Kent State University Press, 1971.

———. *F. Scott Fitzgerald: A Life in Letters.* Ed. Matthew J. Bruccoli and Judith S. Baughman. New York: Scribner's, 1994.

———. *F. Scott Fitzgerald's Ledger: A Facsimile.* Washington, D.C.: Bruccoli Clark/NCR/Microcard Editions, 1973.

———. *The Notebooks of F. Scott Fitzgerald.* Ed. Matthew J. Bruccoli. New York: Harcourt Brace Jovanovich/Bruccoli Clark, 1978.

———. *This Side of Paradise.* 1920. Ed. James L. W. West III. Cambridge: Cambridge University Press, 1995.

Hemingway, Ernest. *A Moveable Feast*. New York: Scribner's, 1964.

Mayfield, Sara. *Exiles from Paradise: Zelda and Scott Fitzgerald*. New York: Delacorte, 1971.

Milford, Nancy. *Zelda: A Biography*. New York: Harper and Row, 1970.

Mizener, Arthur. *The Far Side of Paradise: A Biography of F. Scott Fitzgerald*. Boston: Houghton Mifflin, 1951.

FITZGERALD IN HIS TIME

F. Scott Fitzgerald, Professional Author

James L. W. West III

From 1919 until 1940, F. Scott Fitzgerald was a successful professional writer in America, a country in which full-time authorship has always been a precarious occupation. During those years, the extent of his working life, he earned his living altogether with his pen. He did nothing else: he had no other vocation and drew on no private source of income. Fitzgerald produced novels, short stories, personal essays, and the occasional poem; he attempted drama and wrote for the movies. He made his way on talent, ambition, self-discipline, and luck. Fitzgerald's good fortune ran out toward the end of his career, but he still had a fine run as an author, especially during the 1920s. He was hampered by personal problems and bad habits, but he was also working within a system not designed (even today) to support full-time professional writers.

There has never been a true "profession" of authorship in America. Many white-collar workers in the United States have organized themselves by profession, a considerable advantage in a capitalistic economy, but authors have never been able to do so. True professionals, such as physicians and attorneys, control who is allowed to enter their ranks. Candidates must be trained for entry and must pass qualifying examinations. They are also required to serve apprenticeships; doctors, for example, spend time as interns before they are admitted to full professional status, and attorneys prove themselves as junior members of law firms before they are taken in as partners. College professors, like doctors and lawyers, earn advanced degrees and are judged on their talents as teachers and scholars before being granted tenure. Doctors, lawyers, and pedagogues work within hierarchies and strive to earn titles; they are expected to join professional associations and to adhere to codes of ethics. Violation of those codes can result in expulsion, though this does not often happen. The real purpose of such codes is to protect the professionals, not the clients.

Professionals, especially physicians and attorneys, use specialized vocabularies and command bodies of information that are unfamiliar to their clients. The relationships between true professionals and clients are *fiduciary*, which is to say that the knowledge and power reside entirely with the professionals, whom the clients must trust to handle their education, health, and legal affairs. Professional status provides an enormous advantage in a capitalistic marketplace. A true profession is in effect a monopoly; in most cases (medicine and law, for example) a legislative body makes it illegal to practice that profession without a license. Professionals are thereby protected from the pressures of a free-enterprise economy. They minimize competition by controlling who is admitted into their ranks, and they fix fees by common consent—and, discreetly, through their professional groups.[1]

Obviously, Fitzgerald was not entering any such occupational structure when he decided, in July 1919, to quit the only full-time job he ever held—as an advertising copywriter at the Barron Collier agency in New York City. He took the train back to his native St. Paul, moved in with his parents, and finished writing his first novel. That novel—*This Side of Paradise*, published by Charles Scribner's Sons in 1920—was a considerable success and made him an overnight literary celebrity, but it did not give him entry into an established profession. Then as now, anyone could be an author. One simply picked up pencil and paper and tried one's luck. Authors were not required to hold advanced degrees nor to pass certifying examinations; they served no formal apprenticeships and were not awarded slots as law partners or positions as tenured professors. They commanded no arcane terminology or body of expertise, and they certainly did not have a monopoly on the written word.

Authors did not have clients; indeed, as Fitzgerald quickly learned, they were themselves more nearly the clients of publishers, editors, and agents—people within the literary marketplace who deliberately took on many of the characteristics of the professionalized classes. Nor could writers be considered members of the working proletariat; they belonged to no unions, had no guarantees of work, and enjoyed no fringe benefits. Writers were more nearly piece-workers or cottage laborers who produced individual items for sale on the literary marketplace and thus were vulnerable to most of the dangers of naked capitalism. Fitzgerald was certainly not thinking about these matters when he left New York for St. Paul in the summer of 1919, but they would influence him throughout his professional life. He was taking up a vocation in which, essentially, he would live hand to mouth.

Fitzgerald worked under another disadvantage: he had few opportunities to recycle his writings in order to produce income over the long term. He enjoyed substantial immediate returns for his early novels and, throughout most of his career, good money for short stories sold to mass-circulation magazines such as the *Saturday Evening Post*, *Redbook*, and *Collier's*. What he really needed, though, was continuing money from republication of his earlier writings in other forms, or from adaptation of his novels and stories into other commercial vehicles. Successful professional writers, he learned, had to regard the initial composition of a literary work as an investment—of time, energy, material, and imagination. Would the investment yield only one-time payment, or could it be made to produce steady money over many years, as he grew older? During Fitzgerald's career, we must remember, there was no paperback market to keep his earlier titles alive. Virtually all books were published first in hard covers; successful novels, after their initial runs in the bookstores, usually were available only in cheap clothbound reprints issued by such firms as A. L. Burt, Grosset and Dunlap, Blue Ribbon Books, and the Modern Library. These operations used the original printing plates for the texts, issued the books on inexpensive paper, manufactured them in large print runs, sold them at modest prices through department stores or newsstands, and paid reduced royalties or flat fees to the authors. Such emoluments amounted to little more than pin money for Fitzgerald.

The paperback industry as we know it today did not begin in the United States until 1939 with the launching of Pocket Books, followed in the 1940s by the Bantam, Avon, Dell, Popular Library, New American Library, and Ballantine imprints. Fitzgerald, alas, died in 1940. What a boon it would have been to him during the 1920s and 1930s if his early novels, *This Side of Paradise* and *The Beautiful and Damned*, and his short-fiction collections *Flappers and Philosophers* and *Tales of the Jazz Age*, all published between 1920 and 1922, could have had continuing sales as paperbacks, generating income throughout his career.[2]

Book clubs likewise were not a significant feature of the American literary marketplace during Fitzgerald's years as a working author. The Book-of-the-Month Club was founded in 1926, followed by the Literary Guild later that same year, but neither operation gathered much steam until after the Second World War. Fitzgerald only received one book-club offer during his career—for *Tender Is the Night* to be an alternate selection of the Literary Guild in 1934, an offer which he turned down. Book clubs reached their audiences through the U.S. mail system, rather than through established retail bookstores. They served readers in large areas of the country that had no bookshops. In truth, the American publishing industry marketed its wares effectively only in the Northeast and in some urban areas of the West Coast. There were plenty of potential customers in other parts of the country during the 1920s and 1930s, especially in the South and Midwest, but most New York publishers let these areas take care of themselves. Book clubs stepped into the gap, advertising their titles in national mass-circulation magazines and sending volumes to subscribers via parcel post. The clubs would have enlarged Fitzgerald's readership significantly but, in the 1920s and 1930s, were not yet a strong enough force in the book business to do him significant good.[3]

Fitzgerald did have at least some success in recycling his work.

Two of his four novels were serialized in magazines before publication—*The Beautiful and Damned* in *Metropolitan Magazine* in 1922 and *Tender Is the Night* in *Scribner's Magazine* in 1934. Serialization of novels was a good way to make literary labor pay twice, once for the magazine run and again for clothbound publication. Fitzgerald also selected the best of his magazine fiction and recycled it in hardbound collections published by Scribner's. His most welcome source of secondary income came from the sale of subsidiary rights for stage productions and for movie versions of his works. The great windfall of his career came in 1926 when his agent, Harold Ober, in two separate deals, sold stage and screen rights for *The Great Gatsby*, putting a total of $26,000 into Fitzgerald's bank account—and the author did not have to lift a finger to collect the money. But that was Fitzgerald's only big score; drama and cinema rights to his other works yielded small change.

Fitzgerald's book contracts with Scribner's contained sketchy statements about subsidiary rights. Money from the sale of such rights was to be split fifty-fifty between author and publisher, a standard arrangement for that time. The rights were not named in the contracts; a blanket statement covered everything.[4] A book contract drawn up today, by contrast, would be much more specific about "sub-rights," as they are now called, naming not only paperbacks, book clubs, uniform editions, and stage / cinema rights, but devoting attention to television and radio adaptations, audiotape or compact disc versions, Websites, translations into foreign languages, syndications, abridgments, musical renderings, and toy, T-shirt, and video-game rights. Many of these ways of recycling a literary work, or images drawn from it, did not even exist in Fitzgerald's time. Certainly he would have benefited from such forms of extra income if they had been available to him.[5]

Who among his colleagues and competitors did better than Fitzgerald? As it turns out, almost no one. Many of the serious writers of fiction and poetry who were Fitzgerald's exact or near contemporaries had to rely on other sources of income or support. Edith Wharton's clothbound novels sold in dependably large numbers, and she collected numerous checks for serial and movie rights, but for much of her career she lived on family money. Ernest Hemingway's first two wives had private incomes; indeed, his second wife, Pauline Pfeiffer, was from a genuinely wealthy family. Robert Frost had significant early help from a grandfather; Frost lived frugally, something that Fitzgerald seemed incapable of doing, and benefited from academic and writer-in-residence appointments. (Frost's royalties from his books of poetry were slim until late in his career.) Theodore Dreiser and H. L. Mencken, both older than Fitzgerald, had to earn continuing income from journalism. Mencken's expenses were minimal: for most of his life he lived with his mother in the Baltimore house in which he had been reared. Dreiser, too, had to keep a close eye on his bank account. He had two big paydays in his life, both for movie rights, but even in his fifties he was still quite careful about day-to-day expenditures and parsimonious with tips to waiters and taxi drivers. Thomas Wolfe trained himself to write for the magazine market but found the process difficult: exercising the kind of self-discipline needed to write a salable magazine story went against his instincts as an author. William Faulkner also learned to write popular stories for the *Post* and the *American Mercury*, but Faulkner's biggest paychecks came from Hollywood scriptwriting, which he hated.

Fitzgerald's friend Edmund Wilson subsisted on journalism, advances from book publishers, and money extracted from his widowed mother. E. E. Cummings made almost nothing from editions of his poetry; he collected a few dollars by selling some of his paintings and drawings, but his main source of income, other than his parents, was from public readings and lectures. The serious writer of Fitzgerald's time who was most successful was the novelist Sinclair Lewis. The high sales figures in the 1920s for *Main Street, Babbitt, Arrowsmith*, and *Elmer Gantry* were attributable to the undivided attention of his publisher, Alfred Harcourt, whose fledgling house was essentially a one-author operation. Harcourt devoted nearly all of the resources of his imprint to Lewis, even advertising Lewis's novels on roadside billboards. Lewis also collected significant income from the magazine market for his short stories and essays, and he received large sums from Hollywood studios for the cinema rights to his novels.

Compared to the records of these contemporaries, Fitzgerald's achievement was by no means small. All of these authors, even Lewis and Wharton, went through lean stretches, and all of them scrambled to find ways in which to make their writings yield long-term income.

Fitzgerald's career as a professional writer can be divided into four overlapping periods. By reviewing them one by one, we can get an idea of his progress. During the first period, from 1919 to 1925, he served his apprenticeship (a brief one) and enjoyed much early popularity. The second period, covering the years 1925–1934, was spent largely in Europe, living as a literary expatriate and writing regularly for large-circulation magazines. Fitzgerald's most difficult period was the third, from 1934 to 1937, during which he lost the knack of writing salable magazine fiction and went through his famous crack-up. In the fourth period, 1937 to 1940, he was rescued by a scriptwriting contract with Metro-Goldwyn-Mayer and went to Hollywood. He died there, well into the composition of *The Last Tycoon*, which might have been his best novel, had he lived to finish it.

Fitzgerald served an apprenticeship during his initial period, though it was a literary tutorial, not a true professional apprenticeship. His ambitions to be an author during his years at Princeton were vague; certainly he worked hard at his writing there, producing poetry, fiction, and musical comedy scripts, but he did not consciously set his cap for literary success until near the end of his time at the university. His attitude was changed by the First World War. Fitzgerald left Princeton to become a young officer in the infantry; he was convinced that he would fight in Europe and be killed in the trenches. He was determined to leave something literary behind, in the manner of the English poet Rupert Brooke, one of his heroes. Fitzgerald therefore spent much of his time in army training camp writing a novel called "The Romantic Egotist," only fragments of which survive. That novel was rejected twice by Scribner's, but substantial parts of it were reworked for *This Side of Paradise*.[6]

After the war, while laboring by day at his advertising job in New York, Fitzgerald put himself through an apprenticeship in writing for the magazines. He revised old college work and wrote new stories and one-act plays; these he submitted to popular magazines, almost entirely without success, but he learned what these magazines wanted, both by reading what they did publish and by trying to understand why his own work was being turned down. It is probable that Fitzgerald was still deciding what genre to specialize in during this period. His most visible successes at Princeton had been with the Triangle Club, a musical comedy group that mounted yearly all-male touring productions. If Fitzgerald had possessed an entrée to the New York theater world (as did his near-contemporary Oscar Hammerstein II) he might well have turned his talents to the stage.[7] Fitzgerald decided on fiction, though, and made his initial strike with *This Side of Paradise* in the spring of 1920.

Was Fitzgerald well served by his publisher? Certainly that is the received wisdom, but the matter needs to be examined in commercial terms. Charles Scribner's Sons, as it turns out, might not have been the best house to publish a popular success like *This Side of Paradise*. Scribner's was a conservative firm—not in politics but in business strategy. Other imprints in American publishing at the time (Liveright and Doubleday come to mind) had a more pronounced gambling mentality and might have followed up the excellent early reviews of *This Side of Paradise* with a single massive print run, designed to flood bookstores with copies for display and sale. Scribner's, however, took a much more cautious approach. Company records reveal that it manufactured a string of separate printings of from 2,000 to 3,000 copies, supplying orders as they came in, being careful not to be caught with a warehouse full of unsold stock should Fitzgerald's sudden celebrity vanish. Probably as a consequence, *This Side of Paradise* sold only about 50,000 copies, a respectable figure but hardly large enough to qualify the book as a bestseller.[8] Fitzgerald did not object: he liked the prestige of being a Scribner's author, and he could sense that in Maxwell Perkins, his editor there, he had found an ally for life. Besides, his work and name were in demand with New York magazine editors, and he had learned by now how to manufacture short fiction for them.[9]

What the clamoring editors wanted, he knew, was a character

he had virtually invented, a strong, willful, selfish, beautiful, alluring, independent, and ruthless young woman based on his wife, Zelda, and on other young women whom he met during the postwar period. It seemed not to matter how hackneyed the plot or how flat the male protagonist—Fitzgerald's famous heroine could carry almost any story into print. He would eventually come to feel trapped by this heroine, unable to write about her with conviction, but during these early years she fascinated him, and he wrote about her not only in the stories from this period for which we remember him—"Bernice Bobs Her Hair" and "The Offshore Pirate," for example—but in now-forgotten narratives such as "Myra Meets His Family" and "The Popular Girl."

Fitzgerald was savvy enough to recognize that steady writing for the magazines would blunt his talent and keep him from finishing the novels on which his reputation would eventually depend. He therefore learned to use the stories as workshops for the novels, trying out characters, scenes, and themes in his stories and then reusing them (even carrying over some descriptive passages nearly verbatim) in his novels. This was a habit of authorial thrift that he would follow throughout his career. One sees it first in several stories written between 1922 and 1924: "Winter Dreams," "Dice, Brass Knuckles & Guitar," "Diamond Dick and the First Law of Woman," "'The Sensible Thing,'" and "John Jackson's Arcady." All of these narratives foreshadow the characters and themes of *The Great Gatsby*, published in 1925.

Fitzgerald's practice with such stories was to copy the memorable phrases, sentences, and paragraphs from their published texts into his notebooks. These gleanings he then considered eligible for reuse in his novels. Tearsheets of the stories (the printed texts, torn from the magazine issues) would be placed in his files with the legend *"Positively not to be republished in any form!"* written across the top of the first page. The title of the story would be logged into his *Ledger*, a record he kept of his earnings for tax purposes, and the designation *"Stripped and permanently buried"* would be set down as its final fate.[10]

During this first period of his career, Fitzgerald had not abandoned his ambition to write for the stage. He invested a great amount of labor in 1923 on *The Vegetable*, a three-act farce that flopped in tryouts at Atlantic City and never made it to Broadway. Fitzgerald was immensely disappointed; his contract with the producer, Sam Harris, would have paid off handsomely if the show had been presented in New York and had lasted for a minimum of fifty performances. He would also have drawn later and continuing income from touring, stock, amateur, and repertory versions, and from a possible movie spin-off.[11] The failure of *The Vegetable* in the fall of 1923 caused Fitzgerald, who was by then in considerable debt, to shut himself in a stuffy room over a garage in Great Neck, New York, and write himself out of the red by turning out ten short stories for the magazine market. His fees for these stories totaled more than $16,000. Rescuing himself in this way became a habit for Fitzgerald throughout his writing life; magazine money was always there for the taking, if he could summon the stamina and inventiveness to produce salable stories.

The culmination of this first period came with the composition and revision of *The Great Gatsby*, carried out while Fitzgerald was living in France and Italy in 1924 and early 1925. We think of that novel today as Fitzgerald's signature work and as a landmark in twentieth-century American literature. It is therefore surprising to learn that he was dissatisfied with *Gatsby*, largely because he thought it a commercial failure. Indeed, the novel only sold some 21,000 copies, less than half of what *This Side of Paradise* and *The Beautiful and Damned* had recorded. The sales for *Gatsby* did little more than balance Fitzgerald's account with Scribner's, earning back the advances he had drawn while writing the novel. Fitzgerald saw that he would again have to turn out stories for the magazine market if he were to finance the expensive habits that he and Zelda were developing abroad.

During the second period, from 1925 to 1934, Fitzgerald reached his professional peak. Initially he did not have to produce short fiction because he received the money from stage and screen rights for *Gatsby*. Perhaps it would have been better for Fitzgerald if those payments had come to him in small increments, but most of it came in two lumps, and he set about spending it rather than writing. This was typical behavior for Fitzgerald. Anyone who gives careful study to his professional ca-

PATRONS ARE REQUESTED TO FAVOR THE COMPANY BY CRITICISM AND SUGGESTION CONCERNING ITS SERVICE Form 1281

CLASS OF SERVICE
This is a full-rate Cablegram unless its deferred character is indicated by a suitable sign preceding the address.

WESTERN UNION
CABLEGRAM

NEWCOMB CARLTON, PRESIDENT J. C. WILLEVER, FIRST VICE-PRESIDENT

SIGNS

	Full-Rate Cablegram
LCO	Deferred Cablegram
NLT	Cable Letter
WLT	Week-End Letter

Received at 40 Broad Street (Central Cable Office,) New York, N. Y. ALWAYS OPEN

FCH PS364 LE.

PARIS 20

JUL 2 1928

WLT CARBONATO PAUL R REYNOLDS

NYK 599 FIFTH AVE

STORY FINISHED WILL TRY CATCH MONDAY BOAT WITH IT CAN YOU POSSIBLY DEPOSIT FIVE HUNRDRED IMMEDIATELY

FITZGERALD

THE QUICKEST, SUREST AND SAFEST WAY TO SEND MONEY IS BY TELEGRAPH OR CABLE

Fitzgerald to the Paul Revere Reynolds literary agency, July 1, 1928, sent from Paris. During this period of his career, Fitzgerald often conducted transatlantic business with his agents, asking for advances on unsold work that he was sending via surface mail. The handwritten notation at the bottom right reads, "500 deposited July 1, 1928." The manuscript that Fitzgerald had just completed was probably "He Thinks He's Wonderful," a story in the Basil Duke Lee series; it appeared in the Saturday Evening Post *for September 29, 1928. Reproduced from the original, courtesy of the Lilly Library, Indiana University, Bloomington, Indiana.*

reer comes to the conclusion that he was at his most productive when he worked under financial pressure, not when he had money in hand. Fitzgerald seems to have needed the prodding of debt, with an attendant dose of guilt, to move him to his writing table. In his most fecund periods he always maintained a negative balance with his agent, and sometimes with Scribner's as well—then charged off each magazine sale or book royalty check to the amounts that were outstanding.[12] The money for the subsidiary rights to *Gatsby* did not finance the composition of Fitzgerald's third novel, as he had hoped. He did make some progress on that

67

Record for 1931

Stories	Indecision	$ 4000.	Com 10%	3600	00
	A New Leaf	4000.	"	3600	00
	Flight and Pursuit	4000.	"	3600	00
	Emotional Bankruptcy	4000.	"	3600	00
	Between Three and Four	4000	"	3600	00
	A Change of Class	4000.	"	3600	00
	Half a Dozen of the Other	3000	"	2700	00
	A Freeze Out	4000.	"	3600	00
	Diagnosis	4000.	"	3600	00
	Total			31,500	00
Other Items	Treatment Metro Goldwyn Mayer	6000.	"	5400	00
	Echoes of the Jazz Age	500.		500	00
	Vegetable Performance	25.00	"	22	50
	New Leaf (English)	£17	"	59	00
	Flight & Pursuit (English)	Guineas 35	"	126	00
	John Jackson's Arcady	2.21	"	2	00
	Total			6109	50
Books	This Side of Paradise			12	90
	Flappers & Philosophers			4	30
	The Beautiful & Damned			4	40
	Tales of the Jazz Age			3	90
	The Vegetable			1	13
	The Great Gatsby			17	90
	All the Sad Young Men			7	90
	Advance against Bk.			44	15
	Total			100	00
	Less: Not paid in 1931 by Metro	173.72	"	−155	35
	Grand Total			37,559	00
	New Yorker sketch	50.00		45	00
				37,599	00

Leaf 67 from Fitzgerald's Ledger, *a financial record that he kept for tax purposes. This leaf shows his income for 1931, the peak earning year of his career—and, incidentally, one of the bleakest years of the Great Depression. Nearly all of Fitzgerald's money in 1931 came from short fiction written for large-circulation magazines and from a movie treatment that he prepared for MGM. Earnings from the seven books he had published with Scribner's totaled only $52.43. Reproduced with permission from the original in the F. Scott Fitzgerald Papers, Princeton University Library, Princeton, New Jersey.*

narrative, setting down much of the writing that would eventually go into Book 1 of *Tender Is the Night*, but for the most part 1926 was a wasted year for him professionally.

During the rest of this period Fitzgerald struggled to keep his head above water. This was a difficult time for him and his wife: his drinking increased, and his public behavior became increasingly erratic; her determination to become a serious dancer became an obsession, and she descended into mental illness. Fitzgerald did, though, turn out some of his finest short stories during these years, drawing on his own experiences to produce

"The Rich Boy," "Jacob's Ladder," "Outside the Cabinet-Maker's," "The Last of the Belles," "One Trip Abroad," and "Babylon Revisited." In 1928 and 1929 he wrote the Basil Duke Lee stories, which are among his finest achievements.[13] He hit his stride as a magazine writer in the late 1920s and early 1930s; Ober sold his manuscripts to top markets almost without effort, and Fitzgerald's regular fee from the *Post* reached $4,000 per story, big money for the time. After returning to the United States he finally managed in 1934 to complete *Tender Is the Night*, though that novel, like *Gatsby*, was a commercial disappointment, at least in his eyes. It sold only 13,000 copies and failed to generate interest either from drama producers or movie studios. Serial money for the novel from *Scribner's Magazine*, the house publication for Charles Scribner's Sons, wiped out his debt to the firm but left him with no money in hand for current expenses. Fitzgerald found himself in difficult straits in 1935, depressed and in bad health, heavily in debt, and obliged to earn money quickly for his daughter's school expenses and for Zelda's mental health treatments.

Fitzgerald therefore did what he had always done: he turned to the magazine market for immediate income. He tried to manufacture stories in his old bright manner for dependable outlets like the *Post* but found, to his dismay, that his knack for writing this kind of short fiction had deserted him. The records at Ober's agency prove that Fitzgerald was trying hard, but the few stories that made it into print, together with others that he aborted and saved in manuscript among his papers, show that his talent for writing popular short stories had largely vanished. The familiar matter is there, but the manner is forced, and the characters are unconvincing. Fitzgerald was finding it particularly hard to write about his heroine. Her moment had probably passed in any case; in the mid-1930s America was deep into the Great Depression, and readers were less interested in the romantic escapades of Jazz Age debutantes than they had been ten years before.

Frustrated by his inability to write about this heroine, Fitzgerald took revenge. He wrote a story in which he filled her with dynamite and blew her up. The female character in question, whose name is Gwen Davis, appears in a story called "A Full

Life," which Fitzgerald never published. The plot is improbable: we first see Gwen testing an inflatable flying suit, then watch her dive into the water from the deck of an ocean liner and perform in a circus as a human cannonball. In this last incarnation Fitzgerald dubs her "The Human Shell," an appropriate moniker, since she is a thoroughly empty character. At the end of the story (in what must have been a private gesture, since one cannot imagine any magazine publishing the narrative), Fitzgerald has Gwen admit that she had always been "full of dynamite." Then he detonates her, killing a few bystanders who had moved too close. This grisly little drama, played out on Fitzgerald's work table, reveals how frustrated he was during this period of his professional career (West, "Fitzgerald Explodes His Heroine," 159–65).

Fortunately there was still one magazine open to him: *Esquire*, then in its earliest years of publication and edited by Arnold Gingrich, who admired Fitzgerald's writing and flattered him into becoming a contributor.[14] The pay was small, only $250 per story, but Gingrich took almost everything that Fitzgerald sent him, including the now-famous trio of *Crack-Up* essays, which appeared in *Esquire* in February, March, and April 1936. These essays drew much publicity, not all of it favorable, but Fitzgerald was at least back in the public eye, and he seems to have recognized that he could seize the opportunity to reshape his image as a writer. During the 1920s he had been the enfant terrible of American literature, the self-proclaimed prophet of the Jazz Age. Perhaps now he could refashion himself as a chronicler of loss and regret, an image more in keeping with the temper of the times. He could identify his own fall with the country's decline. His bust period, like America's, had begun after the boom of the 1920s had ended.

Fitzgerald needed to publish a book of personal essays in order to bring about this reinvention of himself. He proposed that book twice to Perkins, once in May 1934 and again in April 1936, but both times Perkins turned him down (*Dear Scott/Dear Max* 195–98, 228–30). From Fitzgerald's letters to Perkins, one of which contains a tentative table of contents, we can see what kind of book he had in mind: a retrospective collection of personal writings that would show his transition from early facile cleverness through a middle period as a young husband and father to his present position as a mature, thoughtful writer. The plan seems sound, but in the second proposal Fitzgerald told Perkins that he wanted to include the three *Crack-Up* essays. Perkins was by nature private and guarded about emotional matters; he was uncomfortable with the self-revelation and confessionalism in the *Crack-Up* pieces and did not want Fitzgerald to reprint them. He therefore stiff-armed Fitzgerald's proposal. He did suggest an alternate book—a reminiscence of the Jazz Age, written from scratch—but Fitzgerald was in no position in the mid-1930s to undertake a new writing project from the ground up, especially one that did not have especially high sales potential. Thus Fitzgerald's plan to recycle some of his personal essays, to create an altered public image, and to give a new direction to his career died in 1936. In the years that remained to him, Fitzgerald did not bring up the proposition again in his letters to Perkins.

During those last years, from 1937 to 1940, Fitzgerald lived and worked in Hollywood. From July 1937 until the end of 1938 he wrote screenplays on contract for MGM. In 1937 he earned $1,000 each week from the studio, a figure that was raised to $1,250 in 1938. He was not the highest-paid scriptwriter in town, but he was certainly in the top bracket. This money allowed him to pay off most of his old debts (which he estimated at $40,000) and to feel financially secure for the first time in almost a decade. Fitzgerald went to Hollywood with high ambitions: he wanted to learn the screenwriting trade, to produce serious scripts, and eventually to have significant control over the movies that he conceived. He was disappointed in those aims; he found that his talent was not particularly well suited to cinema writing, and he hated the atmosphere of the movie production lot and was not a willing collaborator with other writers.

When MGM did not renew his contract at the end of 1938, Fitzgerald turned back to the only source of ready income on which he had ever been able to depend—the magazine market. He began to write short stories again with some success, selling a series about a Hollywood hack writer named Pat Hobby to *Esquire* and marketing other work successfully to *American Caval-*

cade, *Liberty*, and *Cosmopolitan*. Toward the end of his life he began composing *The Last Tycoon*; his initial thought, as a professional, was to sell the novel first as a serial. He sent an outline of the book to Kenneth Littauer, editor of *Collier's*, asking for an agreement that would pay him money as each installment of the serial was delivered, with a final sum due when the last chapters were completed (*Correspondence* 539–40, 545–51, 561–62). Fitzgerald's plan was to live on the serial payments while he wrote the narrative, chapter by chapter, and then to collect book royalties when the novel was published by Scribner's in hard covers. He must also have been thinking about movie rights: surely a good novel about Hollywood would interest one of the major studios. Littauer, alas, would not commit to the plan, and Fitzgerald had to write *The Last Tycoon* as a speculative venture. He was deeply involved in its composition when he died; what he had completed was published, as an unfinished fragment, by Scribner's in 1941. Many students of American literature think that it is our finest novel about Hollywood, even in unfinished form.

It is a great shame that Fitzgerald did not live into the postwar 1950s, when the American publishing industry finally matured and the literary marketplace boomed. The returning GIs went to college; the consequent rise in textbook sales (and the boom in the book business generally) gave publishers a firm footing to back up their gambles on fiction, poetry, biography, and other belletristic writing. Paperback houses came to wield much power in the publishing equation; book clubs became a major force in distribution. Movie money increased, both for cinema rights and for authors who wrote screenplays. Television caused the old market for magazine short stories to wither away, but the magazines continued to publish personal essays and other forms of nonfiction.

All of these developments have benefited Fitzgerald's literary estate, which has remained remarkably active. Indeed, it can be said that his posthumous literary career has been an enormous success. His record during his life, however, was hardly shabby. In just over two decades of full-time writing, he earned almost

$300,000. It is difficult to calculate the current buying power of that money, but one would have to multiply by at least a factor of ten. Fitzgerald overcame the disadvantages of full-time authorship in the America of the 1920s and 1930s and earned significant money during his stint as a professional. Even more important, he left behind a body of writing that continues to generate much admiration, and a great deal of money, to this very day.

NOTES

1. The standard study of the professions in America is Bledstein's *The Culture of Professionalism*. Also valuable are Carr-Saunders and Wilson's *The Professions* and Vollmer and Mills's *Professionalization*.

2. Standard histories of softcover publishing are Schick's *The Paperbound Book in America* and Bonn's *Under Cover: An Illustrated History of American Mass-Market Paperbacks*.

3. A good history of BOMC is Lee's *The Hidden Public*. Two more recent treatments of the book clubs are Rubin's *The Making of Middle/brow Culture* and Radway's *A Feeling for Books*.

4. The contracts for Fitzgerald's first four novels are available in facsimile in Bruccoli's *F. Scott Fitzgerald: A Descriptive Bibliography*, 332–39.

5. A good recent example is John Berendt's bestseller *Midnight in the Garden of Good and Evil*, first published in cloth by Random House in 1994. In addition to a paperback edition, a documentary film, and a Hollywood movie, Berendt's book has generated coffee mugs, photographs, stationery, postcards, watercolor prints, pins, earrings, bracelets, T-shirts, audiotapes, posters, molded candles, cookies, drinking glasses—and horse-drawn buggy tours through Savannah, Georgia (the setting of the book), so that tourists can see the houses, cemeteries, and other locations mentioned in Berendt's narrative.

6. The extant leaves of *The Romantic Egotist* are reproduced in Bruccoli's *F. Scott Fitzgerald Manuscripts*, vol. 1, part 2. For discussion of the fragments, see chapter 2 of West, *The Making of "This Side of Paradise."*

7. Hammerstein, one year older than Fitzgerald, had been a friendly rival at Columbia University, where he wrote book and

lyrics for the Varsity Shows, all-male musicals similar to the productions mounted by the Triangle Club. Fitzgerald mentions Hammerstein's 1917 Varsity Show *Home James!* in his 1920 short story "Head and Shoulders"; see the explanatory note on 357–58 of the Cambridge edition of *Flappers and Philosophers*. Hammerstein, from a family of theater impresarios, producers, and managers, began his career as a librettist in 1919 and 1920 by writing the musical plays for three Broadway productions: *Jimmie*, *Always You*, and *Tickle Me*.

8. See West, "Did F. Scott Fitzgerald Have the Right Publisher?" for a fuller analysis of this question.

9. An excellent study of Fitzgerald as an author of magazine fiction is Mangum's *A Fortune Yet: Money in the Art of F. Scott Fitzgerald's Short Stories*. Mangum includes a record of money earned for each story in appendix A of his volume.

10. See *F. Scott Fitzgerald's Ledger: A Facsimile*. Fitzgerald's tearsheet files are among his papers at Princeton University Library.

11. For details of Fitzgerald's contract for *The Vegetable* with producer Sam Harris, see West, *American Authors and the Literary Marketplace since 1900*, 135–36. The contract is in the files of the American Play Co., Berg Collection, New York Public Library.

12. This pattern is readily apparent in *As Ever, Scott Fitz——: Letters between F. Scott Fitzgerald and His Literary Agent, Harold Ober, 1919–1940*.

13. The stories are collected in *The Basil and Josephine Stories*.

14. See West, "Fitzgerald and *Esquire*."

WORKS CITED

Bledstein, Burton J. *The Culture of Professionalism: The Middle Class and the Development of Higher Education in America*. New York: Norton, 1976.

Bonn, Thomas L. *Under Cover: An Illustrated History of American Mass-Market Paperbacks*. New York: Penguin, 1982.

Bruccoli, Matthew J. *F. Scott Fitzgerald: A Descriptive Bibliography*. Rev. ed. Pittsburgh, Pa.: University of Pittsburgh Press, 1987.

Bruccoli, Matthew J. Ed. *F. Scott Fitzgerald Manuscripts*. 18 vols. New York: Garland, 1990–1991.

Carr-Saunders, A. M., and P. A. Wilson. *The Professions*. Oxford: Clarendon, 1933.

Fitzgerald, F. Scott. *As Ever, Scott Fitz——: Letters between F. Scott Fitzgerald and His Literary Agent, Harold Ober, 1919–1940*. Ed. Matthew J. Bruccoli and Jennifer McCabe Atkinson. Philadelphia, Pa.: Lippincott, 1972.

———. *The Basil and Josephine Stories*. Ed. Jackson R. Bryer and John Kuehl. New York: Scribner's, 1973.

———. *Correspondence of F. Scott Fitzgerald*. Ed. Matthew J. Bruccoli and Margaret M. Duggan. New York: Random House, 1980.

———. *Dear Scott/Dear Max: The Fitzgerald-Perkins Correspondence*. Ed. John Kuehl and Jackson R. Bryer. New York: Scribner's, 1971.

———. *Flappers and Philosophers*. Ed. James L. W. West III. Cambridge: Cambridge University Press, 2000.

———. *F. Scott Fitzgerald's Ledger: A Facsimile*. Ed. Matthew J. Bruccoli. Washington, D.C.: NCR/Microcard, 1973.

Lee, Charles. *The Hidden Public: The Story of the Book-of-the-Month Club*. Garden City, N.Y.: Doubleday, 1958.

Mangum, Bryant. *A Fortune Yet: Money in the Art of F. Scott Fitzgerald's Short Stories*. New York: Garland, 1991.

Radway, Janice A. *A Feeling for Books: The Book-of-the-Month Club, Literary Taste, and Middle-Class Desire*. Chapel Hill: University of North Carolina Press, 1997.

Rubin, Joan Shelley. *The Making of Middle/brow Culture*. Chapel Hill: University of North Carolina Press, 1992.

Schick, Frank L. *The Paperbound Book in America: The History of Paperbacks and Their European Background*. New York: Bowker, 1958.

Vollmer, Howard M., and Donald L. Mills. Eds. *Professionalization*. Englewood Cliffs, N.J.: Prentice-Hall, 1966.

West, James L. W., III. *American Authors and the Literary Marketplace since 1900*. Philadelphia: University of Pennsylvania Press, 1988.

———. "Did F. Scott Fitzgerald Have the Right Publisher?" *Sewanee Review* 100 (Fall 1992): 644–56.

———. "Fitzgerald and *Esquire*." In *The Short Stories of F. Scott*

Fitzgerald: New Approaches in Criticism. Ed. Jackson R. Bryer. Madison: University of Wisconsin Press, 1982. 149–66.

———. "Fitzgerald Explodes His Heroine." *Princeton University Library Chronicle* 49 (1988): 159–65.

———. *The Making of "This Side of Paradise."* Philadelphia: University of Pennsylvania Press, 1983.

Fitzgerald's Intellectual Context

Ronald Berman

There were concentric circles of intellectual influence around Fitzgerald, beginning with the critical ideas about literature transmitted from friends and mentors like Edmund Wilson and H. L. Mencken. After that was the constant flow of opinions and ideas from the literary marketplace in which he was located. Finally, but no less important, was the outermost circle of those who analyzed the world in which that marketplace was located.

In a 1923 interview with the *Richmond Times-Dispatch*, Fitzgerald spoke of books old and new that mattered to "the present generation." He made lists of such books often, and, as we can see from the following, he was a first-class judge of novels:

> Will James Joyce be to the next two generations what Henry James, Nietzsche, Wells, Shaw, Mencken, Dreiser and Conrad have been to the present generation? F. Scott Fitzgerald, the prophet and voice of the younger American smart set, says that while Conrad's *Nostromo* is the great novel of the past fifty years, *Ulysses* by James Joyce is the great novel of the future. In his list of "The Books I Have Enjoyed Most," Scott Fitzgerald places *A Portrait of the Artist as a Young Man* (Huebsch) as third from the top and avers that Joyce is to be "the most profound literary influence in the next fifty years."

> . . . Samuel Butler, Friedrich Nietzsche, and Anatole France were the intellectual influences which molded Fitzgerald's mind. He says this in making up his list of books he enjoyed most. (*On Authorship* 91)

These were not offhand judgments. As to James Joyce, Fitzgerald benefited from the advice of Edmund Wilson, who had helped him formulate this opinion. To express it was to state allegiance to new ideas about form and substance, leaving behind stories about flappers and undergraduates. H. L. Mencken had become editor, friend, and mentor to Fitzgerald. It was probably through Mencken that Fitzgerald developed his ideas about Nietzsche and other aspects of philosophy. He seems to have taken certain ideas from Mencken's essays on our national life, including some plots for his fiction. Joseph Conrad was not only admired by Fitzgerald but imitated by him. Conrad's work, like that of T. S. Eliot, is subcutaneously within *The Great Gatsby*. As to Dreiser, Fitzgerald prided himself on having outdone him.

Fitzgerald was an inveterate list maker, and not only of novels. He thought movies were important, admiring in particular Charlie Chaplin, Ina Claire, and Greta Garbo. He respected the work of D. W. Griffith, who had directed *The Birth of a Nation*. He called attention to the social effects of big movies like *Flaming Youth* and to controversial novels like *Lady Chatterley's Lover* (*Crack-Up* 17). He used individual authors such as Booth Tarkington as a backboard for his own stories of 1920s youth culture (*On Authorship* 86, 142). In short, as a man of letters, Fitzgerald kept abreast of both high culture and popular culture, learning how to integrate both into his work.

Fitzgerald's list making was characteristic, not idiosyncratic, of his contemporaries. Ezra Pound's *ABC of Reading* (1934) and *Literary Essays* (1935) cite classical and medieval writers and remind us that novelists like Stendhal, Flaubert, and Henry James were models for modernists. Pound was himself a direct, personal source of ideas for Ernest Hemingway. T. S. Eliot's famous apparatus of notes to *The Waste Land* (1922) sent a generation of readers back to the library. And, like other modernists, Eliot praised music-hall dance and comedy. In that he was like Edmund Wilson, who described at length lyrics, songs, and dialogues from vaudeville. In some respects, "modern" came to mean the reading of old genres as well as new.

In 1934, in his introduction to the Modern Library reprint of *The Great Gatsby*, Fitzgerald reviewed the literary situation of the recent past. He pointed out that Mencken had done a great service for literary criticism in the 1920s. Mencken had read more, knew more, and was able to apply more knowledge of literature than anyone else. He had formulated criticism as a technique based upon knowledge, not on taste. He had taken on the hitherto forbidden subjects of booze, sex, politics, and religion. In so doing Mencken had made it possible for others to produce books of lasting value rather than books of the month. Writers such as Joseph Wood Krutch and Edmund Wilson knew Mencken as the "civilized consciousness of modern America," a man who was important not only because of his satirical gifts but because he was not afraid to attack respectability (Hobson 218).[1] Nor was he shy about describing the way things were. This line from Mencken's essay "American Culture" (1920) is typical: "What one beholds, sweeping the eye over the land, is a culture that, like the national literature, is in three layers—the plutocracy on top, a vast mass of undifferentiated human blanks bossed by demagogues at the bottom, and a forlorn *intelligentsia* gasping out a precarious life between" (*Mencken Chrestomathy* 181). It was funny, exaggerated, and true enough to be a one-sentence explanation of expatriate lives.

As editor (along with George Jean Nathan) of the *Smart Set*, Mencken was able to publish writers of the younger generation like Fitzgerald. "The Diamond as Big as the Ritz" was rejected by the *Saturday Evening Post* and other midcult magazines, but Mencken ran it in June 1922. The story is a major piece of work, and Mencken showed some backbone in giving it a place in American letters. Mencken also reviewed Fitzgerald's work, corresponded with him, advised him, and made it plain that he regarded him as one of the best new young writers. However, Fitzgerald did not believe everything that Mencken had to say, while Mencken did not like everything that Fitzgerald wrote. Mencken had strong opinions about novelists, whom he thought should be realistic and satirical. That made him altogether too happy with minor leaguers like James Branch Cabell and Joseph Hergesheimer. He approved of Sinclair Lewis, who was a considerably larger figure, but Mencken was not at ease with modernists. By the mid–1920s, Mencken had managed to make two stunning mistakes: he ignored the work of Hemingway, and he failed to see that *The Great Gatsby* was above his standards. When the great American novel came to him, he did not recognize it.[2]

Mencken was useful to Fitzgerald in defining the differences between good writing and marketplace writing and, possibly most important, for providing small narratives of mental life in the cities and provinces. Many of Mencken's essays that date from 1917 to 1925 echo throughout Fitzgerald. But we want to remember that the relationship between Mencken and Fitzgerald was that of a grindstone to the knife.

Fitzgerald borrowed from Mencken's coverage of national anxieties throughout the 1920s and 1930s. Both writers addressed the great debate on "civilization," Mencken in his essays, Fitzgerald in *The Great Gatsby*. This debate was a set of opposing arguments about two connected subjects. First, how was the United States, after the Great War the world's most powerful nation, going to prove its right to preeminence? How would it surpass Europe in the sciences, industries, and arts? Second, how was it going to retain those aspects of life that originally made the United States what it was? Both Mencken and Fitzgerald were interested in the latter, because that was the issue sending off the most sparks. One side—it is beautifully represented by Tom Buchanan in *The Great Gatsby*—wanted to go back to the past. It valued race, social class, and nativism. It worried about foreigners—and also about new ideas. Here is how one writer on that side put the matter in the early 1920s: "America has suddenly been called upon to carry forward the work of civilization"—but that work will not be helped by "the latest shipment of released Ellis Islanders" who will make their homes "among the neglected residences of your own grandfathers" (Van Loon 41). In the first passage below, from thc essay "The Anglo-Saxon" (1923), Mencken formulates some problems of national identity, while in the second (from *Gatsby*) Fitzgerald gives them dramatic form:

> Whenever the Anglo-Saxon, whether of the English or of the American variety, comes into sharp conflict with men of other stocks, he tends to be worsted, or, at best, to be forced back upon extraneous and irrelevant aids to assist him in the struggle. Here in the United States his defeat is so palpable that it has filled him with vast alarms. . . . In the fine arts, in the sciences and even in the more complex sorts of business the children of the later immigrants are running away from the descendants of the early settlers. To call the roll of Americans eminent in almost any field of human endeavor . . . is to call a list of strange and often outlandish names. . . . The most elementary facts about the visible universe alarm him. (*Mencken Chrestomathy* 171, 177)

> "Civilization's going to pieces," broke out Tom violently. "I've gotten to be a terrible pessimist about things. Have you read 'The Rise of the Coloured Empires' by this man Goddard?"
>
> "Why, no," I answered, rather surprised by his tone.
>
> "Well, it's a fine book and everybody ought to read it. The idea is if we don't look out the white race will be—will be utterly submerged. It's all scientific stuff; it's been proved. . . . Well, these books are all scientific. . . . This idea is that we're Nordics. I am and you are and—" After an infinitesimal hesitation he included Daisy with a slight nod and she winked at me again, "—and we've produced all the things that go to make civilization—oh, science and art and all that." (14)

Fitzgerald took exactly the kind of list of strange and outlandish names described by Mencken and turned it into a list of those who went to Gatsby's parties—in other words, of all those who came to America and became part of it. As for Tom, the issue isn't entirely political—those "elementary facts about the visible universe" really do prey on his imagination: "It seems that pretty soon the earth's going to fall into the sun—or wait a minute—it's just the opposite—the sun's getting colder every year" (92). The reader should be aware that Mencken connected the matter of American identity with that of fake aristocracy. Tom Buchanan desperately aspires to patrician leadership: he wants to know the right people and to make sure that his wife doesn't know the wrong people. He wants everyone to listen to his "ideas," a phrase often on his lips. Yet in almost every respect he fails to live up to the criteria of real social leadership that had been stated by Henry Adams and affirmed in the 1920s by Mencken and George Santayana. The heart of aristocratic leadership is honesty, Mencken insists in "American Culture," followed by courage and freedom. It is not plutocracy, the rule of money (*Mencken Chrestomathy* 81).

One of the best places to look at this debate and also at the intellectual marketplace is through the pages of *Civilization in the United States* (1922), edited by Harold E. Stearns. This collection has become a classic of our intellectual history. Its essays on our culture range from architecture to psychology to writing; the job of its contributors was to determine what books and ideas might be useful to American writers, and what might have to be discarded. As to the latter, Lewis Mumford rejected most books about our cities, advising readers simply to look at their streets in order to see how well or badly American ideas were embodied. Mencken added that there was no self-respecting study of national politics; it was best to trudge through the pages of the *Congressional Record* and then make up one's own mind. Joel Spingarn pointed out that literary criticism was at times "pathetically inadequate" (532, 535). But there was much about America to praise. Harold Chapman Brown's notes to his essay in *Civilization in the United States* remind us that "Royce, Dewey, James, and Santayana" had just been the subjects of recent pieces in the *New Republic* (540). In fact, John Dewey and Walter Lippmann often published their own essays in its pages: Lippmann's influential *Public Opinion* (1922) first ran in *New Republic* installments. We may have to reconstruct their influence today, but William James, Dewey, Lippmann, and other public philosophers were then our best-known critics of America's condition and character. They taught at our leading universities, had great debates among themselves, delivered enormously popular public lectures, wrote for the leading journals, and were covered by the leading newspapers. Their critique of American life was the gold standard for intellectuals. As the historian Henry Steele Commager put the matter, "It is scarcely an exaggeration to say that for a generation no issue was clarified until Dewey had spoken" (qtd. in Ryan 19).[3] That was doubly true of what might be called the reincarnation of William James. James's *The Will to Believe* was published in 1919, his *Collected Essays* in 1920, *Some Problems of Philosophy* in 1921, *Talks to Teachers* in 1922, *The Varieties of Religious Experience* in 1923. The 1925 Modern Library edition of his works officially introduced him to the men and women of a new generation.

This edition was of interest for two reasons. The first was its inclusion of James's famous essays on the nature of American life; the second was its analysis of James's work on problems of modern thought. The editor of this collection, Horace M. Kallen, was determined to show how Jamesian ideas might be newly useful in the 1920s. His introduction tells its readers how William James stated the issues *of their own lives*. We draw from James, Kallen wrote, the idea that we are "separate and distinct individuals" (6), an idea that was by no means self-evident to, say, George Babbitt or the cast of characters in Sinclair Lewis's *Main Street*. A related point: our individual experience is to be valued fully as much as any doctrine we may have inherited, whether religious or political. Just how important was this idea to become in the era of modernism? A recent history reminds us of what might reasonably be called the tyranny of the past, the "overbearing deterministic formal systems of nineteenth-century historicism" that told us in minute detail what truth was or might be—or should be. Of more immediate importance was the modern rejection of lives "regulated by social conventions" from the past (Kern 63). Once James had asserted the uniqueness of human experience, the conditions for modern ideas of personal freedom were set.

But James also told the next generation that life in our world would be difficult. He understood that the scientific advances that took place from 1880 on would establish a sense of relativity and even of discontinuity. That conception, too, was due to become part of modernism. Kallen put it this way: a free life is governed by "hazard of belief and hazard of enterprise" (8–9). The idea was to be developed by John Dewey in his essays on alienated national life in the 1920s—and it was certainly one of the underpinnings of Ernest Hemingway's idea of the way things were.

Life, James said, may have been *granted*, but it really needed to be *won*.

As for Fitzgerald, behind the conception of Jay Gatsby lay the Jamesian belief that the energy of individual desire is a social good. The story of Jay Gatsby is also the story of how Nick Carraway comes to understand what he sees. Perhaps James can best tell us about the hard job of being a witness to humanity: "An unlearned carpenter of my acquaintance once said in my hearing: 'There is very little difference between one man and another; but what little there is, *is very important*.'" James himself added, "*Everything* we know and are is through men. We have no revelation but through man. Every sentiment that warms your gizzard, every brave act that ever made your pulse bound and your nostril open to a confidant[*sic*] breath was a man's act. However mean a man may be, man is *the best we know*" (242–43, 249). These ideas matter in Fitzgerald; they force us to ask why Jay Gatsby became great.

When we look back (it is now the better part of a century since Fitzgerald began his writing career) we see how complex and interrelated ideas then were. The word "great" is not often used today to describe character, but it was often in use then. James took it as a matter of course that Americans should admire greatness, and the Modern Library edition brought together many of his statements on the subject. He wrote, for example, that it is only by witnessing greatness that "each one of us may best fortify and inspire what creative energy may lie in his own soul." There is an awful lot of criticism in our own time that devalues Jay Gatsby because he is impulsive, immature, and passionate beyond measure. Yet critics have not examined James's essays for a full understanding of idealism from the turn of the twentieth century through the 1920s. This is the model James gave to writers whose subject was their country and its character: "God bless the American climate, with its transparent, passionate, impulsive variety and headlong fling. There are deeper, slower tones of earnestness and moral gravity here, no doubt, but ours is more like youth and youth's infinite and touching promise" (246, 252). This resonates nowhere more plainly than in a passage on youthful belief in American greatness from Fitzgerald's first novel, *This Side of Paradise*:

> People try so hard to believe in leaders now, pitifully hard. But we no sooner get a popular reformer or politician or soldier or writer or philosopher—a Roosevelt, a Tolstoi, a Wood, a Shaw, a Nietzsche, than the cross-currents of criticism wash him away. . . . We *want* to believe. Young students try to believe in older authors, constituents try to believe in their Congressmen, countries try to believe in their statesmen, but they *can't*. Too many voices, too much scattered, illogical, ill-considered criticism. It's worse in the case of newspapers. Any rich, unprogressive old party with that particularly grasping, acquisitive form of mentality known as financial genius can own a paper that is the intellectual meat and drink of thousands of tired, hurried men too involved in the business of modern living to swallow anything but predigested food. For two cents the voter buys his politics, prejudices and philosophy. (199–200)

Even the no-nonsense literary critic Van Wyck Brooks had written shortly before *This Side of Paradise* appeared that "we above all peoples need great men and great ideals" (99). It is difficult and I think pointless to criticize Gatsby's obsession with love after learning from Brooks that we need to lose our sense of material selves and gain instead "spiritual experience in our blood" (120). The public philosophy of which James was the major figure was concerned not only with ideas but with character.

Here is what Josiah Royce pointed out in 1908, when a young Fitzgerald was just beginning to pick up ideas:

> What do we live for? What is our duty? What is the true ideal of life? What is the true difference between right and wrong? What is the true good which we all need? Whoever begins seriously to consider such questions as these soon observes certain great truths about the moral life which he must take into account. . . . We all of us first learned about what we ought to do, about what our ideal should be, and in general about the moral law, through some authority external to our own wills. Our teachers, our parents, our playmates, society, custom, or perhaps some church,—these taught us about one or another aspect of right and wrong. (2:864)

We remind ourselves of the deep ethical structure of Fitzgerald's fiction—and, I think, of his own life. Throughout his stories and novels, there are choices that are either right or wrong. We are asked in "The Diamond as Big as the Ritz" whether it is possible for great wealth to make its own rules—a question that reverberates in *The Great Gatsby*. In "Babylon Revisited" there are burning questions that need to be answered by Charlie Wales before he can get his daughter back from the custody of her aunt. When Charlie considers the meaning of his life, both past and present, we see realistic moral imagination. Nowhere is Fitzgerald's mind shown to better advantage than in the closing pages of *Gatsby*, in which Nick Carraway realizes that he has to take a stand and finally separate himself from the soft and comfortable world of no decisions. He understands that resolve takes the form of an act—which necessarily produces a consequence. In order to do justice to Gatsby—simply in order to give him a decent burial—Nick has to lose a great deal. Love and friendship give way to loyalty and self-respect, the moment of decision reminding us of the scripts that the books and essays of the public philosophy had so often provided.

Fitzgerald's novels have important passages in which major characters ask each other what they are going to do with their lives. In *The Beautiful and Damned*, Anthony Patch resists that question. He does not want to exert the force of consciousness required to answer. In *The Great Gatsby*, Daisy Buchanan must ask what people do with their lives because she does not know how to get through her own. From the beginning of *Gatsby* to the end, Daisy is depicted as beautiful, charming, even overwhelming—but without the power of decision. The narrative tells us that she married Tom Buchanan perhaps for love, perhaps for money—and certainly because she needs some outside "force" to shape her life (118). Fitzgerald drew many such characters in his fiction. One important reason was the abrupt change of social context during the first quarter of the twentieth century. Walter Lippmann, who updated the public philosophy for the new generation, had argued in two important books that our national character had developed in ways that few were able to foresee. In *Drift and Mastery* (1914) he outlined a new sense of national character—weak, dependent, unable to assert consciousness or will. In so doing he provided writers with a new view of their subject. One of the best-known passages of *Drift and Mastery* concerns the problem of individual freedom, which was to be accentuated during the 1920s:

> Effort wells up, beats bravely against reality, and in weariness simmers down into routine or fantasy. . . . This abandonment of effort is due, I imagine to the fact that the conscious mastery of experience is, comparatively speaking, a new turn in human culture. The old absolutisms of caste and church and state made more modest demands than democracy does: life was settled and fantasy was organized into ritual and riveted by authority. But the modern world swings wide and loose, it has thrown men upon their own responsibility. And for that gigantic task they lack experience, they are fettered and bound and finally broken. . . . No wonder then that those who win freedom are often unable to use it; no wonder that liberty brings its despair. (331, 333)

Specifically, Lippmann meant that anyone interested in understanding his own time would first have to understand that icons of the past no longer existed. The family was no longer sacrosanct; religion, community, and other forms of social authority had disappeared. As he put the matter in *Public Opinion* the young (1922), were guided by new habits, not by old morals. One recalls that Fitzgerald invariably illustrates the social context in terms of failed connections between past and present. In Fitzgerald, those who are part of that "youth culture" have no older people whose opinion they respect and no sacred texts to invoke. They are, as Lippmann suggested, alone in history (xvii–xviii). In fact, in "The Scandal Detectives" (1928), one of his best stories, Fitzgerald describes a mother at one end of the "infinite and unbridgeable" gap between generations. Her own thoughts "would have been comprehensible to her great-grandmother" but are unintelligible to her own children (*Stories* 309).

Lippmann's *Public Opinion* appeared in 1922. Among the points made in that volume is the rejection of the Idea of Progress—

more accurately, of the current social version of that idea. We remind ourselves of the trajectory of lives described by Fitzgerald, Hemingway, and even by Lewis. In a culture in which everyone seems to be going somewhere, in which the watchword is success and in which progress is confused with upward social mobility, these authors' characters seem often to be moving in reverse. Even George Babbitt, who actually believes in the idols of the marketplace, finds that "success" may carry a price too high to pay. Fitzgerald's stories and novels in particular are about the *ending* of dreams, not their fulfillment. His two best novels (*Gatsby* and *Tender Is the Night*) end in self-imposed exile, not in success. In short, writers with a tragic view of life had something to learn from the analysis of America provided in Lippmann's *Public Opinion*:

> The stereotype represented by such words as "progress" and "perfection" was composed fundamentally of mechanical inventions. And mechanical it has remained . . . to this day. In America more than anywhere else, the spectacle of mechanical progress has made so deep an impression, that it has suffused the whole moral code.
>
> Not every American, of course, sees the world this way. Henry Adams didn't, and William Allen White doesn't. But those men do, who in the magazines devoted to the religion of success appear as Makers of America. They mean just about that when they preach evolution, progress, prosperity, being constructive, the American way of doing things. . . . the ideal confuses excellence with size, happiness with speed, and human nature with contraption. (71–72)

Fitzgerald wrote a great deal about one material form that the idea of progress took in America, that of great houses and many not so great. It might take a considerable time to collate his architectonic images. He has provided the many houses in his fiction with their provenance, and they have known marketplace value.[5] He describes the acquisition of places built to express wealth and confidence in "The Diamond as Big as the Ritz" and *The Great Gatsby*. But these places do not last long. They endure just about every fate known to man and realty, from aging to being blown up by explosives. Towns, neighborhoods, buildings, and even a certain billboard in *Gatsby* take on heavily symbolic values, suggesting at first confidence, success, and that elusive idea of progress, then suggesting the far greater natural powers of entropy. Among the lively arts, Fitzgerald was attuned to music, movies, and design. He understood the use of the latter in fiction: it was the largest source of imagery in the public realm. The spirit of American place is captured by the alkali dust drowning the village of Fish, the billboard of Dr. Eckleburg, the wreckage of the palace of the Washingtons in "Diamond," and, finally, by the dark and empty house of Jay Gatsby.

The following passages, the first from "Dice, Brass Knuckles & Guitar" (1923) and the second from "Two for a Cent" (1922), demonstrate the extent to which Fitzgerald used landmark design to express his own ideas about the idea of Progress:

> Here and there lie patches of garden country dotted with old-fashioned frame mansions, which have wide shady porches and a red swing on the lawn. And perhaps, on the widest and shadiest of the porches there is even a hammock left over from the hammock days, stirring gently in a mid-Victorian wind. When tourists come to such last-century landmarks they stop their cars and gaze for a while and then mutter: "Well, thank God this age is joined on to *some*thing." (*Short Stories* 237)

> Bungalows . . . were reproducing their species . . . as though by some monstrous affiliation with the guinea-pig; it was the most common type of house in the country. For thirty years such dwellings had satisfied the canons of the middle class; they had satisfied its financial canons by being cheap, they had satisfied its aesthetic canons by being hideous. It was a house built by a race whose more energetic complement hoped either to move up or move on. (*Price* 34)

These passages represent what should be called Fitzgerald's provincial strategy. The first, set in New Jersey, shows us American history left behind. We bear in mind that the phrase "Victorian" is not always pejorative in Fitzgerald: as the passage suggests, we are connected to something deeply meaningful. The second passage describes the experience of the South, which has unwillingly come to follow the northern ideology. Fitzgerald often invoked the South's resistance to change as a symbol of historical and personal *strength*. He did so against the national grain—Mencken and others were busy trying to prove that southern traditionalism led only to decline. But Fitzgerald's connection to the South, personal and professional, argues the opposite. For example, the color gold often appears in his southern stories, suggesting a haunting beauty that deserves to be remembered. Particularly in "The Ice Palace" (1920), Fitzgerald thinks in images: "the sunlight dripped over the house like golden paint over an art jar and the freckling shadows here and there only intensified the rigor of the bath of light" (*Stories* 48). We are looking at more than a historical reference. The extended description of Tarleton, Georgia, reflects the debate on "civilization" but is stated in more compelling form. I note that Fitzgerald is not being simply "poetic" but also dialectical. There were *two* mythologies of American life, that of the golden future and that of the golden past. One mythology was northern, the other belonged to the South. And *both were fictions*.[6]

Fitzgerald was a fluent translator of public ideas. He understood that the nature of American issues in his time was more cultural than political. When they find expression in his work, they tend to be more acutely stated than they had been before he thought about them. One doesn't want to think of him the way that Mencken and Edmund Wilson did, as a great talent with superficial intelligence. The men who said that are no longer on our map. Fitzgerald succeeded because he deployed ideas about national character and life in a more convincing way than his opposition. One might think of his connection to that life in the terms framed by his great contemporary, Ludwig Wittgenstein: "I believe my originality (if that is the right word) is an originality belonging to the soil rather than to the seed. . . . Sow a seed in my soil and it will grow differently than it would in any other soil" (qtd. in Stroll 5).

NOTES

1. Hobson reprints Fitzgerald's remark that Mencken had "done more for the national letters than any man alive." But see the sixth chapter of *The Sun Also Rises* for Hemingway's very different opinion.

2. For Mencken's assessment of Fitzgerald, see *My Life as Author and Editor*, 256–66.

3. See also Commager's *The American Mind* for more on the role of public philosophers in shaping American ideas. For the relevance of James and Dewey to Fitzgerald, see Berman, *"The Great Gatsby" and Fitzgerald's World of Ideas*, 29–30. Finally, Posnock succinctly interprets James's influence on twentieth-century intellectuals.

4. For the relevance of Lippmann's ideas to this keystone year of modernism, see North.

5. For an assessment of both the provenance of these houses and their value, see O'Meara 11–21.

6. For more on this distinction, see Brooks's *William Faulkner: Toward Yoknapatawpha and Beyond*, 272.

WORKS CITED

Berman, Ronald. *"The Great Gatsby" and Fitzgerald's World of Ideas*. Tuscaloosa: University of Alabama Press, 1997.

Brooks, Cleanth. *William Faulkner: Toward Yoknapatawpha and Beyond*. New Haven, Conn.: Yale University Press, 1978.

Brooks, Van Wyck. *America's Coming-of-Age*. 1934. Garden City, N.Y.: Doubleday, 1958.

Commager, Henry Steele. *The American Mind: An Interpretation of American Thought and Character since the 1880s*. New Haven, Conn.: Yale University Press, 1950.

Fitzgerald, F. Scott. *The Crack-Up*. Ed. Edmund Wilson. New York: New Directions, 1945.

———. *F. Scott Fitzgerald on Authorship*. Ed. Matthew J. Bruccoli and Judith S. Baughman. Columbia: University of South Carolina Press, 1996.

———. *The Great Gatsby*. 1925. Ed. Matthew J. Bruccoli. Cambridge: Cambridge University Press, 1991.

———. *The Price Was High: The Last Uncollected Stories of F. Scott*

Fitzgerald. Ed. Matthew J. Bruccoli. New York: Harcourt Brace Jovanovich / Bruccoli Clark, 1979.

———. *The Short Stories of F. Scott Fitzgerald*. Ed. Matthew J. Bruccoli. New York: Scribner's, 1989.

———. *The Stories of F. Scott Fitzgerald*. Ed. Malcolm Cowley. New York: Scribner's, 1951.

———. *This Side of Paradise*. 1920. Ed. James L. W. West III. New York: Cambridge University Press, 1995.

Hobson, Fred. *Mencken: A Life*. New York: Random House, 1994.

James, William. *The Philosophy of William James, Drawn from His Own Works*. Ed. Horace M. Kallen. New York: Modern Library, 1925.

Kern, Stephen. *The Culture of Time and Space 1880–1918*. Cambridge, Mass.: Harvard University Press, 1983.

Lippmann, Walter. *Drift and Mastery: An Attempt to Diagnose the Current Unrest*. New York: Mitchell Kennerley, 1914.

———. *Public Opinion*. 1922. New York: Free Press, 1997.

Mencken, H. L. *A Mencken Chrestomathy*. New York: Knopf, 1949.

———. *My Life as Author and Editor*. Ed. Jonathan Yardley. New York: Knopf, 1992.

North, Michael. *Reading 1922: A Return to the Scene of the Modern*. New York: Oxford University Press, 2000.

O'Meara, Lauraleigh. *Lost City: Fitzgerald's New York*. New York: Routledge, 2002.

Posnock, Ross. "The Influence of William James on American Culture." In *The Cambridge Companion to William James*. Ed. Ruth Anna Putnam. Cambridge: Cambridge University Press, 1997. 322–42.

Royce, Josiah. "The Philosophy of Loyalty." In *The Basic Writings of Josiah Royce*. 2 vols. Ed. John J. McDermott. Chicago, Ill.: University of Chicago Press, 1969. 855–1014.

Ryan, Alan. *John Dewey and the High Tide of American Liberalism*. New York: Norton, 1995.

Stearns, Harold E. Ed. *Civilization in the United States*. London: Cape, 1922.

Stroll, Avrum. *Wittgenstein*. Oxford: Oneworld, 2002.

Van Loon, Hendrik Willem. "The American Naissance." *Vanity Fair* 18 (May 1922): 41.

Fitzgerald's Consumer World

Kirk Curnutt

> You resemble the advertisement of the man. . . .
> You know the advertisement of the man—
> —Daisy Buchanan to Jay Gatsby

The February 22, 1929, issue of the *Princeton Alumni Weekly* features one of the oddest autobiographical vignettes that F. Scott Fitzgerald ever wrote. Commissioned for an issue on media images of the exalted Ivy League institution, "Ten Years in the Advertising Business" purports to be a dialogue between "Mr. Fitzgerald," a copywriting drudge, and an employer with the Dickensian name of "Mr. Cakebook." When the former complains that he cannot subsist on his paltry salary, the latter reprimands him as "too temperamental" and "too fancy, too imaginative" and suggests that his talents would be better utilized if he loaned his picture and name to a beauty contest that the company is sponsoring. Mr. Fitzgerald reluctantly complies, and the conversation takes an odd, melancholy turn prompted by Mr. Cakebook's inquiry into the young man's personal life:

> "Did I understand you to say you're about to get married?" he asked.
>
> "Oh, no, I've been married ten years. That was back before those little dots [the ellipsis in the text]."

"It must have been some other couple."

"It was," I assured him. "Only the names were the same. The tissues change every decade. Good-bye, Mr. Cakebook."

"Good-bye, Mr. Fitzgerald." (*Afternoon of an Author* 126)

The sketch makes little sense without knowledge of the two biographical events it conflates. The first half of the story refers to a pivotal moment in the Fitzgerald legend when, in July 1919, the then twenty-two-year-old college dropout and discharged army officer quit his job as a composer of trolley-card jingles for the New York advertising agency Barron Collier. With neither money nor prospects, Fitzgerald repaired to his parents' home in St. Paul, Minnesota, where he hurriedly revised a manuscript already twice rejected by the publisher Charles Scribner's Sons into his first novel, *This Side of Paradise*, which Scribner's went on to publish to great notoriety in March 1920. By 1929, the story of Fitzgerald abandoning a dead-end career for one final shot at both literary eminence and the girl of his dreams—Zelda Sayre had refused to marry him until he proved he could support her in style—was a familiar one; it had been told and retold in virtually every newspaper and magazine account of the writer's rise to fame, and a fictional version of it appears in *This Side of Paradise*. The tale no doubt inspired envy if not resentment among former colleagues at Barron Collier. As the industry journal *Printer's Ink* noted at the time, many copywriters fancied themselves "unappreciated poets and unstaged dramatists" who found catering to the whims of clients reduced them to the role of "literary courtesans." "It would be interesting to watch some of these morons edit Shakespeare's copy!" one indignant contributor groused. While such men may have daydreamed of quitting work to "write The Great American Novel" (qtd. in Marchand 43, 40), most spent their lives inventing slogans like the one Mr. Fitzgerald submits to Mr. Cakebook: "We Keep You Clean in Muskateen."

The second story to which "Ten Years in the Advertising Business" refers was neither celebrated nor well known. Throughout 1929, the likeness of the then *thirty*-two-year-old Fitzgerald appeared along with those of actor John Barrymore and socialite

Cornelius Vanderbilt, Jr., in ads in *Ladies' Home Journal* promoting a beauty contest sponsored by the Woodbury Soap company. (Ostensibly, the trio judged the competition, although no extant evidence suggests that any of them participated in the selection process.) That Fitzgerald was embarrassed by his affiliation with Woodbury Soap is evident from the resentful tone with which he tells the story in the *Princeton Alumni Weekly*: "It's understood," he admonishes Mr. Cakebook, as if clinging to his last shred of artistic integrity, "that I'm in no sense to endorse this product" (*Afternoon of an Author* 125).[1] The point seems to be the author's remorseful recognition that he never escaped the advertising business; during the decade to which the title alludes, the commodity he has sold has merely been himself, not Muskateen Laundry.[2] His closing assertion that he and his wife are not the same people they were in 1919 ("only the names were the same") seems an admission that his complicity in this trade has cost him the naïveté that allowed him to become a professional writer. His subsequent comment about the tissues changing every ten years is doubly resonant: while evoking Fitzgerald's grief over the marital strife, drinking, and money woes that impeded his work and derailed the couple's glamorous life, it also suggests the unceasing cycles of new products like facial tissue (which Kleenex first introduced to the marketplace in 1924) whose consumption advertising was designed to stoke. And just as these goods were made to be thrown away rather than preserved, so, too, Fitzgerald insinuates, his willingness to cash in on his brand name compromises the durability of his work. When viewed as commerce rather than literature, his writing and reputation amount to little more than a fad or fashion doomed to disposability—a fear no doubt keenly felt in a year that saw his commercial fiction fetching maximum prices of $4,000 per story while progress stalled on the long-delayed follow-up to *The Great Gatsby* (1925), which he hoped would revive his flagging artistic reputation.[3]

However sketchily, "Ten Years in the Advertising Business" conveys the disdain for what Malcolm Cowley called "the stultifying effects of a civilization ruled by business" that many writers cultivated between the two world wars (58). America's slavish devotion to commerce in this period, as historian Michael E. Parrish writes, occurred because its citizens enjoyed "a rising standard of living and luxury unknown on their continent or to the human race generally . . . [for] in this decade they experienced something that eluded virtually all later generations: full employment and low inflation" (30).[4] But while the Great Boom inaugurated an era of prosperity unmatched until the late 1990s bull market, it also inspired criticism for its indifference to intellectual and artistic life. This was a time, after all, when President Calvin Coolidge praised business with a reverence once reserved for religion: "The man who builds a factory builds a temple. The man who works there, worships there" (qtd. in Dumenil 28). Accordingly, as Fitzgerald portrays him, Mr. Cakebook is not only unimaginative but antiliterary, his disregard for creativity reminiscent of the decade's most famous philistine, Sinclair Lewis's George F. Babbitt, to whom all art is an anathema if it does not advance the economy. Fitzgerald's satire of advertising lingo—Mr. Cakebook revises the doggerel cadence of "We Keep You Clean in Muskateen" into the purely descriptive "Muskateen Laundry—We Clean and Press"—also recalls contemporaries like James Joyce and John Dos Passos, who incorporated actual ad slogans into *Ulysses* (1922) and *U.S.A.* (1929–1936) to demonstrate how commerce steals the poetic soul of words, reducing them to barren banalities. Finally, the gloomy awareness that authorship is not immune to salesmanship reflects the central complaint that the modernist generation leveled against American culture: it provided no autonomous space outside of the closed circuit of buying and selling for the literary arts to flower. Not surprisingly, a dominant theme of American writing between 1900 and 1940 is the artist's need to resist commodification and to work outside of marketplace constraints. Such is the plot of innumerable novels, stories, and poems, from Willa Cather's *The Troll Garden* (1905) and Theodore Dreiser's *The Genius* (1906) to Sherwood Anderson's *Windy McPherson's Son* (1916) and Ezra Pound's *Hugh Selwyn Mauberly* (1920), to name an eclectic quartet.

At first glance, Fitzgerald might seem an unlikely ally in the literary critique of 1920s consumer culture, for few writers reveled so blatantly in the "greatest, gaudiest spree in human history" that was the postwar boom (*Crack-Up* 87). As early as 1921, Edmund Wilson rebuked his fellow Princetonian for his materialism, which in Wilson's view made him incapable of appreciating the Old World aestheticism that modernists idealized: "You are so saturated with twentieth-century America, bad as well as good—you are so used to hotels, plumbing, drug stores . . . and the commercial prosperity of the country—that you can't appreciate those institutions of France, which are really superior to American ones" (*Letters* 63). This saturation was evident not only in the notorious profligacy with which Fitzgerald conducted his personal affairs; it was prominent, too, in the spendthrift image he promoted in self-deprecating essays such as "How to Live on $36,000 a Year" and "How to Live on Practically Nothing a Year," both of which appeared in the *Saturday Evening Post* in 1924. Most important, his consumerist fascinations are everywhere evident in his fiction, which luxuriates in the tints and textures of consumable goods. So packed with accoutrements of decor and leisure are many of his descriptive passages that his prose radiates the extravagance of detail that one associates with the catalog copy of high-end retailers. One thinks, for instance, of the famous moment in *The Great Gatsby* when the eponymous hero showers Daisy Buchanan with tailor-made shirts "piled like bricks in stacks a dozen high" in his patent cabinets:

> He took out a pile of shirts and began throwing them one by one before us, shirts of sheer linen and thick silk and fine flannel which lost their folds as they fell and covered the table in many-colored disarray. While we admired he brought more and the soft heap mounted higher—shirts with stripes and scrolls and plaids in coral and apple green and lavender and faint orange with monograms of Indian blue. Suddenly with a strained sound Daisy bent her head into the shirts and began to cry stormily. (97–98)

Shirts are but one item upon which Fitzgerald lavishes his prodigious lyricism. Elsewhere, he describes cut-glass bowls, blue porcelain bathtubs, yellow roadsters, chiffon dresses and silk stockings, saffron hats, pink-shaded lamps with blackbirds painted on them, Circassian leather lounges, tortoise-shell eyeglasses (a badge of "slickerhood," according to *This Side of Paradise*), as well of jewels of all varieties, from emeralds to rubies to diamonds—including at least one as big as the Ritz Hotel.

The prominence of such objects has for decades led Marxist critics to debate whether Fitzgerald encouraged or critiqued commodity fetishism. The question suggests the complexity of his attitude toward consumerism. Precisely because Fitzgerald labored in the ambiguous interstices of commerce and art by seeking to amass a financial and critical fortune, his insights into the effects of "the most expensive orgy in history" (*Crack-Up* 21) are more varied and nuanced than those of his chief rivals. Ernest Hemingway cloaked his heroes in a veil of asceticism meant to dramatize their resolve to not succumb to modern excesses; Dos Passos's leftism led him to flatten his characters into satiric ciphers symbolizing capitalist corruption. Fitzgerald, by contrast, appreciated the pros and cons of commodity culture, and, as a result, his oeuvre reverberates with both the giddy opportunities and somber pitfalls posed by the expanding American marketplace. In general, his ambivalence can be measured through the prism of three important concerns that consumerism brought to the forefront of cultural debate: (1) whether the marketplace offered individuals new opportunities for self-definition or whether it trapped them in mechanistic spending habits; (2) whether the abstraction of financial values occasioned by the proliferation of stock speculation and consumer credit occasioned a concomitant abstraction in ethical values; and (3) whether the normalization of wastage engineered through the planned obsolescence of goods was an inconsequential by-product of a demand for cultural progress (epitomized by the advertising cachet of "new and improved") or whether it marked a darker, more troublesome aesthetic of squandering that celebrated disposability as a privilege of abundance.

The Marketplace of Self-Making: Consumerism, Identity, Gender

The changes wrought by consumerism in the early twentieth century were writ most visibly in conceptions of identity. Selfhood before the modern age had been defined by such comparatively deterministic criteria as class, race, regionalism, and morality. Yet the explosion of consumable goods provided individuals with new tools for packaging their personalities in vibrant and captivating ways, which fell under the general rubric of *style*. As Stuart Ewen writes, "Style was a way of saying who one was, or who one wished to be. The emerging market in stylized goods provided consumers with a vast palette of symbolic meanings, to be selected and juxtaposed in the assembling of a public self" (*Images* 79). This assemblage, it should be noted, was not presumed to be an imagistic collage of the kind we today think of as postmodern; rather than a *simulacra* or semblance, to use terms popularized by Jean Baudrillard, consumer goods facilitated the externalization of an authentic self inhibited by confusion and timidity. Advertising insisted that consumption would eventuate "wholeness," a term that designated the integrated sense of health, well-being, and happiness necessary for individuals to survive the fractures of modernity and to maximize their full psychological and economic potential. "Every man is a combination of many different personalities, a battlefield in which the fighters are his different selves," advertising guru Bruce Barton wrote in a 1928 *Good Housekeeping* article. "The best self is the real self" (58). For the captains of industry, consumption was not a means of constructing a false personality but of manifesting the "real" person.

Barton belonged to a prominent coterie of advertising chieftains who proselytized the benefits of consumption with evangelical glee. The religious rhetoric here is appropriate, for the cofounder of Batten, Barton, Durstine, and Osborn (BBD&O), one of the top five American advertising agencies in the 1920s, was best known for *The Man Nobody Knows* (1925), a book whose message Fitzgerald's editor, Maxwell Perkins, summarized while trying to convince Charles Scribner to publish it: "It treats Christ as a supersalesman, a go-getter, a man with a talent for business. Of course it might sell" (qtd. in Berg 135). Perkins's instinct was correct, for by the decade's end more than a quarter-million copies of Barton's rereading of the Gospels were in print—much to the chagrin of Scribner's, which, despite Perkins's enthusiasm, had declined the manuscript.

The Man Nobody Knows owed its success to its vision of Christ as a bold, charismatic leader, the "founder of modern business" (v) and the ultimate example of "executive success" (23). For contemporary readers, the virile and magnetic managerial personality described here can seem laughably hypermasculine, for Barton's intent, as he outlines in his preface, is to redeem Jesus from generations of dowdy Sunday school teachers responsible for a "sissified" image of the Son of God (ii). Yet, however excessive, the entrepreneurial initiative and talent for persuasion attributed to Christ soothed 1920s fears about the morality of consumption by assuring audiences that Christianity and capitalism were compatible. In a strikingly literal bit of exegesis, Barton spends an entire chapter hammering home this point by sermonizing on the moment in Luke 2:49 when a preadolescent Jesus answers his mother's rebuke for quizzing Jerusalem priests on God's wisdom. As Jesus responds, "How is it that ye sought me? Wist ye not that I must be about my father's business?" "He thought of his life as *business*," Barton declares before insisting that the word's spiritual and secular connotations are synonymous:

> Ask any ten people what Jesus meant by his "Father's business," and nine of them will answer "preaching." To interpret the words in this narrow sense is to lose the real significance of his life. It was not to preach that he came into the world; nor to teach; nor to heal. These are all departments of his Father's business, but the business itself is far larger, more inclusive. For if human life has any significance it is this—that God has set going here an experiment to which all His resources are committed. He seeks to develop perfect human beings. . . . No single kind of human talent or effort can be spared if this experiment is to succeed. The race must be fed and

> clothed and housed and transported as well as preached to, and taught and healed. Thus *all* business is his Father's business. (179–80)

Commerce is thus God's work, too, because it is part of the process of "develop[ing] perfect human beings"—and it is every bit as essential a part as ministerial or devout actions. Interestingly, Fitzgerald also refers to Luke 2:49 in *The Great Gatsby* when describing James Gatz's transformation into the titular hero, whose magnetism approximates the Bartonesque ideal:

> The truth was that Jay Gatsby, of West Egg, Long Island, sprang from the Platonic conception of himself. He was a son of God—a phrase which, if it means anything, means just that—and he must be about His Father's Business, the service of a vast, vulgar, meretricious beauty. So he invented the sort of Jay Gatsby that a seventeen year old boy would be likely to invent, and to this conception he was faithful to the end. (104).

Obviously, Fitzgerald satirizes the entrepreneurial appropriation of the Gospels for which Barton would become famous, yet the coincidental allusion dramatizes how ingrained the business ethos was in modern ideas of selfhood. The calibrating of salesmanship and salvation was even made iconographic at the height of Barton's popularity with an ad described by Perkins, still lamenting Scribner's missed opportunity, in a letter to Fitzgerald: "Did you see that [ad] of Bruce Barton's 'The Man Nobody Knows' headed 'Christ the Executive' illustrated with two pictures, in juxtaposition, of groups of men around a table? One showed Christ and the twelve apostles; the other a twentieth century 'Chairman of the Board' and the directors of a corporation." The image, Perkins noted, captured the business-minded mood of America; it gave off "a genuine whiff of the U.S.A." (*Dear Scott/Dear Max* 143).

As Simone Weil Davis has argued, Barton's Jesus epitomized a paradigm shift in which "masculine selfhood" was defined by "the persuasive impact one had on others, rather than in the monadic integrity of self-reliance" (2) advanced by such nineteenth-century exemplars of rugged individualism as Emerson and Thoreau. In both advertising and self-improvement literature, the equation of "male subjectivity [with] effective salesmanship" (46) conferred agency upon the ideal man, creating the illusion that his consumer habits were their own mode of production. Fashioning a personal style out of items offered by the marketplace was not a decorative act but a functional one, for it was essential to the successful negotiation of everyday transactions, whether commercial or romantic.[5] As one might expect, such was not the case for women. The dominant model of female self-making emphasized objectification, with women encouraged to discover their true selves through beautification rather than assertive extroversion. This does not mean they were reduced to passive vessels, however—far from it. The diversity of consumable goods meant that the marketplace empowered female consumers with variety, so that feminine self-realization involved not just adornment but the discrimination and discipline required to make informed purchases. Armed with these attributes, women—at least as advertisers depicted them—became "the repository of choice and freedom that mass-marketed goods were said to encompass. Women were invested with a high degree of political and social determining power—a formation which linked the expanding commodity market with the political climate born out of suffrage" (Ewen, *Captains*, 168).[6] Thus, according to the marketplace, men achieved their ultimate embodiment by selling, women by buying.

The relevance of this gendered dynamic to Fitzgerald's fiction becomes clear when we recall that his prototypical story involves "a young man devis[ing] an elaborate plot . . . in order to win an imperious girl" (Bruccoli 130). In more commercial variations on this story line, buying and selling are the constituent metaphors of romance, with commodities playing no small part in brokering the exchange. In *This Side of Paradise*, for example, Amory Blaine woos Isabelle Borgé (a character based on Ginevra King, whom Fitzgerald courted in his adolescence) by donning "a close-fitting dress suit and a silk ruffled shirt of the kind that women still delight to see men wear, but men were just beginning to get tired of" (66). Isabelle proves a formidable challenge, for mass culture has minted her romantic expectations, whether through its imagery (she is initially disappointed that Amory is not "dark and of garter-advertisement" slenderness) or its rhythms (Jerome Kern's popular song "Babes in the Woods," which plays in the background as Amory steals a first kiss, functions as a virtual aphrodisiac). Significantly, when Fitzgerald describes Isabelle's fantasies of love, Amory is the most expendable element in the tableau: "The future vista of her life seemed an unending succession of scenes like this. Under moonlight and pale starlight, and in the backs of warm limousines and in low, cosey[*sic*] roadsters stopped under sheltering trees—only the boy might change" (71). Isabelle conducts her affairs with just the kind of shrewdness attributed to women in such proconsumerist tracts as Carl Naether's *Advertising to Women* (1928), Paul Nystrom's *Economics of Fashion* (1928), Christine Frederick's *Selling Mrs. Consumer* (1929), and Elizabeth Hurlock's *Motivation in Fashion* (1929): she knows what she wants, and she is shopping for the right supplier.

Because *This Side of Paradise* depicts adolescent love as a game of poses, it is not surprising that Amory and Isabelle's affair ends abruptly. What is surprising is the cause of the breakup: during a "petting" session, Amory's shirt stud pinches Isabelle's neck, causing an "Old Nick" (flapper slang for a "hickey"). For Isabelle, the sudden intrusion of function over fashion destroys her image of Amory as a debonair figure; he is merely a boy whose fondness for sartorial ostentation has now marked her, literally, as a "speed," a flapper with a reputation for indiscriminate kissing. Isabelle's sudden coolness excites Amory's desire: "He wanted to kiss her, kiss her a lot, because then he knew he could leave in the morning and not care. On the contrary, if he didn't kiss her, it would worry him. . . . It would interfere vaguely with his idea of himself as a conqueror" (90). In the economy of teenage seduction, the kiss "seals the deal," so to speak, the sign of a successful transaction. When Amory realizes that Isabelle no longer "buys" his image, he cannot accept the possibility that she can resist him, and he fantasizes of overwhelming her with sheer pushiness—*not*, again, to reassure her of the genuineness of his affection but to confirm his own entrepreneurial prowess. In effect, Amory imagines abandoning the soft approach to give Isabelle the "hard sell."

This Side of Paradise is atypical of Fitzgerald's fiction in that Amory's varied attempts to create a personality through style detour his journey to self-discovery. More commonly, the persuasive tactics that beaux employ to win over the objects of their affection enable the realization of their true selves—even, paradoxically, when seduction requires them to assume actual disguises. In "The Offshore Pirate" (1920), Toby Moreland adopts the piratical persona of outlaw Curtis Carlyle to capture the affections of Ardita Farnam. As Toby knows, Ardita has no interest in meeting him, for he has already sought an audience with her through his uncle, a friend of Ardita's family. The plot is thus an effort to demonstrate that, despite appearances, he is passionate and exciting. Indeed, in one passage, Fitzgerald even suggests that Toby needs to convince himself as much as Ardita that he possesses these qualities: "Ardita scrutinized him carefully—and classed him immediately as a romantic figure. He gave the effect of towering self-confidence erected on a slight foundation—just under the surface of each of his decisions she discerned a hesitancy that was in decided contrast to the arrogant curl of his lips" (*Short Stories* 78). We have here an intimation of the "battlefield of selves" that Barton describes in his *Good Housekeeping* article. If Ardita's impression can be trusted, Toby suffers from uncertainty and self-doubt, which he can only overcome by slipping into his Curtis Carlyle persona. By casting off the guise at the story's end, Toby reveals that the "vividness of imagination" (*Short Stories* 79) for which Carlyle is known is an authentic personality trait of his own. It has taken this challenge of selling himself to Ardita to externalize the agency he latently possessed. And Toby's reward for enacting this real self is the same one that advertising promised male consumers in the 1920s: he gets the girl.[7]

The most explicit evocation of the rhetoric of selling and buying occurs in the romantic lark "Rags Martin-Jones and the Pr–nce of W–les" (1924), whose plot recycles the scenario of "The Offshore Pirate." Here the Ardita Farnam figure is a celebrity heiress who returns to New York after five years in Europe to dash the romantic aspirations of John M. Chestnut, the successful businessman who lacks the charisma of more stellar personalities such as the Valentinoesque Roderigo Minerlino, "the movie and face-cream star" (*Short Stories* 280). When Rags demands to know what Chestnut thinks he can possibly offer her, his simple reply—"Love"—inspires a lecture on the economics of romance:

> Life to me is a series of glistening bazaars with a merchant in front of each one rubbing his hands together saying "Patronize this place here. Best bazaar in the world." So I go in with my purse full of beauty and money and youth, all prepared to buy. "What have you got for sale?" I ask him, and he rubs his hands together and says: "Well, Mademoiselle, to-day we have some perfectly bee-*oo*-tiful love." Sometimes he hasn't even got that in stock, but he sends out for it when he finds I have so much money to spend. Oh, he always gives me love before I go—and for nothing. That's the one revenge I have. (*Short Stories* 277)

Rags's speech bespeaks not only the critical sophistication of the discriminating female consumer; also emphasized here is an ancillary trait that advertising theorists attributed to her. As Christine Frederick claimed, the "average woman" was "a born bargainer [who would] not be fooled by inferior goods, no matter how successfully trademarked or camouflaged" ("Advertising Copy" 233). Whether advertisers believed this is another matter, yet they flattered female audiences by claiming that age-old stereotypes of feminine gullibility and impulsiveness were wrong and that women actually exercised the cutthroat economic cunning associated with successful entrepreneurs. Rags's "revenge"—her ability to deploy her wiles and attain her desire "for nothing"—is indicative of the power to transcend their commodification that women were encouraged to believe they possessed, allowing them to feel that they could turn the tables on the marketplace.

Facing Rags's consumer incredulity, Chestnut must prove that he has "got the goods" by concocting a Barnum-style hoax involving a murder charge, an attempted escape across the Canadian border, and a mock shoot-out with the police—not to mention an elevator boy disguised as the Prince of Wales. Upon learning the spectacle has been staged for her benefit, Rags exhibits yet a third characteristic of the average female consumer, the desire to feel personally catered to, both in terms of intimacy and entertainment (Naether 31): "Was the whole thing just *mine*? . . . Was it a perfectly useless, gorgeous thing, just for me?" Chestnut assures her the extravagance was indeed for her benefit, and the two set off to City Hall to marry. As the story ends, the rhetoric of selling and buying confirms that love is indeed a marketing venture. Chestnut, "rubbing his hands together in a commercial gesture," begs his lover: "Patronize this place, lady. Best bazaar in the city!" To which Rags, now sold, replies, "Wrap it up, Mr. Merchant. . . . It looks like a bargain to me" (*Short Stories* 288).

Such stories are ironic but not satirical; because Fitzgerald's lovers *knowingly* conflate love and commerce, the comedy is not orchestrated at their expense as it is in *Babbitt* and other caricatures of American commercial culture. This is not to say that Fitzgerald was averse to mocking the business mindset à la Sinclair Lewis. The duplicitous salesman, for example, is a stock emblem of modern anxieties toward unregulated entrepreneurism. Although his presence in American literature can be traced back to such antecedents as the eighteenth-century Yankee peddler and the nineteenth-century confidence man, he is notable in *Babbitt, Main Street*, and other 1920s novels for his exuberant sermonizing on the mantra of self-perfection through salesmanship. Fitzgerald's second novel, *The Beautiful and Damned* (1922), includes a motivational speech by salesman Sammy Carleton, author of the self-help guide *Heart Talks*, which promises to reveal "the principal reasons for a man's failure and the principal reasons for a man's success—from John D. Rockerfeller [*sic*] to John D. Napoleon" (379). The joke is that the "senile bromides" (382) that Carleton passes off as "principles of success" are as phony as the stock scam he pushes. Such characters ridiculed consumer advocates' insistence that the salesman ethos would prove ineffective if not guided by innate sincerity. Throughout *The Man No-*

body Knows, Barton (whose style resembles that of the fictional Carleton) argues that Christ's most persuasive trait was his sincerity: "We speak of personal magnetism as though there were something mysterious about it—a magic quality bestowed on one in a thousand and denied to all the rest. This is not true. The essential element in personal magnetism is a consuming sincerity—an overwhelming faith in the importance of the work one has to do" (19). Yet the emphasis Barton and others placed upon *displaying* earnestness only exacerbated doubts about its authenticity. As T. J. Jackson Lears notes, consumers suspected that "for advertising men . . . truth was insufficient and sometimes irrelevant. The important job was . . . making the Truth 'Sound True.' Sincerity had become at once a moral stance and a tactic of persuasion" ("Rise" 157). For critics of the salesman persona, including Nick Carraway, the narrator of *The Great Gatsby*, the more effort expended on appearing sincere, the more likely the personality behind it would prove to be a façade.

Even as minor characters, Sammy Carletons are rare in Fitzgerald's oeuvre. In dissecting this model of masculine self-making, he focuses more on the salesman's own gullibility, his tendency to deceive *himself* by falling for the "central appeal of style[:] its ability to create an illusory transcendence of class or background" (Ewen, *Images*, 77). In stories such as "Winter Dreams" (1922) and "Dice, Brass Knuckles & Guitar" (1923), entrepreneurial young men discover that, despite a talent for mimicking the fashions and leisure of the wealthy, they are not accepted by that class but can only achieve instead what Thorstein Veblen in *The Theory of the Leisure Class* (1898) calls "pecuniary emulation," in which "purposeful effort comes to mean . . . effort directed to or resulting in a more creditable showing of accumulated wealth" (22).

Of course, Jay Gatsby stands as Fitzgerald's richest emblem of the self-deception of pecuniary emulation. As Scott Donaldson has noted, Gatsby's personal style, from his fondness for pink suits, silver shirts, and cream-colored cars to his affected salutations (he calls Nick "old sport"), is so gauche as to mark him nouveau riche: "Given an opportunity, Gatsby consistently errs in the direction of ostentation. His clothes, his car, his house, his parties—all brand him as newly rich, unschooled in the social graces and sense of superiority ingrained not only in [Daisy's philandering husband] Tom Buchanan but in Nick" (188). James Gatz may have fashioned his persona from a Platonic conception of himself, but few others in the novel accept it as authentic, least of all Nick, who often points out its more contrived aspects. Upon meeting Nick, for example, Gatsby greets him with a supercilious smile that "understood you just so far as you wanted to be understood, believed in you as you would like to believe in yourself and assured you that it had precisely the impression of you that, at your best, you hoped to convey" (53). Later, while reuniting with Daisy for the first time in five years, Gatsby strikes a nonchalant pose, "reclining against the mantelpiece in a strained counterfeit of perfect ease, even of boredom" (91)—a stance undermined when in his nervousness he knocks a clock off the mantel. Significantly, Nick links his intrigue with Gatsby's transparency to the allure of mass-culture images: "My incredulity was submerged in fascination. . . . It was like skimming hastily through a dozen magazines" (71). Daisy makes the same point shortly before her husband denounces Gatsby as "Mr. Nobody from Nowhere" (137): "You always look so cool. . . . You resemble the advertisement. . . . You know the advertisement of the man—" (125).[8] Noticeably, Gatsby does not respond to this compliment, which to him would not be complimentary at all, for to suggest that his identity is constructed out of commodified images is to impugn the very mechanism of his self-realization. Ronald Berman has made the marvelous observation that, unlike fellow characters, Gatsby "is not a very good actor because he often gives way to sincerity" (113). His tragedy, in other words, is that he assumes style indeed makes the man. Despite his enviable commitment to his romantic ideals, Gatsby is an ironic inversion of the 1920s fear of consumer deception: he is the salesman duped by his own powers of persuasion.

The main anxiety surrounding female consumerism was willpower, not sincerity. The marketplace may have extended to women the power of choice through its diversity of available colors, patterns, flavors, and aromas, yet it also sought to instill a degree of perpetual dissatisfaction that would encourage their continued spending. Critics of consumerism warned that female spending was susceptible to the lure of false wants. In *Middletown* (1929), one of the most influential critiques of modernity's effects on American life, Robert and Helen Lynd blamed mass culture for pressuring women to conform to a commodified standard of living: "Through these periodicals [*Good Housekeeping, McCall's, Pictorial Review*], as well as through the daily press, billboards, and other channels, modern advertising pounds away at the habits of the Middletown housewife. Whole industries mobilize to impress a new [consumer] habit upon her" (158). The Lynds typify the anticonsumerist stance that insisted that the average woman lacked the ability to resist the "accusing finger" that "makes her acutely conscious of her unpolished fingernails, or of the worn place in the living room rug, and sends [her] peering anxiously into the mirror to see if *her* wrinkles look like those that made Mrs. X—— in the ad 'old at thirty-five'" (82). Advertising manuals said much the same thing. Christine Frederick's *Selling Mrs. Consumer* asserts female pliability even as it insists that women wish to see themselves as discerning shoppers:

> The average consumer . . . does not want to visualize herself as an automaton told what to do by advertising. . . . But nevertheless the American woman has struck up a closer *entent cordiale* and co-partnership with industry and trade (even if it is largely unconscious), than has ever been known in the history of trading. . . . She has developed a "consumer acceptance" spirit,—a readiness to follow where she is led. (334)

Fitzgerald's fiction includes many women who exhibit this readiness. For every Rags Martin-Jones who drives a hard bargain, there is a Yanci Bowman, heroine of "The Popular Girl" (1922), who fantasizes about frequenting "smart not-to-be-entered-without-a-card women's shops" where she can "spend the morning hours acquiring and acquiring, ceaselessly and without thought of expense" (*Before Gatsby* 485), or her even more spoiled counterpart, Fifi Schwartz of "The Hotel Child" (1931), who is "as thoroughly equipped for beauty by man as by God" in her designer dresses, whose palette of colors includes "cerise for Chanel, mauve for Molyneux, pink for Patou" (*Short Stories* 599). An even more tragic example is Myrtle Wilson, Tom Buchanan's mistress in *The Great Gatsby*. The novel's second chapter details the panoply of consumer items Myrtle gathers around her to convince herself she leads a glamorous and exciting life. In fewer than five pages this lowly mechanic's wife changes clothes three times, switching from crepe de chine to muslin to chiffon. "With the influence of the dress her personality had also undergone a change," Nick reports. "The intense vitality that had been so remarkable in [her husband's] garage was converted into impressive hauteur" (35). This observation substantiates consumer psychologist Paul Nystrom's explanation of why apparel creates such a pronounced effect on the female demeanor: "Change in dress gives the illusion of change in personality. . . . If after completing her work [the housewife] makes a change to an afternoon dress or a street garment, the change makes a lady of her" (78). Yet Fitzgerald questions whether Myrtle is indeed a lady or if she mimics marketplace tastes. From her excessive use of perfume to her fondness for trashy novels and gossip magazines, her interests are not only petit bourgeois but imperiously impulsive: she refuses to ride in a taxi unless it is "lavender-colored with grey upholstery" and hectors Tom into buying a dog for the simple reason that "they're nice to have—a dog" (31). In this way, Myrtle symbolizes the female consumer who derives more pleasure from the accruing of possessions than from the possessions themselves.

In more empathic instances, Fitzgerald depicts female characters' attempts to break their dependency on commodities. In the supernatural "The Cut-Glass Bowl" (1920), a series of personal crises inspires Evylyn Piper to smash a gift given her years earlier by a spurned suitor. In the suitor's estimation, the bowl symbolizes Evylyn's haughty personality, for it is "as hard . . . and as beautiful and as empty and as easy to see through" as she is (*Flappers* 126). After the showy item precipitates several family disasters, she recognizes its baleful influence on her life, and she tries to destroy it. Whether the effort is successful remains ambiguous: as Evylyn goes to hurl the bowl, she slips and falls onto it, perhaps (the ending is ambiguous) killing herself. A less melodramatic version of a similar effort appears in the nonfiction essay "Auction—Model 1934," written by Zelda but published under a joint by-line with Scott in *Esquire*. In an attempt to unburden themselves of the past, the Fitzgeralds inventory the possessions accumulated over their marriage. The pathos is that the knickknacks they propose to auction off, from a moth-eaten Patou suit to a pair of stolen salt and pepper shakers, have no value beyond the memories of their attainment. Their worth, in other words, is not to be found in their utility but in what they reveal about the impulsive and undisciplined nature of the couple's lifestyle. Written at the nadir of the Fitzgeralds' marriage as they contemplated divorce, "Auction" finds the pair questioning what they have to show for their adulthood. In the end, they decide they must retain the items, for they are the only evidence that any work at all has been accomplished during the couple's years together: "We shall keep it all—the tangible remnant of the four hundred thousand we made from hard words and spent with easy ones" (*Crack-Up* 62).

If Jay Gatsby is Fitzgerald's most complex representative of masculine salesmanship, his most ambiguous portrait of the female consumer is Nicole Diver in *Tender Is the Night* (1934). The novel's twelfth chapter includes a tour-de-force scene in which Nicole escorts ingenue Rosemary Hoyt on a Paris shopping spree. While Rosemary's purchases are practical (two dresses, two hats, four pairs of shoes), Nicole's run the gamut from the expensive (a guest bed, a pair of "chamois leather jackets of kingfisher blue") to the absurd (a rubber alligator). Not only are many of the items impulse buys, but several are intended as gifts, for "everything she liked that she couldn't possibly use herself, she bought as a present for a friend." The elaborate list culminates in an editorial commentary that dismisses Nicole as precisely what Christine Frederick wrote women did not wish to view themselves as—a consumer "automaton":

> Nicole was the product of much ingenuity and toil. For her sake trains began their run at Chicago and traversed the round belly of the continent to California; chicle factories fumed and

> link belts grew link by link in factories; men mixed toothpaste in vats and drew mouthwash out of copper hogsheads; girls canned tomatoes quickly in August or worked rudely at the Five-and-Tens on Christmas Eve; half-breed Indians toiled on Brazilian coffee plantations and dreamers were muscled out of patent rights in new tractors—these were some of the people who gave tithes to Nicole, and as the whole system swayed and thundered onward it lent a feverish bloom to such processes of hers as wholesale buying. . . . She illustrated very simple principles, containing in herself her own doom, but illustrated them so accurately that there was grace in the procedure. (65)

For many critics, the passage is Fitzgerald's most explicit critique of capitalism, for in addition to depicting Nicole's shopping as conditioned behavior it exposes the labor exploitation required to serve her whims.[9] There is more than a little hindsight here in Fitzgerald's narrative perspective: writing in the thick of the Great Depression, he could look back to his mid–1920s time frame to recognize that the "very simple principle" of creating a consumer demand in women commensurate with the industrial capacity to produce goods was too frivolous an engine to propel such an intricate economy.

Yet whether Nicole's consumerism is as robotic as this chapter insists is questionable. At the novel's end, her purchases provide her the tools that allow her to break her dependency on her husband, Dick Diver, the once vibrant psychologist ruined by drink and dissipation. Fitzgerald employs religious rhetoric to dramatize the rebirth of sensuality Nicole feels as she prepares to consummate her attraction to Dick's nemesis, Tommy Barbans: she "anoint[s] herself with powder" and "cross[es] herself reverently with Chanel Sixteen" (312). Nicole's actions belie the matrix of conflicting motives that define women's relationship to the marketplace. On the one hand, her desire "to have [possessions] like this, to be worshipped again, to pretend to have a mystery" arises from her "jealousy of youth," her need to compete with the "myriad faces of girl-children" like Rosemary whom the culture upholds as the ideal of femininity. And yet Nicole effects this awakening not for the reason that Frederick laments the cosmetics industry coveted women consumers: "As a 'feminist' I hate to say it, but the bare truth is that woman's chief business in life still appears to be to charm and hold a man" (*Selling* 189). Because Nicole knows Barbans can be as cruel and callous as Dick—upon greeting her, he points out the crow's feet around her eyes—she roots her self-esteem in her own confidence, not in the attention of any particular man. Indeed, accepting the marketplace truism that beauty is a woman's best currency, Nicole derives empowerment from the same discriminating power of choice wielded by Rags Martin-Jones: "She had a thrill of delight in thinking of herself in a new way. New vistas appeared ahead, peopled with the faces of many men, none of whom she need obey or even love" (315). If Gatsby's tragedy is that he mistakes style for sincerity, Nicole's freedom seems determinedly opportunistic—she is taking the best deal the market has to offer. Her actions may not challenge the female obligation to appear attractive, but they at least provide her the opportunity for variety that consumerism taught women to believe was their most advantageous mode of social power.

Prosperity and Prodigality: Disembodied Abundance and Vaporizing Values

In addition to selfhood, Fitzgerald's writing confronts 1920s concerns over how consumerism transformed conceptions of work, cost, and worth. The dual challenge that consumer engineers faced in their effort to normalize and routinize the buying habits required for economic growth revolved around connotations of the word *value*. On the one hand, consumers had to be taught to regard frugality as outmoded and to celebrate spending as a pleasurable leisure activity. The 1920s thus witnessed a vilification of financial restraint, with editorials such as "Thrift—The New Menace" and "The Dilemma of Thrift" a staple of newspapers and periodicals. The miser also became a figure of popular-culture ridicule, appearing in such Fitzgerald stories as "A Penny Spent" (1925), where his Victorian niggardliness impedes the *joie de vivre* of younger, modern characters. Few avatars of consumption went as far as advertising publicist Garet Garrett, who insisted that because "there is no limit to prosperity—to the satisfaction of human wants," Americans should gorge themselves to "this side of satiety" (84)—a phrase Fitzgerald undoubtedly would have appreciated. The moderate stance argued that consumption was a hallmark of cultural evolution because it offered immediate compensation for hard work. In the words of economist Simon Patten, whose *The New Basis of Civilization* (1907) can be read as a rejoinder to Veblen's more critical *Theory of the Leisure Class*, material attainments served as a civilizing influence by offering the working and middle classes access to aesthetic pleasures once limited to aristocracies: "Leisure and work may supplement each other so fully that every family may have the culture that is the product of one, and the efficiency that is acquired by the other" (63).

By promising these cultural pleasures, consumerism also redefined the value of the commodities providing them. Previously, a product's worth was tied to its utility, to what it did. In a consumer economy, however, a concrete, practical measure of value such as usage is detrimental to continuous buying, for it teaches people that the item should only be replaced when it can no longer serve its narrow purpose. What was needed was a more mutable sense of value whose chief criterion was fashion, not function. Accordingly, the marketplace measured worth by more abstract, transitory indices such as how a commodity looked, felt, tasted, or smelled—in other words, by the symbolic yardstick of style.

In devaluing thrift and practicality, manufacturers had to confront another formidable roadblock, this one having to do more with economics than morality: few Americans could afford to indulge their consumer whims to the degree that business wanted them to. Automobiles, refrigerators, furniture, and even radios were prohibitively expensive for many families, even many middle-class ones. The need for new forms of financing led to expanding credit extended through a variety of institutions, including

> installment sales finance companies (such as the General Motors Finance Company), retail installment lenders (particularly department stores), licensed consumer finance companies (such as Beneficial Loan Company), and a number of other lenders, such as "industrial" banks, remedial loan societies, credit unions, and personal loan departments of commercial banks. (Calder 19)

Despite a preponderance of morality tales about the fiscal irresponsibility that "easy payments" and "monthly installments" encouraged, the availability of credit ameliorated the notion of living in the red. Once a mark of impecuniousness, debt became a badge of bourgeois pride as securing credit meant that one had not only been deemed a reliable borrower but that one possessed value in the marketplace. By 1929 the consumer debt load in the United States exceeded $7 billion, while the percentage of disposable income that the average family saved fell by one-third from the preceding decade. As one economic historian notes, "Such a sharp decline in the personal savings rate is astounding, particularly since the 1920s were rather prosperous years and we usually expect the savings rate to climb, not fall, during periods of prosperity" (Olney 49).

Two recurring motifs suggest the consequences of these shifting values. The first is indicated by a phrase from Patten's argument that consumerism enhances the community life of the proletariat: "Industrial efficiency . . . brings the [working] class to a plane where family life is desired and possible. The horizon of wants and consumption widens. The satiety of primitive desires[,] which follows increased income, urges men to displace crude individual gratifications with grouped pleasures" (*New Basis* 137). The "horizon of wants" was a popular image for both pro- and anticonsumerist voices; one often finds it literalized to a point where nature is no longer represented as a paradise of resources but as a landscape of ready-made goods ripe for consuming. Walter Lippmann conjures up a protosurreal panorama in *Drift and Mastery* (1914) to vivify his concerns about advertising creating a "deceptive clamor that disfigures scenery": "The eastern sky [is] ablaze with chewing gum, the northern with toothbrushes and underwear, the western with whiskey, and the southern with petticoats, the whole heavens . . . [are] brilliant with monstrously flirtatious women" (52–53). Note the complete absence of production in this vision: America is no longer the land of milk and honey, for milk and honey must be harvested. Instead, the world becomes a kind of celestial shop where manufactured goods wait to be snatched off the shelves of stars. Of course, Lippmann's vision is an admonitory one, but more celebratory examples also abound. In the popular folk song "The Big Rock Candy Mountains"—first recorded around 1910, but best known today for its inclusion on the soundtrack to the film *O Brother, Where Art Thou?* (2000)—Harry McClintock envisions the world as a vast buffet, enjoyable precisely because it does not require any labor: "O—the buzzing of the bees in the cigarette trees / Round the soda-water fountain / Where the lemonade springs and the blue bird sings. . . . I'm going to stay where you sleep all day / Where they boiled in oil the inventor of toil / In the Big Rock Candy Mountains." As Lears argues, such imagery reveals how the consumer revolution occasioned the "disembodiment of abundance":

> Popular notions of abundance were moving away from their origins in the rhythms of agrarian life and bodily existence. . . . What was obscured was any sense that abundance could be the result of patient cooperation between the human mind and the material world. In a disembodied discourse of abundance, enjoyment of the fruits of one's labors became less important than the pursuit of disposable goods. (*Fables* 117)

A comparable evocation of disembodied abundance appears in a notebook fragment that Fitzgerald intended for inclusion in a story: "In children's books forests are sometimes made out of all-day suckers, boulders of peppermints and rivers out of gently flowing, molasses taffy. Such books are less fantastic than they sound, for such localities exist, and one day a girl, herself little more than a child, sat dejected in the middle of one" (*Crack-Up* 117). While surreal landscapes of this sort are rare in his work,

Fitzgerald does convey disembodied abundance in another important way. Throughout the 1920s, advertising theorists such as Earnest Elmo Calkins advocated innovative uses of color and design to add value to commodities: "Beauty is introduced into material objects to enhance them in the eyes of the purchaser. The appeal of efficiency is nearly ended. Beauty is the natural and logical step. . . . When choice rests between two articles of equal utility, it veers toward the more attractive" (149). The attractiveness of a product would transform consumers' experiential interaction with the world. No longer would the aesthetic and the industrial exist in opposition, Calkins argued; they would be, rather, inseparable elements of a mass-marketed standard of taste: "We are just on the threshold of creating a new world on top of our modern industrial efficiency, a world in which it is possible through the much criticized machines to replace the beauty that the machines originally displaced" (150).

What Calkins describes here is what, from a far less enthusiastic perspective, Marxist critics call "reification," the process by which commodities come to so dominate perception that individuals are incapable of registering phenomena without reference to them. It is a process upon which Edmund Wilson also commented in a 1925 *New Republic* note when he listed the names of some three dozen hues prevalent in women's apparel, even though they did not exist in the natural spectrum, including "skynn," "tanbark," and "sauterne." As Wilson wryly suggested, "The people who make women's hosiery must be employing poets" ("Current Fashions" 76). While Calkins would have been delighted by such an observation—he encouraged advertisers and manufacturers to study and mimic modern art—most modernists would have been appalled by the appropriation of their aesthetic ideals, which they believed should operate autonomously from the commercial world. Yet Fitzgerald's own descriptive habits bear the stamp of reification. When, for example, the opening sentence of "The Offshore Pirate" describes the sea as "a blue dream, as colorful as blue silk-stockings" (*Short Stories* 70), he implies that the baseline of that color is no longer found in nature but in the marketplace. *The Great Gatsby* includes several comparable similes and metaphors, most famously Gatsby's comment that Daisy's "voice is full of money" (127). In each case, Fitzgerald dramatizes the modern impossibility of envisioning life through anything but the refracting lens of consumerism.

The second, related motif involves what Ewen calls the "vaporization of values," which results from disembodied abundance. Once any demonstrable link between a commodity's function and worth is severed, notions of value lose their material anchorage and become instead ever more abstract. As Ewen explains, the resulting glorification of the ephemeral over the tangible in the modern age was apparent not only in the rampant stock and bond speculation that came to a screeching halt on October 29, 1929 ("Black Tuesday") with the Wall Street crash; it was the dominant trend in the period's style, as well, which displayed a marked preference for "representation divorced from matter":

> With the global dominance of finance capital, a "state of mind" which could comprehend wealth independent of matter began to be monumentalized in style. The iconography of Western cultures was shifting, reflecting the glory of intangibility, evanescence, and uninhibited motion. If the aesthetics of feudalism were rooted in a tactile appreciation of nature, the new capital aesthetic began to explore a conception of value and desire that transcended nature, which operated by its own immaterial laws of physics. (*Images* 163)

In this way, images of immateriality, much like disembodied abundance, reflected the new reified world of experience.

Throughout his writing, Fitzgerald moralizes upon the pursuit of disembodied prosperity and the resulting loss of tangible measures of value. The downward trajectory of Anthony and Gloria Patch in *The Beautiful and Damned*, for example, is a direct result of the joint dissolution of concrete economic and ethical standards. As the scion of a wealthy Wall Street family, Anthony lacks appreciation for the moral salubriousness of work, while Gloria is a born consumer with a voracious appetite for ostentation. Without purpose or direction in life, the couple seeks contentment by squandering Anthony's allowance on houses, cars, clothes, and parties, all the while amassing debts that they can only hope to settle through an impending inheritance. The Patches' precarious finances are built upon ephemeral forms of capital: with little cash on hand, Anthony must write "bum" checks (425) and borrow against bonds (225) to pay for basic necessities. At his lowest ebb, after his grandfather disinherits him and he is forced to take a job, he participates in Sammy Carleton's stock-selling scheme, albeit halfheartedly (385). Yet even after the bank closes Anthony's account, he boasts of having "paper worth eighty thousand dollars at par," which the couple can liquidate for "about thirty thousand on the open market." Straining for a last semblance of *carpe diem* affluence, Gloria encourages her husband to cash out: "Let's sell all the bonds and put the thirty thousand in the bank. . . . We can live in Italy for three years and then just die" (426–27). The disparity between Anthony and Gloria's paper wealth and the reality of their reduced circumstances (between them they can scrounge together two dollars in coins) is a pungent commentary on the immateriality of Jazz Age prosperity.

As critics have noted, Fitzgerald's moral stance in *The Beautiful and Damned* is not always clear, for as often as he rebukes the Patches for their profligacy, he "credits [them] with a certain integrity of irresponsibility" by glorifying their wastrel ways (Bruccoli 179). Elsewhere, however, he more consistently questions the intangibility of modern values. The satirical plot of "The Diamond as Big as the Ritz" twists upon the homicidal extremes to which Braddock Washington must go to maintain his status as the world's richest man. The Washington family lives on a mountain-sized diamond in the Montana Rockies; the diamond is so large, however, that "there was no valuing it by any regular computation. . . . If it were offered for sale not only would the bottom fall out of the market, but also, if the value should vary with its size in the usual arithmetical progression, there would not be enough gold in the world to buy a tenth of it" (*Short Stories* 193). To prevent a panic that would plummet the market and wipe out his fortune, the billionaire must either imprison or kill anyone who happens upon the secret source of his affluence, be they the architects who design his lavish estate, aviators who fly over it, or his children's vacationing schoolmates. Although "The Diamond as Big as the Ritz" ranks among his most accomplished stories, Fitzgerald discovered that its lampoon of the volatility of economic and moral values depreciated its own market worth. The *Saturday Evening Post* and several other "slick" magazines rejected the story, forcing its author to place it with the smaller-circulation *Smart Set*, which paid a paltry $300 for contributions. In the probusiness environment of 1922, few periodical editors were prepared to question the reality of the new prosperity.

This does not mean that American culture was averse to moralizing against prodigality. As vigorously as they encouraged spending, consumer advocates warned against the overextension of credit and the crippling effects of excess debt. The message was that consumerism was appropriate when it enabled "better living" but inappropriate when its goal was "keeping up with the Joneses."[10] Typical of such advice was the 1922 *Post* article "Debtor's Cowardice"—it appears in the same issue that features Fitzgerald's "The Popular Girl"—in which an anonymous contributor laments his lack of fiscal discipline and cautions readers against succumbing to the "mad race to keep up with the times and the styles and the fashions" (93). Fitzgerald's "How to Live on $36,000 a Year," which appeared in the *Post* two years later, makes much the same point in much the same tone. The piece is as critical of ephemeral capital as "The Diamond as Big as the Ritz," particularly when Fitzgerald invests in a bond that promises to pay a 7 percent return, only to discover that its lack of cash value for all practical purposes renders it worthless: "In all financial crises I dig it out and with it go hopefully to the bank, supposing that, as it never fails to pay the proper interest, it has at last assumed a tangible value. But as I have never been able to sell it, it has gradually acquired the sacredness of a family heirloom. . . . It was once turned in at the Subway offices after I left it by accident on a car seat" (*Afternoon of an Author* 89).

What no doubt made this piece palatable to the *Post* is the solution to which the Fitzgeralds turn when they discover they cannot account for nearly a third of their annual income: they institute a budget. Throughout the 1920s, commentators viewed this remedy to unregulated household expenditures as a means of balancing compulsive consumerism and the miserly thrift associated with crotchety Victorians. "Debtor's Cowardice" recommends this practice, as did essays in other middle-class periodicals such as *Good Housekeeping* and *American Magazine*. The conclusion of "How to Live on $36,000 a Year" parodies the rigorous accounting methods typical of this discourse: "Our allowance for newspapers should be only a quarter of what we spend on self-improvement, so we are considering whether to get the Sunday paper once a month or to subscribe to an almanac. According to the budget we will be allowed only three-quarters of a servant, so we are on the lookout for a one-legged cook who can come six days a week" (*Afternoon of an Author* 99). Such humor suggests how observers doubted the argument that financial discipline alone could stabilize an economy in which values were so fluid and transitory.

After the onset of the Great Depression, Fitzgerald produced a cluster of stories in which reversals of fortune force characters to confront prosperity's corrupted values. In more regrettable instances, such as "A Change of Class" (1931), his moralizing is heavy-handed and didactic. When the stock market crash wipes out the fortune of former barber Earl Johnson, he happily returns to work. Local millionaire Philip Jadwin, who provided Earl the tip that allowed him to prosper, is relieved to learn that Earl does not blame him for his losses. Jadwin is so grateful, in fact, that unbeknown to Earl, he covers the check Earl writes to open his own shop, which will otherwise bounce because the barber's philandering wife has absconded with his remaining cash. The story goes to extremes to assure readers that Earl's and Jadwin's morals have remained stable despite the economic volatility: the latter's generosity proves his beneficence, while Earl is content to remain at his station in life. Gratuitously, the closing sentence dismisses leftist incredulity toward the story's happy ending: "The soul of a slave, says the Marxist. Anyhow that's the sort of soul Earl has, and he's pretty happy with it. I like Earl" (*Price* 368).

A far less sentimental exploration of this theme occurs in "Babylon Revisited" (also 1931), Fitzgerald's best-known short story. When American expatriate Charlie Wales returns to Paris after an emotional breakdown to reclaim his daughter, he must reconcile his nostalgia for the heady days of the bull market with its tragic consequences. Charlie's wife, Helen, died from "heart trouble" attributed to the couple's indulgent lifestyle, and Charlie's own subsequent confinement in a sanitarium has forced him to place his child with Helen's sister. The story offers Fitzgerald's most explicit delineation of the parallel between evanescent economics and morality. As a stockbroker, Charlie could finance extravagance, which in turn eroded his stability. The same unmoored impulses that allowed him to tip "thousand-franc notes . . . to an orchestra for playing a single number, hundred-franc notes . . . to a doorman for calling a cab" (*Short Stories* 620) were the same ones that allowed him to lock Helen out of their apartment after an argument, stranding her in a snowstorm and contributing to the illness that killed her. As Charlie must recognize, affluence impugned his sense of reality: "The snow of twenty-nine wasn't real snow," he thinks, haunted by his callousness toward Helen. "If you didn't want it to be snow, you just paid some money" (*Short Stories* 633). Yet complicating this moral accounting is the ambiguity of Charlie's remorse. Unlike Earl in "A Change of Class," he does not cheerfully embrace the austerity of the Depression. Rather, he regrets that irresponsibility is no longer fashionable. "We were a sort of royalty, almost infallible, with a sort of magic around us," he reflects (*Stories* 619). As J. Gerald Kennedy has written, Charlie's "visit to Paris forces him to confront the results of his carelessness, but . . . he remains too deeply enamored of the pleasures of Babylon to recover his [daughter] or to escape the condition of spiritual exile" (326). In this way, "Babylon Revisited" is not a parable about the inevitability of the "correction," the deflation of the market that balances its overvaluation. It recognizes, rather, that even in a hobbled economy, consumers are less apt to right their values than they are to pine for new opportunities to indulge their irrational exuberance.

Wastage as Never Before: Disposability and the Privileges of Abundance

In addition to selfhood and values, consumerism transformed attitudes toward conservation by making disposability an essential component of the marketplace exchange. Key to economic expansion, business proponents insisted, was the consistency of consumer spending, which could only be ensured by conditioning people to derive as much pleasure from depleting commodities as from acquiring them. Without the satisfaction of "using up" an item, they reasoned, consumers would have little motivation to spend their disposable income on a continuous basis. Simon Patten was one of the first to celebrate the cyclical nature of procuring and expending: "The standard of life is determined, not so much by what a man has to enjoy, as the rapidity with which he tires of the pleasure," he wrote in *The Consumption of Wealth* (1889). "To have a high standard means to enjoy a pleasure intensely and to tire of it quickly" (34). The challenge manufacturers faced was to develop methods for ensuring this rapid dissatisfaction. According to Earnest Elmo Calkins, "The [goal] is to make the customer discontented with his old type of fountain pen, kitchen utensil, bathroom or motor car, because it is old-fashioned, out of date. The technical term for this idea is obsoletism. We no longer wait for things to wear out. We displace them with others that are not more effective but more attractive" (qtd. in Ewen, *Images*, 243). As this quote suggests, Calkins was an early articulator of what would become known as "planned obsolescence"—although in the 1920s, again in deference to the entrenched Victorian regard for thrift, advertisers were apt to use the terms "creative" or "progressive" obsolescence (Frederick, *Selling*, 246–47). As this lingo implied, the unceasing changes in commodity design and packaging would not glorify novelty for its own sake but would instead provide customers the illusion of riding the cusp of cultural evolution.

The downside of planned obsolescence can be seen in what Ewen describes as the rampant "aestheticization of waste" that occurred throughout the 1920s (*Images* 239). As advertisers sang the pleasures of disposability, other arenas of popular culture began to revel in the human capacity to exhaust and destroy. Perhaps the most awe-inspiring medium to dramatize this impulse was the cinema. Beginning with such pioneering efforts by Georges Méliès as *Collision and Shipwreck at Sea* (1898) and *The Catastrophe of the Balloon 'Le Pax'* (1902), the film industry strove to overwhelm audiences with its technological ability to fabricate intense scenes of orchestrated devastation. Whether in the popular Italian imports *The Last Days of Pompeii* (twice filmed, once in 1908 and again in 1913) or in Hollywood productions such as D. W. Griffith's *Intolerance* (1916) and Irving Cummings's *The Johnstown Flood* (1926), moviemakers spared little expense in constructing elaborate sets designed for imminent decimation. The pleasure derived from these displays of simulated ruin was no different than what contemporary purveyors of action/adventure films enjoy. In Martin Jay's words, such films promised "kinaesthetic amusement" by "producing a sensation of immediacy and involvement that narrowed the gap between spectator and spectacle. Instead of disciplining the viewer to sit quietly and contemplate the scene from a safe distance . . . they produced a viscerally excited, sometimes libidinally aroused, sometimes violently terrorized body that was more than a passive eye" (102–3). In Jeffrey T. Schnapp's estimation, the thrill generated by exposure to destruction was evident as well in modern amusement-park rides such as roller coasters, loop-de-loops, and vertigo machines, all of which recreated the dangers of wreckage by transforming "passengers into . . . whirling dervishes who, once passed through a sort of spatialized centrifuge, could be expected to wander about as if drugged, trembling with fear and giddy with excitement." As Schnapp notes, these new entertainments often teased consumers with "the threat/promise of accident" both by publicizing themselves with slogans such as "An Automobile Dash for Death Down a Mountain at One Thousand Miles an Hour" and by integrating their machinery within painted scenes of destruction that illustrated the perils of modern velocity (30–31).

Fitzgerald's fiction contains several scenes that convey wonder at the wastage that modern technology made possible in the

1920s. Some cases are relatively minor, as when Nick in *The Great Gatsby* halts his narration to note the "pyramid of pulpless halves" left by the "machine in [Gatsby's] kitchen which could extract the juice of over two hundred oranges in half an hour, if a little button was pressed two hundred times by a butler's thumb" (44). Elsewhere, Fitzgerald describes spectacles of destruction in filmic images that evoke the "kinaesthetic amusement" of the movies mentioned above. "The Diamond as Big as the Ritz" ends with Braddock Washington dynamiting his estate rather than allowing a group of marauding aviators to capture it. The explosion, which immolates Washington along with his enemies, is graphically depicted:

> The whole surface of the mountain had changed suddenly to a dazzling burning yellow, which showed up through the jacket of turf as light shows through a human hand. For a moment the intolerable glow continued, and then like an extinguished filament it disappeared, revealing a black waste from which blue smoke arose slowly, carrying off with it what remained of vegetation and human flesh. Of the aviators there was left neither blood nor bone—they were consumed as completely as [Washington and his minions]. (*Short Stories* 214)

Although this passage ranks as one of Fitzgerald's goriest, it is not his most famous image of destruction. That distinction belongs to the valley of ashes in *Gatsby* that Long Islanders pass on the road into Manhattan. Fitzgerald describes the eerie vista through an ironic agricultural metaphor that suggests the underside of disembodied abundance: this "desolate area" is "a fantastic farm where ashes grow like wheat into ridges and hills and grotesque gardens, where ashes take the forms of houses and chimneys and rising smoke and finally, with a transcendent effort, of men who move dimly and already crumbling through the powdery air" (27). Critics have noted the influence of T. S. Eliot's *The Waste Land* (1922) on this passage. Just as Eliot views the refuse polluting the banks of the Thames as symbolic of humanity's alienation from nature, so, too, Fitzgerald portrays debris as indicative of modernity's capacity to exhaust experience. But while Eliot employs concrete (though fragmented) imagery, Fitzgerald's evocation is more hallucinatory, the "grey land and the spasms of bleak dust which drift over it" imply an almost apocalyptic portent of ecological disaster.

Another motif testifying to the modern fascination with wastage involves the many automobile wrecks found throughout Fitzgerald's work. From the moment it emerged in the marketplace to transform American life, the automobile inspired a bizarre fascination with accidents and injuries. Although couched as cautionary tales about the perils of motorized travel, essays such as Elizabeth Jordan's "Automobile Collisions," which the *Saturday Evening Post* published in January 1926, luxuriated in describing the gruesome wounds that resulted from crashes. "I shall never cease to hear ringing in my ears the horrible groans of a man with a fractured skull, lying near me in a pool of blood after the truck collision," Jordan wrote before detailing the cut head and bloodied eyes she herself suffered during the most serious of the *five* wrecks she was involved in since obtaining her driver's license (16). The frequent evocation of "pools of blood" in such articles suggests a rhetorical effort to titillate readers with a voyeuristic view of body and car parts so mangled and intertwined that the distinction between the human and the machine is lost. Long before Andy Warhol transformed accident-site photos into pop art with "Five Deaths on Orange" and "Ambulance Disaster" in the early 1960s, or J. G. Ballard explored the erotic fetishization of wrecks in *Crash* (1973), a cultish black market for images and urban legends involving car wreckage flourished in 1920s America. As Mikita Brottman has argued, this intrigue was especially concentrated when the accident victim was a celebrity such as Pauline Flood, "better known as silent-movie star Baby Sunshine [who was] run over by a truck in Los Angeles when she was only one year old," or the dancer Isadora Duncan, strangled and dragged along a cobblestone street in the French Riviera when her flowing silk scarf tangled around the rear wheel of the convertible taxi in which she was riding (xv–xvi). Such macabre stories suggest that "if the automobile signifies wealth, movement, progress, and all that is venerated in America, then vehicular death embodies its counterpart—that violent rage toward destruction that lies beneath the surface of the proverbial 'pioneer spirit.' If the car is the symbol of America, then the car wreck is the nation's bloodstained sarcophagus" (xxxvi). Similarly, if the car was the ultimate consumer status symbol in the 1920s, the car wreck became a totem of consumer destruction, representing the loss not only of a significant monetary investment but of human life.

Fitzgerald's depiction of auto wreckage, as with his treatment of disembodied abundance and evaporating values, reflects a tension between moralizing against transgression and indulging in it. On the surface, a humorous essay such as "The Cruise of the Rolling Junk," an account of a 1920 road trip from Connecticut to Alabama published in *Motor* magazine in 1924, details the difficulties travelers faced in the early days of interstate driving. Plagued by blown tires, dead batteries, and overheated engines, the Fitzgeralds find themselves servants of their finicky "Expenso" car, which they dub the "Rolling Junk." Beneath the comic treatment of the trip's mishaps lies a desire to liberate oneself from subservience to technology through violence. Upon finally arriving at the Montgomery home of Zelda's parents after losing countless hours (and dollars) in repair shops, Scott daydreams of the Junk's ultimate destruction, imagining it broken down "into its component parts" so it loses its "identity and its mortal soul," its pieces either "perished by fire or . . . drowned in the deep sea" (70). Such humor reflects the frustration of consumers who resented committing significant portions of their income to financing products like the automobile, which the marketplace sought to define as necessities rather than luxuries.

More frequently, however, Fitzgerald, like Jordan, invokes wreckage as an index of morality through the metaphor of the "reckless driver," which recurs throughout his major works. *The Beautiful and Damned* and *Tender Is the Night* both include scenes in which reckless driving symbolizes the downside of Jazz Age exuberance. In the former, Gloria Patch drives a newly purchased roadster over a fire hydrant, ripping out its transmission, causing her husband to judge her "a driver of many eccentricities and of infinite carelessness" (175). In the latter, an unstable Nicole

Diver tests her husband's courage by forcing a car carrying her family off a steep Swiss hillside: "She was laughing hilariously, unashamed, unafraid, unconcerned. . . . 'You were scared, weren't you?' she accused him. 'You wanted to live!'" (211).[11] *The Great Gatsby* contains the most extensive depiction of driving as a metaphor for morality. When Nick's sometime girlfriend, Jordan Baker, nearly careens into a group of workmen, she defends herself against the accusation that she is a "rotten driver" by claiming others will compensate for her incautiousness: "It takes two to make an accident" (63).

Yet an earlier wreck at the initial party of Gatsby's that Nick attends impugns the truth of this aphorism. As the evening ends, a drunken guest rips a wheel off his coupé trying to navigate the drive. For Nick, the sight becomes "bizarre and tumultuous" as guests gather to gawk at the disabled machine: "At least a dozen men, some of them little better off than [the driver] was, explained to him that wheel and car were no longer joined by any physical bond. 'Back out,' he suggested after a moment. 'Put her in reverse'" (60). The driver's inability to comprehend the damage reflects his complete detachment from the car's utility, and he tells the disbelieving crowd, "there's no harm in trying" to run it on only three wheels. The episode foreshadows the tragic moment when Daisy runs over Myrtle after the climactic confrontation between Gatsby and Tom. Here, too, the crowd—including Nick, Tom, and Jordan, who happen upon the accident scene moments after Daisy and Gatsby speed away without stopping—is transfixed by the spectacle. Only this time it is the damage done *by* a car, not *to* it, that captivates. Struck dead in the street, Myrtle becomes an arresting sight, her breast, while not severed like the "amputated" wheel of the coupé, is nevertheless left "swinging loose like a flap" (145). The sight encapsulates the dual appeal that wastage held for Fitzgerald. On the one hand, Myrtle's very public death offers him (through Nick) an opportunity to condemn the immoderation and detachment that causes such accidents: "They were careless people. . . . They smashed up things and creatures and then retreated back into their money or their vast carelessness . . . and let other people clean up the mess" (187–88). Yet the detailed description of Myrtle's corpse, as with similar scenes in "Automobile Collisions" and other essays on the hazards of driving, invites the reader to gaze in spectatorial awe upon the gruesome damage that technologies such as the automobile wreak. Thus, while Fitzgerald recognizes the moral consequences of wastage, he also acknowledges the captivating allure of wreckage that consumerism encourages.

However viscerally arresting are images of car accidents, Fitzgerald's most original contribution to the literature of wastage involves the squandering of psychological and emotional resources rather than material ones. It should be noted that the protagonists of three of Fitzgerald's four novels indulge in spectacular forms of self-destruction that dramatize their moral deterioration. From Amory Blaine to Anthony Patch to Dick Diver, Fitzgerald's heroes not only relieve their unrealized ambitions through forms of excess consumption (usually alcohol)—they turn their dissolution into an exaggerated parody of disposability by exhausting their own potential.[12] Amory articulates this aesthetic most explicitly toward the end of *This Side of Paradise* as he struggles to account for his failures: "Youth is like having a big plate of candy. Sentimentalists think they want to be in the pure, simple state they were in before they ate the candy. They don't. They just want the fun of eating it all over again. . . . I don't want to repeat my innocence. I want the pleasure of losing it again" (239). There is more than a bit of ironic braggadocio in such assertions. In their wholesale indifference to moderation, they are meant to shock audiences by reveling unabashedly in the gluttonous extremes of consumer excess. When a drunken Anthony chides a friend who is encouraging him to seek a productive outlet for his energies by demanding, "Does it bother you particularly that I don't want to work?" (407), or when Dick casually quizzes a former lover, "Did you hear I'd gone into a process of deterioration?" (307), Fitzgerald illustrates an observation that Walter Benjamin makes in his influential essay "The Work of Art in an Age of Mechanical Reproduction": "Mankind's self-alienation has reached such a degree that it can experience its own destruction as an aesthetic pleasure of the first order" (qtd. in Ewen, *Images*, 239). As Fitzgerald implies, if consumerism encourages individuals to view themselves as commodities, it only stands to reason that the same satisfaction to be had in using up and throwing away a marketplace good can be derived by wasting one's own assets.

It would have been interesting, had Fitzgerald not died prematurely in 1940, to gauge his response to the century's next great wave of consumerism in the 1950s, whose momentum was likewise driven by an economic boom occasioned by the winning of a world war. How would he in his fifties have measured the effect of television on his characters, which, not unlike movies in his own time, disseminated idealized images of American life, which spectators were urged to emulate by adopting the fashions and buying the products placed on display? What would he have thought of the backlash against advertising epitomized by exposés such as Vance Packard's *The Hidden Persuaders* (1957), which purported to reveal the quasi-brainwashing techniques by which the heirs of Bruce Barton and Earnest Elmo Calkins shaped consumer desires? Would he have agreed with sociologists such as David Reisman and C. Wright Mills, who in *The Lonely Crowd* (1950) and *White Collar* (1951) argued that the dominance of the corporation in American business meant that the most pressing threat of capitalism wasn't disembodied abundance or evaporating values but consumer conformity? Would he have become a probusiness Republican as Hemingway, Dos Passos, and many others of his generation did in their later years? Or would the leftism he dabbled with in *Tender Is the Night* have grown more pronounced until he sided with Theodor Adorno, Herbert Marcuse, and other members of the Frankfurt School of Marxism, who popularized the term "culture industry" to dramatize the reification of everyday experience? What would Fitzgerald have thought of Levittown, the first prefabricated suburb that arose on Long Island, not far from the site where *The Great Gatsby* was set? How would he have regarded the youth-culture heroes of the Eisenhower era—Holden Caulfield, Sal Paradise, Dean Moriarty—who, like his own Amory Blaine and Anthony Patch, indulge in spectacles of self-wastage? Would he have dismissed teen icons like James Dean and Elvis Presley as idols of mass consumption, or would he have recognized that they excited the same consumer desire to package personality that he himself had in his flapper fictions?

Such questions invite speculation that, in the end, only confirms the complexity of Fitzgerald's attitude toward consumerism. As a social observer, one of his best-appreciated talents was what scholars have called his "double perspective"—his (and his characters') ability to at once participate in a phenomenon while stepping back to objectively assess its consequences. Indeed, as a topic of literary exploration, the booming marketplace elicited the best in Fitzgerald: its variegated styles and colors invited him to exercise his lyrical skills to capture the plush and dazzle of its products, while the change in values it engineered incited his instinct to editorialize. As a result, his fictions remain fully human, capturing both the giddy delight consumers felt when freed from Victorian animadversions against indulgence and the unease of critics who forecasted the excesses encouraged by the modern lack of restraint. "In those days life was like the race in *Alice in Wonderland*," he wrote in "Echoes of the Jazz Age" (1931), a Depression-era reminiscence of the preceding decade. "There was a prize for everyone" (*Crack-Up* 21). But as his work demonstrates, there was a cost to prosperity, too, and the toll was moral, not economic.

NOTES

1. Davis notes that the J. Walter Thompson archive at Duke University contains interesting background on this campaign, including speculation as to why the contest failed to meet the Thompson agency's expectations. See 193n.35.

2. The company's name was actually Muscatine; Fitzgerald was obviously attempting to avoid legal problems by spelling it differently.

3. Fitzgerald's frustrations are evident in a September 1929 letter to Ernest Hemingway, in which he complains about the stalled progress on his novel while confessing the new premium his commercial fiction brings: "Here's a last flicker of the old cheap pride:—the *Post* now pay[s] the old whore $4000. a screw. But now its [*sic*] because she's mastered the 40 positions—in her youth one was enough" (*Life in Letters* 169).

4. Parrish provides several statistics to illustrate the economic uniqueness of the 1920s boom: the American gross national product rose roughly 2 percent a year throughout the decade, while the unemployment rate never broke 4 percent. At the same time, annual income rose "on average a whopping thirty percent," allowing consumers to "lavish a rising fraction of their personal incomes on self-improvement and recreation" (30).

5. Marchand also notes how the salesman is the dominant masculine image of this period: "Among hundreds of thousands of advertisements in the 1920s and 1930s, I have yet to discover a single one in which the husband or the ambitious young man is defined as a factory worker, policeman, engineer, professor, architect, or government official. . . . As a *McCall's* advertisement put it, in an offhand manner that reflected the conventionality of the advertisement stereotype, 'The average man is just a businessman'" (189).

6. One notorious example of how consumerism offered women the illusion of "determining power" was the Torches of Freedom march held in New York on Easter Sunday 1929, when a group of women led by feminist Ruth Hale paraded up and down Fifth Avenue puffing on cigarettes. Ostensibly, the march protested the supposed immorality of female smoking; the women hoped to demonstrate that cigarettes could be every bit the sophisticated fashion accessory for women that they were for men. In reality, however, the march was a clever marketing campaign organized by Edward L. Bernays, one of the founding fathers of modern public relations, at the behest of the American Tobacco Company, which was trying to expand its middle-class distaff market. See Bernays 386–87.

7. For a fascinating study of the rhetoric of eroticism in 1920s advertising, see Reichert. Examining ad campaigns by Woodbury's Facial Soap and Jergen's Lotion, he shows how beneath appeals to intimacy and self-perfection "advertisers advanced the subtle argument that women, if they bought the product, could become the object of the right kind of men's desire" (95).

8. The advertising icon Daisy has in mind is likely the Arrow Collar Man, the ultimate 1920s symbol of "cool." Created by illustrator J. C. Leyendecker, this fictional spokesman appeared in shirt ads between 1905 and 1920. As Kitch notes, the Arrow Collar Man's "predominant characteristic was *class*. In society, [he] appeared with a sophisticated female partner with similarly long body lines and chis-

eled nose and chin. . . . As a couple, they embodied elitism and affluence, conveyed by their facial expressions, their formal poses . . . and their setting. And of course these attributes were conveyed by their clothing. In that sense, 'class' was not a rigid set of social categories but rather something that was for sale, available to people who did not have it but could afford to buy it" (162–63)—someone, in other words, like Gatsby.

9. To appreciate the point of this passage it is helpful to know that, as Donaldson points out, by the time Fitzgerald wrote *Tender Is the Night* in the early 1930s his "political convictions had moved him sharply and programmatically to the left" (195).

10. The phrase "keeping up with the Joneses" comes from the title of a popular early twentieth-century comic strip that featured stories about parental "efforts to restrain fashionable extravagance among the sons and daughters (the 'heirastocracy') of the affluent middle class" (Calder 214). The inspiration for the strip was a pair of bestselling novels by Irving Bacheller, *Keeping Up with Lizzie* (1911) and *"Charge It!" or, Keeping Up with Harry* (1912). Bacheller's characters also provided the nickname for Henry Ford's Model T, which was known as the "Tin Lizzie."

11. *This Side of Paradise* also depicts a gory car wreck when Amory Blaine's Princeton friend Dick Humbird is killed on the road into New York.

12. For a fuller exploration of this theme, see Curnutt, "Youth Culture and the Spectacle of Waste: *This Side of Paradise* and *The Beautiful and Damned*."

WORKS CITED

Barton, Bruce. *The Man Nobody Knows*. Indianapolis, Ind.: Bobbs-Merrill, 1925.

———. "The Prodigal Son." *Good Housekeeping* 80 (July 1928): 58, 192, 194.

Berg, A. Scott. *Maxwell Perkins: Editor of Genius*. 1977. New York: Riverhead, 1997.

Berman, Ronald. *"The Great Gatsby" and Modern Times*. Urbana: University of Illinois Press, 1994.

Bernays, Edward L. *Biography of an Idea: Memoirs of a Public Relations Counsel*. New York: Simon and Schuster, 1965.

Brottman, Mikita. Introduction to *Car Crash Culture*. Ed. Mikita Brottman. New York: Palgrave, 2001. xi–xliii.

Bruccoli, Matthew J. *Some Sort of Epic Grandeur: The Life of F. Scott Fitzgerald*. 1981. Rev. ed. New York: Carroll and Graf, 1991.

Calder, Lendol G. *Financing the American Dream: A Cultural History of Consumer Credit*. Princeton, N.J.: Princeton University Press, 1999.

Calkins, Earnest Elmo. "Beauty—The New Business Tool." *Atlantic Monthly* 140 (Aug. 1927): 145–56.

Cowley, Malcolm. *Exile's Return: A Literary Odyssey of the 1920s*. 1934. New York: Viking, 1951.

Curnutt, Kirk. "Youth Culture and the Spectacle of Waste: *This Side of Paradise* and *The Beautiful and Damned*."In *F. Scott Fitzgerald in the Twenty-First Century*. Ed. Jackson R. Bryer, Ruth Prigozy, and Milton R. Stern. Tuscaloosa: University of Alabama Press, 2003. 79–103.

Davis, Simone Weil. *Living Up to the Ads: Gender Fictions of the 1920s*. Durham, N.C.: Duke University Press, 2000.

"Debtor's Cowardice." *Saturday Evening Post* 194 (Feb. 11, 1922): 23, 89–90, 93–94.

Donaldson, Scott. "Possessions in *The Great Gatsby*." *Southern Review* 37 (Spring 2001): 187–201.

Dumenil, Lynn. *The Modern Temper: American Culture and Society in the 1920s*. New York: Hill and Wang, 1995.

Ewen, Stuart. *All Consuming Images: The Politics of Style in Contemporary Culture*. New York: Basic, 1988.

———. *Captains of Consciousness: Advertising and the Social Roots of the Consumer Culture*. New York: McGraw Hill, 1976.

Fitzgerald, F. Scott. *Afternoon of an Author: A Selection of Uncollected Stories and Essays*. New York: Scribner's, 1958.

———. *The Beautiful and Damned*. New York: Scribner's, 1922.

———. *Before Gatsby: The First Twenty-Six Stories*. Columbia: University of South Carolina Press, 2001.

———. *The Crack-Up*. Ed. Edmund Wilson. New York: New Directions, 1945.

———. *The Cruise of the Rolling Junk*. 1924. Bloomfield Hills, Mich.: Bruccoli Clark, 1976.

———. *Dear Scott/Dear Max: The Fitzgerald-Perkins Correspondence.*

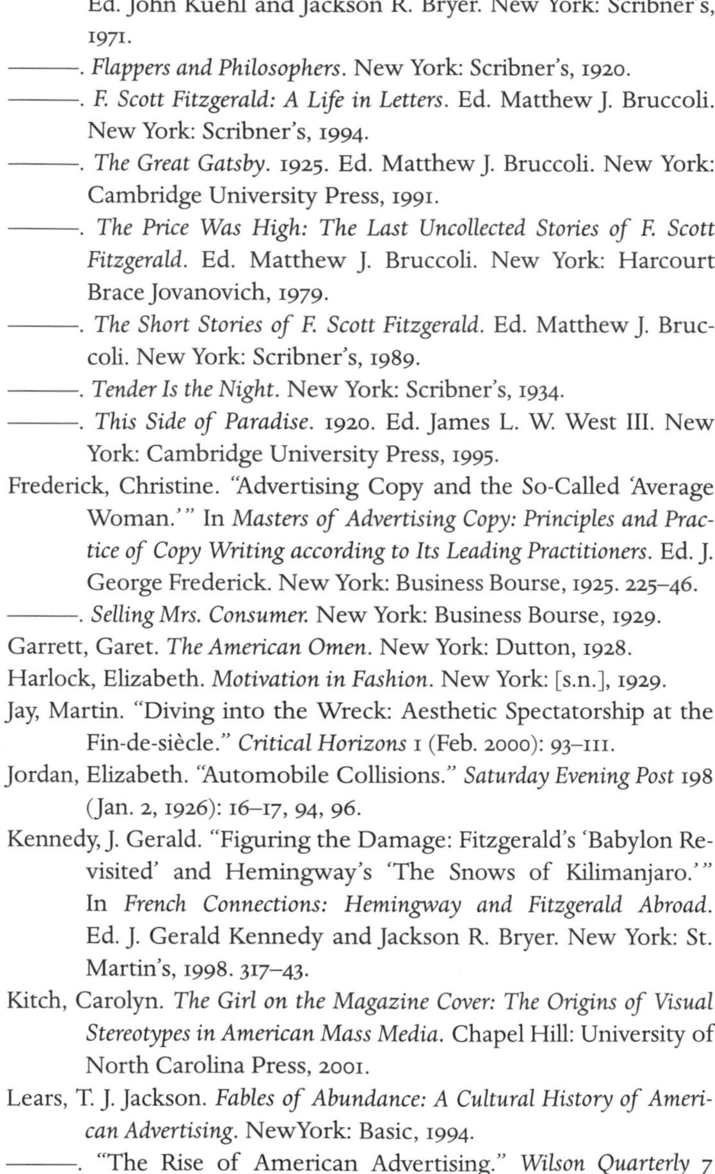

Ed. John Kuehl and Jackson R. Bryer. New York: Scribner's, 1971.
———. *Flappers and Philosophers*. New York: Scribner's, 1920.
———. *F. Scott Fitzgerald: A Life in Letters*. Ed. Matthew J. Bruccoli. New York: Scribner's, 1994.
———. *The Great Gatsby*. 1925. Ed. Matthew J. Bruccoli. New York: Cambridge University Press, 1991.
———. *The Price Was High: The Last Uncollected Stories of F. Scott Fitzgerald*. Ed. Matthew J. Bruccoli. New York: Harcourt Brace Jovanovich, 1979.
———. *The Short Stories of F. Scott Fitzgerald*. Ed. Matthew J. Bruccoli. New York: Scribner's, 1989.
———. *Tender Is the Night*. New York: Scribner's, 1934.
———. *This Side of Paradise*. 1920. Ed. James L. W. West III. New York: Cambridge University Press, 1995.
Frederick, Christine. "Advertising Copy and the So-Called 'Average Woman.'" In *Masters of Advertising Copy: Principles and Practice of Copy Writing according to Its Leading Practitioners*. Ed. J. George Frederick. New York: Business Bourse, 1925. 225–46.
———. *Selling Mrs. Consumer.* New York: Business Bourse, 1929.
Garrett, Garet. *The American Omen*. New York: Dutton, 1928.
Harlock, Elizabeth. *Motivation in Fashion*. New York: [s.n.], 1929.
Jay, Martin. "Diving into the Wreck: Aesthetic Spectatorship at the Fin-de-siècle." *Critical Horizons* 1 (Feb. 2000): 93–111.
Jordan, Elizabeth. "Automobile Collisions." *Saturday Evening Post* 198 (Jan. 2, 1926): 16–17, 94, 96.
Kennedy, J. Gerald. "Figuring the Damage: Fitzgerald's 'Babylon Revisited' and Hemingway's 'The Snows of Kilimanjaro.'" In *French Connections: Hemingway and Fitzgerald Abroad*. Ed. J. Gerald Kennedy and Jackson R. Bryer. New York: St. Martin's, 1998. 317–43.
Kitch, Carolyn. *The Girl on the Magazine Cover: The Origins of Visual Stereotypes in American Mass Media*. Chapel Hill: University of North Carolina Press, 2001.
Lears, T. J. Jackson. *Fables of Abundance: A Cultural History of American Advertising*. NewYork: Basic, 1994.
———. "The Rise of American Advertising." *Wilson Quarterly* 7 (Winter 1983): 156–67.

Lippmann, Walter. *Drift and Mastery: An Attempt to Diagnose the Current Unrest*. New York: Kennerly, 1914.

Lynd, Robert S., and Helen Merrell Lynd. *Middletown: A Study in American Culture*. New York: Harcourt, Brace, 1929.

McClintock, Harry. "The Big Rock Candy Mountains." *O Brother, Where Art Thou?* Universal CD. 2000.

Marchand, Roland. *Advertising the American Dream: Making Way for Modernity, 1920–1940*. Berkeley: University of California Press, 1984.

Naether, Carl A. *Advertising to Women*. New York: Prentice-Hall, 1928.

Nystrom, Paul. *Economics of Fashion*. New York: Ronald, 1928.

Olney, Martha L. *Buy Now, Pay Later: Advertising, Credit, and Consumer Durables in the 1920s*. Chapel Hill: University of North Carolina Press, 1991.

Parrish, Michael E. *Anxious Decades: America in Prosperity and Depression, 1920–1941*. New York: Norton, 1992.

Patten, Simon. *The Consumption of Wealth*. Philadelphia, Pa.: Johnson, 1889.

———. *The New Basis of Civilization*. 1907. Cambridge, Mass.: Belknap, 1968.

Reichert, Tom. *The Erotic History of Advertising*. Amherst, N.Y.: Prometheus, 2003.

Schnapp, Jeffrey T. "Crash (Speed as an Engine of Individuation)." *Modernism/Modernity* 6 (Jan. 1999): 1–49.

Veblen, Thorstein. *The Theory of the Leisure Class*. 1898. New York: Dover, 1994.

Wilson, Edmund. "Current Fashions." In *The American Earthquake: A Documentary of the Twenties and Thirties*. 1958. New York: Farrar, Straus & Giroux, 1979.

———. *Letters on Literature and Politics, 1912–1972*. Ed. Elena Wilson. New York: Farrar, Straus & Giroux, 1977.

Fitzgerald's Flappers and Flapper Films of the Jazz Age

Behind the Morality

Ruth Prigozy

F. Scott Fitzgerald was born just one year after Auguste and Louis Lumière projected moving pictures onto a screen, forever changing the world of popular entertainment. The achievements of Georges Méliès, Thomas Edison, Sergei Eisenstein, and the master silent-film director D. W. Griffith were milestones in the history of the medium and profoundly affected the aspirations, habits, and even economic conditions of those who came of age in the early decades of the twentieth century.

Although other American writers had brief associations with the movies, no other author of his time was as enraptured with the medium as Fitzgerald. From his childhood in Buffalo where he attended matinees featuring western star Dustin Farnum through his years at prep school in the East and at Princeton, he regularly frequented Broadway movie houses, which were rapidly becoming "palaces." He worshiped Griffith, whose influence on his novel *Tender Is the Night* (1934) was profound.[1]

In 1934, when asked by a newspaper to list his ten favorite plays—or outstanding impressions in the theater—Fitzgerald selected three from films: Charlie Chaplin in *The Pilgrim*, Greta Garbo "in her first big role," and "David W. Griffith's face as I imagine it during the filming of *A* [*sic*] *Birth of a Nation* when he was 'forging in the smithy of his soul' all the future possibilities of the camera." (In that same list, he makes a reference to a stage actress whose name he does not remember, although he knows that Joan Crawford played her role in the film version of *Grand Hotel*. See "My 10 Favorite Plays" 61–62.) In an interview with Thomas Boyd in 1922, Fitzgerald retorted to Boyd's disparagement of movies: "But you might as well protest against a Cunarder or the income tax as to protest against the movies. . . . The movies are here to stay" (Bruccoli and Bryer 249). Yet Fitzgerald's lifelong connection with movies was shifting and frequently ambivalent. He recognized that the industry was a fact of contemporary life, that movies provided opportunities to escape from the mundane and to live, albeit vicariously, in a world illuminated by wealth and beauty.

In 1922, after several experiences with filmmaking, he was pleased that some of his works were being adapted into films, and he noted that his own taste ran to seeing a "pleasant flapper like Constance Talmadge or . . . comedies like those of Chaplin's or Lloyd's. I'm not strong for the uplift stuff. It simply isn't life to me" (Bruccoli and Bryer 245). The movies also provided much-needed income at critical moments in his life. But in his strongest criticism, in 1936, after several failed attempts at his own filmwriting career, he wrote:

> I saw that the novel, which at my maturity was the strongest and supplest medium for conveying thought and emotion from one human being to another, was becoming subordinated to a mechanical and communal art that, whether in the hands of Hollywood merchants or Russian idealists, was capable of only the tritest thought, the most obvious emotion. (*Crack-Up* 78)

Yet the movies remain a thread in his work and in his life. His references to films, film stars, and cinematic techniques (notably in *The Great Gatsby*, where he comments on the sunshine and the "great bursts of leaves growing on the trees, just as things grow in fast movies" [7]) abound in letters, notebooks, stories, and, as above, novels, concluding with his, unfinished novel, *The Last Tycoon* (1941), written in Hollywood where he had been working intermittently as a screenwriter for the three years preceding his death. Despite the many disappointments he endured in Hollywood, he remained convinced of his ability to write for the movies, as he reminded Harold Ober in 1936 when trying to get a contract for a screenplay: "Now it seems to me that the point can be sold that I am equipped to do this treatment which is the whole gist of this letter" (*Life in Letters* 295).

In the early years, Fitzgerald's celebrity status made him a natural contender for movie celebrity. He gave interviews to motion-picture magazines (which frequently described him as looking like a handsome movie star), sold a screenplay of his first successful novel, *This Side of Paradise* (1920)—it was rejected—and succeeded in selling the rights to some of his short stories: "Head and Shoulders" (1920) became *The Chorus Girl's Romance* (1920); "Myra Meets His Family" (1920) became *The Husband Hunter* (1920); and "The Offshore Pirate" (1920) was released as a film of the same name in 1921.[2] These three early adaptations have in common their subject matter and main character. They revolve around the exploits and character of the new woman, the flapper, who had become associated in the public mind with Fitzgerald's short stories.

Fitzgerald wrote stories about the uninhibited, freedom-loving, playful, and sexually responsive (but never promiscuous) young women who seemed to appear almost spontaneously after World War I.[3] The staid *New York Times* analyzed the flapper phenomenon in 1922, describing her different types while praising the independence she represented: "She is shameless, selfish and honest, but at the same time she considers these three attributes virtues. Why not? She takes a man's point of view as her mother never could, and when she loses she is not afraid to admit defeat, whether it be a prime lover or $20 at auction" (qtd. in Mowry 173–74). This same newspaper, in July 1929, linked the end of the flapper with the end of the Jazz Age as new, more sophisticated Parisian types were taking center stage: "And the flappers know it. Voices falter in their stridences and reach for lower notes. . . . To Europe, the emergence of this new-old feminine type symbolizes the end of the post-war jazz age and the recrudescence of values that for years were crowded out by the nervous intensity of speed and the jeering laughter of saxophones" (qtd. in Mowry 185).

Fitzgerald was acutely aware of the public's linkage of him, his wife, and his stories and novels to the fate of the flapper. Unlike the *Times*, when he looked back in his 1932 essay "My Lost City," he announced the demise of the flapper as having occurred as early as 1923: "The flapper, upon whose activities the popularity of my first books was based, had become passé by 1923—anyhow in the East" (*Crack-Up* 29). But in that same year, he also expressed surprise at his association with her:

> I did not know *This Side of Paradise* was a flapper book until George Jean Nathan, who had read parts of it before publication, told me it was. However, I do not consider any of my heroines typical of the average bob-skirted "Dulcy" who trips through the Biltmore lobby at tea time. My heroine is what the flapper would like to *think* she is—the actual flapper is a much duller and grayer proposition. I tried to set down different aspects of an individual—I was accused of creating a type. (Bruccoli and Bryer 167–68)

Although many of Fitzgerald's statements about the flapper are responses to questions in celebrity interviews and thus may indeed be exaggerated, there is no question that Fitzgerald's flapper possesses qualities to which the film flappers can only aspire. For Fitzgerald's flappers are complex young women, but the film embodiments of the type are reflections of the stars who played them wearing the newest styles in dress and makeup and who, most important, beneath the surface remain pure, conventional, and decidedly moral.

Both Fitzgerald and the *New York Times* commentator are correct: the flapper as Fitzgerald describes her was indeed part of the past by 1923, but the flapper would have a new incarnation in movies—and unavoidably, the film flapper would be linked with Fitzgerald's creations. I hope to demonstrate the significant differences between the two, for both were major influences in the 1920s—indeed, although Fitzgerald's flapper was the model, the film flapper became overtly a messenger of conventional morality whose style and antics belied those messages. Fitzgerald did recognize that the flapper films served another purpose for their producers: to advertise clothing, architecture, and home decor. In his story "The Popular Girl" (*Saturday Evening Post*, February 18, 1922), Fitzgerald describes his heroine, Yanci—a sympathetic flapper—going to the movies:

> Sitting alone in one of the magnificent moving-picture theaters . . . Yanci watched Mae Murray swirl through splendidly imagined vistas, and meanwhile considered the progress of the first day. . . . Engrossed for a while in the moving picture, she calculated the cost of the apartment in which its heroine endured her movie wrongs. She admired its slender Italian table, occupying only one side of the large dining room and flanked by a long bench which gave it an air of medieval luxury. She rejoiced in the beauty of Mae Murray's clothes and furs, her gorgeous hats, her short-seeming French shoes. Then after a moment her mind returned to her own drama. (*Before Gatsby* 488)

Years later, in his 1931 essay "Echoes of the Jazz Age," he would look back critically at films like the one Yanci is watching, a reflection of his deep ambivalence about the value and quality of the films of the decade (with the exception of those directed by Griffith):

> Contrary to popular opinion, the movies of the Jazz Age had no effect upon its morals. The social attitude of the producers was timid, behind the times and banal—for example, no picture mirrored even faintly the younger generation until 1923, when magazines had already been started to celebrate it and it had long ceased to be news. There were a few feeble splutters and then Clara Bow in *Flaming Youth*; promptly the Hollywood hacks ran the theme into its cinematographic grave. Throughout the Jazz Age the movies got no farther than Mrs. Jiggs, keeping up with its most blatant superficialities. (*Crack-Up* 17–18)[4]

Fitzgerald's comment on the gulf between the morality of the audience and that of the flapper films is perceptive, indeed, as I hope to demonstrate, incontrovertible. But there is an important corollary to any assessment of these films: although Fitzgerald, despite his reservations about particular films, would frequently indicate his respect for cinematic technique, he does not mention here or in "The Popular Girl" that the flapper films of the Jazz Age demonstrate the technical brilliance and artistry of the medium of motion pictures. Although the plots were hackneyed, the narratives awkward, and the messages retrograde, the flapper movies were visually splendid; the skills of directors and cinematographers kept alive both the glittering world and the transcendent image of the young woman who was so strongly associated with Fitzgerald's novels and stories.

In her study of women in the films of this era, *Virgins, Vamps, and Flappers* (1978), Sumiko Higashi examines flapper films from a political/sociological framework. Because she believes that works on film scholarship are not helpful in such a study, as their focus is on the cinematic, she is primarily concerned with the political implications of the representation of women. Her conclusion is that film is a conservative force with respect both to its image of women and its offering the spectator the opportunity to experience life vicariously, thus serving to "disarm the viewer in confronting life's realities" (v). She places much of the blame for that conservatism on censorship, a position that I believe only partially accounts for the moral conservatism of the flapper films. Another writer on the subject, Lewis Jacobs (*The Rise of American Film*, 1968), believes that films and real life did coincide, but in his 1915 pioneering study, *The Art of the Moving Picture*, Vachel Lindsey celebrated the brilliant, dazzling visual achievements of the new cinematic art, recognizing its power to create a world of illusion. In a recent study of silent film, Paula Marantz Cohen (*Silent Film and the Triumph of the American Myth*, 2001) correctly perceives the films of the period as vessels promoting the new consumerism: immigrants learned from films how to become more American, while all women learned consumerism, which "gave them a leverage in the marketplace that would help them to gain the vote.

The stars acted as representatives and guides for these groups" (160).

Unquestioningly, Fitzgerald would agree with some of these assertions, and this essay will explore the questions they raise, but my concern here is the relation between Fitzgerald's flapper and her popular incarnation in flapper films. Both were products of the era and both provided models for young women and for those affected by their ambitions and social roles. Both express and reflect their contemporary culture—and I believe that by looking first at those Fitzgerald stories adapted for film and then at the most important flapper films themselves, we will have a new understanding of the relationship between F. Scott Fitzgerald and the most important popular medium of the Jazz Age. We will also, perhaps, gain an understanding of the author's gradual disappointment in the art form he celebrated throughout his youth. Film flappers were stars and thus by their very nature prohibited from exhibiting the kind of complexity that literary works allow. Despite the implied connection between his work and images of wildly dancing flappers provided by stock footage for many films and TV documentaries on the 1920s, Fitzgerald's flappers were individuals, often troubled, generally courageous, frequently in conflict with themselves, and never predictable. The films tell another story: we will determine what remained of Fitzgerald's flappers in them and in what way the flapper became a phenomenon exploited by the new medium and the economic development of the 1920s.

Fitzgerald's Flappers

F. Scott Fitzgerald wrote novels and stories featuring the flapper, but because he had become so associated in the public mind with this exciting image of the new woman, he was often asked about the history of the type and about her current status. Thus there are actually two types of Fitzgerald flappers: one that exists solely in his fiction and one that reflects his perception of the actual popular feminine icon. In his early interviews he is concerned for the flapper; in 1923 he declares:

> The flapper is going stronger than ever; she gets wilder all the time. She keeps on doing the things she had done before, and adding to them all the time. She is continually seeking for something new to increase her store of experience. She still is looking for new conventions to break—for new thrills, for sensations to add zest to life, and she is growing more and more terrible. (qtd. in Bruccoli and Bryer 263–64)

He would repeat that cautionary note whenever he spoke of the flapper in the mid– to late 1920s, noting that a movement that had begun as a liberating force for women and society had become a superficial display of personality and style. In 1930, he remembered the birth of the flapper in 1912 when the world-famous dancers Vernon and Irene Castle "brought the nice girl into the cabaret and sat her down next to the distinctly not-nice girl." The fun soon went out of the movement, however—it was no longer an expression of the spirit of youthful rebellion but had become the expected behavior of young women. The "flapper movement was over," the accessibility of the automobile standardizing what was once unconventional behavior (Bruccoli and Bryer 207). Zelda Fitzgerald, too, felt that the flapper's most attractive quality had been her spirited unconventionality—she was never boring—but by 1922, "flapperdom has become a game; it is no longer a philosophy" (*Collected Writings* 391).[5]

In an interview conducted in 1927 after the Fitzgeralds had returned from several years abroad, Fitzgerald was asked about the current status of the flapper, for, as the reporter noted, he had virtually created her in *This Side of Paradise*: "The man's book took the country by, as they say, storm. Girls—all the girls read it. They read about the flapper's deportment, methods and career. And with a nice simultaneousness they became, as nearly as their varied capabilities permitted, flappers. Thus the frequency of the term today" (qtd. in Bruccoli and Bryer 277). The writer then identifies the author as F. Scott Fitzgerald and the first flapper as his wife, Zelda, or Rosalind in the novel. She then mentions his first trip to Hollywood when he wrote his screenplay *Lipstick* for Constance Talmadge. The question for the author is, "Have flappers changed since you first gave them the light of publicity?

For better? For worse?" Fitzgerald replies that there is not much change, except that the flappers of today are "less defiant, since their freedom is taken for granted. . . . In my day . . . they had just made their escape from dull and blind conventionality." He then turns to a discussion of the screen flapper and accurately distinguishes between the flapper in real life and on the screen:

> On the screen, of course, is represented every phase of flapper life. But just as the screen exaggerates action, so it exaggerates type. The girl who, in real life, uses a smart, wise-cracking line is portrayed on the screen as a hard-boiled baby. The Type, one of the most dangerous, whose forte is naivete, approximates a dumb-dora when she reaches the screen. The exotic girl becomes bizarre. But the actresses who do flappers really well understand them thoroughly enough to accentuate their characteristics without distorting them. (Bruccoli and Bryer 279–80)

Fitzgerald's assessments of such screen stars as Clara Bow, Colleen Moore, Constance Talmadge, Alice White, and Joan Crawford are astute and reveal his thorough understanding of films and the phenomenon of stardom. His knowledge and understanding of the medium helped to secure him screenwriting contracts, but although he was frequently drawn into consideration of film career possibilities—most resulting in disappointment—his relationship with Hollywood and the world of the movies was at best conflicted: he wanted the rewards, financial and artistic, that the movies promised, but at the same time, he recognized that he could never become part of the structure of an industry that looked first to box-office receipts. His flappers and Hollywood's versions were inevitably different, and the great irony is that he should be firmly linked with the flapper films of the decade.

"Head and Shoulders" was the first short story Fitzgerald sold to the *Saturday Evening Post* (February 21, 1920), and it was the basis for the first film adapted from his work.[6] Of the three Fitzgerald flapper stories that were filmed, it has the most intri-

Filmdom's leading flappers in the 1920s: Constance Talmadge, Alice White, and Joan Crawford. Courtesy Museum of Modern Art, Film Stills Archive.

cate plot and the most underdeveloped characterization. It well might have been constructed as a scenario, so strongly does it depend on action, comic turns, and convolutions. The ending, however, provides the surprise, for it conveys the pathos of a character who may have gained his true love but has lost his essential self—very unlike the typical Hollywood ending of a romantic comedy. Horace Tarbox is a parody of a prodigy (Fitzgerald said he was based on an actual prodigy and that he introduced the chorus girl who "almost stole the show"; qtd. in *Before Gatsby* 129). Marcia Meadow is the chorus girl, and her daring meeting with Horace, her sprightly straightforward dialogue, her exceptional beauty, and the sheer force of her personality make her an endearing heroine, a model of the fearless flapper. She is irresistible, but for Horace, who loves her passionately, her price is high: to live with Marcia, he must become the antithesis of his former self. Perhaps, Fitzgerald suggests, the flapper's energy is, for those closest to her, enervating, and we are left to wonder if youthful passion is worth the price Horace—and presumably other young educated men (perhaps even the author)—must pay. Despite its amusing premise and vivid accounts of vaudeville performances, Fitzgerald did not regard this story highly, and it does not display his gift for descriptive prose. Marcia Meadow, however, is the literary equivalent of Clara Bow: her lack of education, her bouncy charm, and her sexually charged behavior would become recognizable in the flapper who seduced the world's male population in *It* (1927).

"Myra Meets His Family" (*Saturday Evening Post*, March 20, 1920) is a richer, more polished work with a far more complex heroine. Myra Harper is introduced as a generic flapper—a young woman who has had many opportunities to marry but has found excuses to reject all of her suitors.[7] She is the model for Fitzgerald's dissipated heroine Josephine Perry, who becomes an emotional bankrupt, a near-tragic victim of her own excesses in his Basil and Josephine stories. Because of Myra's reputation as a man-hunter out to snare a wealthy husband, her latest admirer becomes frightened and plays a nasty trick designed to discourage her efforts to marry him. The plot is ingenious, but the most attractive aspect of the story is Myra herself.

With knees and garters blazing, Clara Bow portrayed the flapper as an unrelenting flirt with a gusto for "living." Courtesy Museum of Modern Art, Film Stills Archive.

Fitzgerald has carefully painted Myra's past. She is part of a class or group of young women who "live on the Eastern colleges, as kittens live on warm milk" (*Price* 11). Although Fitzgerald clearly reveals Myra's self-absorption, she is nonetheless appealing in her bravery and determination. She is the quintessential flapper, never boring, looking for fun, but knowing that (at twenty-one!—her "prime" is nineteen) her youth is passing and that she must find a husband and settle down—and in doing so must renounce the pleasures she has come to expect in her daily life. Again, Fitzgerald uses theatrical performances effectively within the story, but in one notable passage, he captures the essence of the flapper whose vitality has been diminished by too much experience in her youth: "I can't seem to get interested. . . . I've played round so much that even while I'm kissing the man I wonder how soon I'll get tired of him. I never get carried away like I used to" (*Price* 13). Fitzgerald's flappers see life as a game and all too often must learn that the price for the freedom they have won is the dull routine of marriage and motherhood.

Although Fitzgerald did not think highly of this story, Myra Harper is an affecting heroine, and Fitzgerald explores—as the flapper films would not—the darker side of youthful antics. Other short stories of the period, such as "The Ice Palace" (1920) and "Winter Dreams" (1922), are more sober explorations of similar themes of the possibility of tragic consequences that may result from decisions made in youth and haste. In *The Beautiful and Damned*, Gloria Patch, again too old—at twenty-nine—to continue as a flapper, is in despair looking at her aging face. Fitzgerald is not disparaging these women: he shows clearly that they have become victims of a social order that values youth, beauty, and wealth, and Gloria's rejection of a dull, mechanical life is not a symptom of her ego but, rather, a manifestation of her courage in pursuing a career that, sadly, is now closed to her.[8] Higashi sees the movie flapper as "basically honest and moral in contrast to the Fitzgerald flapper, who could be destructive in a careless manner" (129), but clearly, Fitzgerald's flappers are often conflicted between their needs and strict social constraints. Destructive behavior simply mirrors the intense conflict these young women experience in an era that has removed the old boundaries and has not offered them the alternatives that the feminist movement would help make available for their granddaughters in future decades.

The third film adapted from an early short story (published in the *Saturday Evening Post*, May 29, 1920), *The Offshore Pirate* was released by MGM in 1921, its title unchanged. From the lush visual opening of the story, its cinematic possibilities are evident, although the entrancing colors would be lost in this pre-Technicolor era: The

> sea . . . was a blue dream, as colorful as blue-silk stockings, and beneath a sky as blue as the irises of children's eyes. From the western half of the sky the sun was shying little golden disks at the sea . . . a white steam-yacht, very young and

> graceful, was riding at anchor and under a blue-and-white awning aft a yellow-haired girl reclined in a wicker settee. (*Flappers* 5)

Clearly, this will be a romantic story, and when the young flapper Ardita Farnam appears, it will become a virtual handbook on the manners and morals of the daring young women with whom Fitzgerald's early fiction was linked. Ardita is impudent, self-assertive almost to the point of recklessness, "a supreme egotist" with "unquestioned charm" who at nineteen "gave the effect of a high-spirited precocious child . . . and in the present glow of her youth and beauty all the men and women she had known were but driftwood on the ripples of her temperament" (*Flappers* 14). But, like all of Fitzgerald's flappers, Ardita is courageous, her "one redeeming feature" is that she is unafraid of "anything in heaven or earth." She values her courage "as a rule of life—a sort of insistence on the value of life and the worth of transient things." Ardita expresses the view that underlay the apparently wild antics of young women of spirit in a decade that was rejecting the manners and morals of the prewar generation: "And courage to me meant ploughing through that dull gray mist that comes down on life—not only overriding people and circumstances but overriding the bleakness of living" (*Flappers* 25). For Fitzgerald, the flapper's egotism, rudeness, and thoughtlessness are redeemed by her willingness to embrace life fully and fearlessly, even if she must confront unforeseen and unwelcome consequences of her actions. Curtis Carlyle, the pseudonymous young man who courts her through trickery (the kind of technique used by Whitney Knowlton in "Myra Meets His Family" to avoid marrying), is Ardita's equal in daring and originality; because he is willing to accept life on her terms, they are ideally suited, and their love blossoms.

Of course, Ardita's courage is firmly linked with her youth—and just as in "Winter Dreams" and so many of Fitzgerald's other stories and novels (*The Great Gatsby* is a notable example), it is evanescent. As the author interjects, "To me the interesting thing about Ardita is the courage that will tarnish with her beauty and youth" (*Flappers* 27). Yet clearly, Fitzgerald implies, if we have lived fully, even for a moment, then we have achieved victory over darkness and death. Curtis asks Ardita to suppose that "before joy and hope and all that came back the curtain was drawn on you for good?" Her reply, "Why . . . then I'd have won!" is Fitzgerald's reply to those who would moralize over the antics of the flapper (*Flappers* 26). The film flappers might look and even speak like Ardita, but her sense of daring life to offer its ultimate reward—despite the moral consequences—is missing from the flapper of 1920s films. The main distinction is that the film flappers want fun and flirtation, but there is never a sense that they are seeking anything deeper than the ultimate reward: money and marriage. That Curtis (or Toby Moreland, his real name) can understand, value, and desire Ardita precisely because of her vital commitment to a life enriched beyond material rewards (Fitzgerald's flappers are usually financially secure, but rich girls can be unfulfilled, he reminds us frequently—Daisy Buchanan is one of them) renders him the perfect suitor, and their dance in the moonlight with "the infinite starry spaces overhead" (*Flappers* 30) is an otherworldly expression of a genuine romance.

Both *The Chorus Girl's Romance* and *The Offshore Pirate* featured one of the most popular female stars of the era, Viola Dana, so clearly, Fitzgerald's stories were produced with care. Viola Dana was an early flapper with less overt sex appeal than Clara Bow or Joan Crawford, but she was a unique screen personality. William Everson in *American Silent Film* regards her as unusual in that, at first glance, she seems plain:

> At her first introduction, often chewing gum or dowdily dressed, it was difficult to believe that we could interest ourselves in this kind of a heroine for the ensuing six reels. And yet within a very short time, a kind of inner beauty began to radiate through (in the dramas) or an inner vivacity (in the comedies), so that we were completely won over by her, well able to understand the devotion and love she inspired in her hero. Few actresses were able to pull off this trick, or would have wanted to try. (117)

Fitzgerald's original screenplay, *Lipstick*, featured a flapper, Dolly Carrol, a reversal-of-fortune theme, and a final sequence that would have demonstrated Hollywood's cinematic sophistication. Commissioned in January 1927 by John W. Considine, Jr., of United Artists as a vehicle for Constance Talmadge, the screenplay was quickly rejected. On April 23, 1927, Fitzgerald received a wire from Considine notifying him that production would not begin on his screenplay because "everyone thinks the beginning or premise contains exceptionally fine material but that rest of story is weak" (qtd. in *Lipstick* 35). Fitzgerald received $3,500 for his efforts, which would have brought him an additional $8,500 had the film been made. Considine's judgment of the screenplay is accurate: it opens strongly, sets up its characters and conflict quickly, but bogs down under the weight of slapstick comedy, unsuccessful farce, and unbelievable and unnecessary comic types. Ten years later Fitzgerald would look back ruefully on this experience:

> I had been loafing for six months for the first time in my life and was confidant[*sic*] to the point of conceit. Hollywood made a big fuss over us and the ladies all looked very beautiful to a man of thirty. I honestly believed that *with no effort on my part* I was a sort of magician with words—an odd delusion on my part when I had worked so desperately hard to develop a hard colorful prose style. . . . Total result—a great time + no work. I was to be paid only a small amount unless they made my picture—they didn't. (*Life in Letters* 330)[9]

Aaron Latham notes that the "comic flaw" in the script resides in the author's belief that his "hard colorful prose style" would be sufficient to create a good script (58).[10] But more serious than Fitzgerald's literary interpolations—like the opening, which might just as well introduce a short story: "School was over. The happy children, their books swinging carelessly at a strap's end, tripped out into the Spring fields—Wait a minute, that's the wrong story" (6)—is the descent into farce without interesting characters to propel the action.

The plot concerns a young woman who is falsely imprisoned

and a wealthy, handsome, intelligent but judgmental young man who ultimately overcomes his prejudices against what he perceives as her criminal background through the force of her beauty, charm, and courage. The plot gimmick is a magnetic lipstick that is so alluring that men immediately fall in love with the wearer. That Dolly is able to attract Ben Manny without the lipstick is the ultimate test of the authenticity of his love and commitment.

Fitzgerald's screenplay lacks any visual directions, unlike early dramatic efforts like "The Debutante" (1917), which was later incorporated into *This Side of Paradise*; here he would have needed suggestions for the camera. His subtitle is "A College Comedy," which suggests the striking juxtaposition between the prison school where Dolly instructs other inmates and the college classroom. Indeed, although Fitzgerald eschews cinematic guidelines, it is clear that he is thinking of crosscutting between the two locations, with action in the prison paralleling events on a college campus. Thus, the introductions to Dolly and to Ben occur virtually simultaneously, as they would in a film, offering the relationship between the two principals as the focus of the ensuing narrative. As Fitzgerald urges the reader to "look around her cell and you will hear the drums that have beat in her ear on lonely nights. Pictures of debutantes, of society functions, bathing beauties, actresses, golf champions, film stars—people reveling through life, being happy," he is setting up a cue for a cinematic internal monologue, using a montage sequence to dramatize her clippings of the life she yearns for. The shots cut from debutante Mimi Haughton (Ben's fiancée) "*presented to society at dinner dance at the* Plaza" to a "*'Flapper Army' besieging the Mayor for a Mother's Relief*" to a "*contest winner gets the lead role in* Amorous Love," and finally to "*'Necking parties on wane' say Club Women*" (7). At the end of the first four of the six sequences of the screenplay, Fitzgerald states, "This is the end of the first [second, etc.] sequence." He is trying to conform to the demands of a screenplay, but this effort is a curious amalgam of his multiple-sequence short stories and a treatment for a screenplay.

Fitzgerald clearly understood parallel action in movies, one of Griffith's most important contributions to the genre years earlier. In the early sequences it creates suspense and anticipation—

notably when Dolly is preparing to leave her prison cell and when Ben, on a college field trip, enters the same building.

Shifting the scene to the "Ritzmore" Hotel, Fitzgerald is attempting to conform to the movies' blatant appeals to consumers. The Russian sable coat, the chauffeured Rolls Royce, the prom with its smartly costumed flappers, and the lavish ballroom all reflect the appeal of films to a public—particularly women—eager to participate, even vicariously, in the world of fun and excitement that was beckoning in the heady days of the Jazz Age. Ironically, the trainload of girls and chaperones arriving for the prom would be replicated thirteen years later in *Winter Carnival* (1940), based on the Dartmouth festival at which Fitzgerald and Budd Schulberg drank themselves into disgrace and (for Fitzgerald) into the hospital.[11]

As the narrative becomes farcically convoluted in parts 4 through 6, the character of the flapper loses her dominance and the screenplay falters badly. Fitzgerald has created in Dolly Carrol a young woman of integrity, strength, beauty, and intelligence—indeed, she is one of his most admirable heroines. Latham is correct in noting the link between Dolly Carrol (he misspells her last name as Carroll) and Kathleen, the heroine of *The Last Tycoon*, a young woman whom life has not always treated kindly. But the descent into plot tricks robs her of the opportunity so clearly given to Ardita Farnam in "The Offshore Pirate"; Dolly becomes simply an illustration of the Hollywood happy ending. As the lovers commence the grand march, climbing the "Wedding Stair" that leads to the "Honeymoon Tower," her conflicts, doubts, and nuances of character disappear.

Fitzgerald knew more about contemporary films than most of the commentators on *Lipstick* suggest, for he built the narrative to a visual crescendo, looking to a set design that would, in the best art-deco manner, present the couple on the tower where "the night is soft as a benediction" (31). His description of the prom from above, as critics have noted, is a forerunner of Busby Berkeley—but as my analysis of other films of this period will indicate, filmmakers were already experimenting with unusual camera placement to achieve remarkable special effects (although Berkeley's genius carried similar sequences to a higher level of sophistication than Hollywood had thus far achieved). Fitzgerald's description is filmic (again, despite his use of color for a black-and-white cinema world), and the view that he was not sufficiently knowledgeable about film technique is questionable:

> Looked at from above the prom resolved itself into a central circle of closely packed stags around which hub revolved the varicolored wheel of dancers. Outside the wheel was a further ring of stags, flanked at each end by a celebrated orchestra from New York. The slow revolution of the wheel and the flashes of black darting out to dance with pink or blue or gold, kept the whole scene in constant, colorful motion. (28)

There is another reason for the failure of *Lipstick*: the era of the flapper was truly over, as Fitzgerald had stated four years earlier. And the flapper of his stories and novels before 1925 was unlike her cinematic counterpart, even the heroine of the 1923 *Flaming Youth*, starring his good friend Colleen Moore. The *New York Times* noted that the censors were lenient with this film, possibly because of its focus on artistic photography and settings. Thus there is a bath sequence with women seen in silhouette with their undergarments clearly visible. The flapper is simply a "saucy . . . jazz-devoted novice. . . . she lives the part of a pert young thing" (qtd. in Pratt 295). The emphasis is on the flapper's sexuality, notably in a scene that would be duplicated by Clara Bow in *It* in which the young woman is pulled out of the sea, her clothes clinging suggestively to her body. It is clear from *Flaming Youth*'s early screen incarnation of the flapper to the later, more polished and sophisticated models that they would be unlike Fitzgerald's flappers—indeed, they would, like Colleen Moore's Pat Fentriss, reflect the personalities, sexual appeal, and publicly molded images of their stars.

The Flapper in Films

The flapper in the films of the late 1920s was a figure who duplicated some of Fitzgerald's heroine's ideals—independence of

The luxurious world of Our Dancing Daughters, *replete with art-deco decor. Courtesy Museum of Modern Art, Film Stills Archive.*

spirit and love of fun—but used them in the service of securing the most desirable middle-class goals: money, husband, home. Indeed, in these films, the flapper is the movie star, attractive on the surface, but with little to suggest of an interior life (perhaps with the exception of Joan Crawford in *Our Dancing Daughters*).

The film flapper is closely defined by the star system that evolved in the second decade of the twentieth century.[12] For filmgoers in the mid– to late 1920s, when the important flapper films were produced, the heroine combined the traits of the vamp and the good girl, both familiar icons of silent film melodramas, and emerged as the sparkling heroine whose pursuit of fun entranced audiences. As Paula Marantz Cohen states, "The stars were not mere placards for the display of commodities but also the embodiment of the public's deepest desires and fears, so that what the stars wore and surrounded themselves with became invested with these feelings" (157). And because the stars of these films were notable for their exhibitionism, whether dancing, drinking, swimming, or simply displaying their wardrobes, they do not achieve the subtle expression of internal conflict that Greta Garbo's performances convey during these years. Instead, their overt sexual allure and flirtatiousness are embedded in morality tales that audiences could easily ignore—as Fitzgerald so accurately observed.

I propose here to examine a select group of films from the late 1920s that deal with this new woman who, as has been noted, was associated in the public mind with Fitzgerald's *This Side of Paradise* and later such short stories as those discussed previously. The two stars of the era most closely associated with the flapper are Clara Bow and Joan Crawford, each with a distinct personality as well as a uniquely characteristic interpretation of the model. Lillian Gish, the ideal Victorian heroine, and Mary Pickford, the spunky child-woman, are unparalleled in their depiction of other types of women of the era, particularly in the melodramas. Yet it is the flapper who is most frequently linked with the Jazz Age spirit and whose on-screen persona reveals much about the interaction between the movies and their audiences. In this brief examination I hope to demonstrate that far from serving as moral tracts as their overt messages so stridently stress, the flapper films were celebrations of modern art, architecture, costume design, dance, and a world of exhilarating aesthetic pleasure expressed in a new medium that was itself both the means and the focus of that pleasure. For film itself by the late 1920s offered sophisticated visual delight, and the banal morality was lost in the sheer joy of spectatorship.[13] For this discussion I will concentrate on two Clara Bow films, *Dancing Mothers* (1926) and *It* (1927), and two featuring Joan Crawford, *Our Dancing Daughters* (1928) and *Our Modern Maidens* (1929). I shall also comment briefly on two films featuring the same stars that reveal how outmoded the flapper had become after the advent of sound, Bow's *Wild Party* (1929) and Crawford's *Our Blushing Brides* (1930), the latter notably affected by the 1929 stock market crash.

In *Dancing Mothers*, Clara Bow plays the aptly named "Kittens" Westcourt, a relentless and unrepentant flirt, who, like her father, Hugh (Norman Trevor), enjoys dancing, dining, drinking, and even tacitly illicit assignations with the opposite sex while their mother and wife, Ethel (Alice Joyce), stays at home. An unusual film for its time (and not particularly successful at the box office), it is remarkable today for its portrait of a modern Ibsen's Nora in Ethel, who ultimately walks out on her faithless husband and self-absorbed daughter to pursue a life of freedom—a goal purposely left vague at the end. Throughout the film the emphasis is on "living," a word whose meaning differs greatly from the aspirations of Fitzgerald's Ardita. For Ethel, the decision to go out on the town to a roof club is clear: "I want to live!" she declares. Later when she flirts with a young man, Naughton, whom Kittens admires, she says, "I'm playing with life." When Hugh appears at Naughton's to confront Ethel, Naughton tells him to stop "playing the heavy." The emphasis throughout is on play—and this new life as a form of amusement-park entertainment, a meaning that the leisure settings reinforce. Thus, although this film has the most unique and serious message of the group I am discussing—Ethel's last line is clearly serious: "You've given me my freedom. My duty is to myself"—the chief attractions for the viewers are Clara Bow, the dance sequences, and the excitement of the nightclub and speakeasy.

The Westcourt home is the first of many mansions that would come to symbolize the world of the wealthy who could afford to indulge their leisure-class whims. Not yet as lavish as the decor in later films, the home is nevertheless notable for its wide staircase, spacious entrance hall, and large, comfortable furnishings. The roof club is likewise the haunt of pleasure seekers: it is a spacious room, with oversized potted plants and stately columns, but an otherwise curiously innocuous decor. But the dancing couples are everywhere—dance is the euphemism for living and for escaping the boundaries of the moral life. The other pleasure haunt, the speakeasy, is constructed like a huge sailing ship, with dancers on the top deck and booths and tables below, with a prow that suggests the dangers of exotic adventure.

Clara Bow flits through the film like a blithe spirit who refuses to rest; she dances, smiles, rolls her eyes, pouts, and throws her body suggestively, challenging the camera to find another person or object as alluring as she. Clearly made on a smaller budget than the other films under discussion, *Dancing Mothers*, despite its remarkable conclusion, was primarily interesting to audiences who saw in Bow the epitome of the fun-loving flapper, attired in the latest fashion, dancing and drinking in the new establishments that no longer were unattainable to a population itself in pursuit of fun.

Bow's star-making film, *It*, was based on Elinor Glyn's book of that name (Glyn has a cameo in the film). Bow is a working girl who exemplifies Glyn's definition of "it"—which behind the film's euphemisms may be defined as sex appeal.[14] (Fitzgerald's flappers were of a higher social class, except for Marcia Meadow of "Head and Shoulders," but Bow's role as a performer places her in an arena beyond class distinctions—as it did all of the new stars of the era.) In this Cinderella saga, the lingerie salesgirl sets her sights on the owner of the department store and after a series of misadventures finally captures him. Although analysts of class distinctions will quickly discern the working girl's desire to achieve leisure-class status, behind the leering flirtations, the unfettered Bow is a miracle of free-spirited fun, showcasing a window of opportunity that may open to the truly daring young woman. And the world of the film is a consumer's paradise, from the opening high-angle long shot of the world's largest department store, to the heroine's friend remaking a daytime dress into a glamorous evening gown, to the lavish boudoir of a wealthy blonde who is after the same man as the heroine, to the uninhibited world of the Coney Island amusement park beach and funhouse, and to the final sequences shot at sea on an elegant yacht. The film is, of course, filled with sexual innuendo, ending with the inimitable Bow clinging to the ship, drenched, with every curve of her body clearly outlined so as to underscore her sex appeal. In a genuine Clara Bow moment, the star plays the banjo and sings for a group of admirers as the love interest approaches to ask for her hand. No audience could possibly take the silly story seriously, but no one in the audience could emerge immune to the considerable charms of the star and to the possibilities awaiting a young woman of beauty and calculation whatever her social class might be. In Bow's films, the vitality of the star overwhelms the world of the film; the decor, architecture, and costumes (although scanty) are less important than the ceaseless energy she brings to the screen. Bow as Kittens is upper class, but not convincingly; as Betty Lou in *It*, she incarnates the working-class heroine who through her sexuality, her wiles, and her innocence—an important component of her charm—achieves the material rewards that appear to lie beyond her reach. The film was enormously successful, primarily because of Bow's undeniable appeal. It broke records throughout the country, achieving twice the gross of every other film that year, even in New York City, where it achieved a 50 percent higher box office than the competition. *Variety* gleefully noted, "This Bow girl certainly has that certain 'It' for which the picture is named, and she just runs away with the film. She can troupe in the front of a camera, and the manner in which she puts it all over the supporting cast in this production is a joy to behold." As Bow's biographer notes, "*It* made Clara the ranking Jazz Baby of the Jazz Age" (Stenn 87).

The Joan Crawford films, on the other hand, effectively merge the glamour, sophistication, and beauty of the star with a world that mirrors her attributes. Crawford's flapper is less overtly sexual than Bow's, and it is clear that her greater refinement was perfectly attuned to the aspirations of the audience, to the world of her films, and to the considerably greater advancement in film technique and visual style of the last years of silent film.

Our Dancing Daughters announces its subject and style from the first shot, a statue of a naked dancing woman, then a quick cut to a woman's feet in dancing shoes, frantically performing the Charleston. The camera retains its focus on the woman's legs as she dons underwear, a fringed skirt, and finally, as it becomes clear that she is no longer nude, the camera pulls back to reveal Crawford in full flapper gear, looking into a set of triple mirrors as she continues the frenetic dance. Then, in a long shot, we are treated to the world of this young woman: an enormous bedroom with high arches, mirrors, art-deco furnishings, and a fur wrap which she carelessly throws over her shoulders. In the first close-up of Crawford, we see a beautiful and sensitive face in soft focus, quiet for a moment, then smiling in anticipation of the evening ahead. She bids good night to her equally elegant parents—"See you at dawn"—as she heads to the yacht club. As she and her parents raise their glasses in a toast, she drinks, "To myself. I have to live with myself until I die—so may I always like myself." These are, of course, coded words of the era: whatever her actions may suggest, she is a virtuous, albeit fun-loving girl—her morality is never in question to the audience. There is never a sense of depth in her yearning for experience, which Fitzgerald's flappers so eloquently affirm. The film then takes up the lives of two other flappers in a morality tale about three women from three very different homes. Joan Crawford, looking back, said the film was "a field day for me—I think it was the first time the script department was told to write strictly for Crawford" (Newquist 70).

As the heroine, Diana, Crawford becomes the model of the flapper, wild on the outside, but inwardly virtuous and sensitive. Although the excuse for the film is the moral contrast among three young women, the real subject is the world of the wealthy flapper, and the film spares no expense in its graphic depiction of that world. The first party at the yacht club is a riotous affair, filmed from high angle, with balloons filling the frame. Diana is in the middle, on a table, dancing wildly for the delectation of the spectators. For these party scenes, director Harry Beaumont's point-of-view editing emphasizes the dancing, costumes, decor, and especially the sexuality of Diana, who is in ceaseless motion until her eyes meet those of the young man who will become her successful suitor. Although her wild ways cause others to doubt her virtue, her declaration, "I'm not a liar and a cheat. I've been decent and I've lost and the others have won," endears her to an audience that has not for a moment doubted her essential morality.

Throughout the film the viewer is afforded glimpses of closets stocked with furs and evening gowns and drawers filled with glittering jewels. But what engages the viewer throughout is the architecture and decor of the mansions, yachts, and clubs. Establishing shots predominate, for they leave no doubt about the kind of world to which the audience has been admitted. In a sequence that foreshadows the ending of a later Crawford success, *Mildred Pierce* (1945), the camera focuses on three scrubwomen cleaning up the ravages of a party. The "bad" girl—scheming and avaricious, she mocks the working women, but intoxicated, she falls down a flight of stairs into their world—embodies a message for those who treat virtue lightly. The scrubwomen, looking at the girl who has died in the fall, state the film's moral: "Jewels won't do her no good now." The obviousness of the words is, however, lost in the conflicting message that this and other films of the genre imply: a world of beauty, elegance, and fun lies out there, and short of committing an irrevocable error, it is available to the clever young woman who knows how to use her charms to achieve the goals so vividly realized by sophisticated cinematography.

Joan Crawford electrified audiences as Clara Bow had, and the opening performance, with a frenetic musical accompaniment, further lessened the film's moral statement. Indeed, the reviewer for the *New York Times* complained about the "several love songs, stentorian cheering, and at the end, a chorus of shrieks." He noted that the drinking, dancing, and dalliance make the film "anything but conservative and points to the too-obvious moral—the bad girl falling down the stairs" (qtd. in Pratt 471). For Crawford, who had already made twenty-five films, her presence in this film, like Bow's in *It*, made her an authentic star.

In *Our Modern Maidens*, director Jack Conway continues the pattern of Crawford's previous success. Crawford noted that this was "the first one that gave the wardrobe department a chance to go all out to make Crawford a clothes horse" (Newquist 70). And she is indeed dressed for every occasion, from the first shot of her dancing in a glittering gown atop a packed automobile celebrating graduation at a prom. With Douglas Fairbanks, Jr., in a splendid performance (he and Crawford subsequently married), Crawford, as Billie, announces that they have to go to live in Paris: "It's got to be Paris. . . . The big brass band for me." Although she matures along the way and finds a man who expects more than dancing in his future, the narrative is once again merely an excuse for a film that is an extraordinary example of what film technology could achieve in 1929.

The house party on the Fourth of July begins with a montage of musical instruments, dancing, drinking; it's a party in full swing, with Billie at the drums. Then the camera pulls back to reveal in long shot an art-deco room, lavishly decorated with white statuary and a massive piano placed in the foreground. As Billie climbs the stairs, the camera stays in long shot, and the intricate, oval-ceilinged architecture captures the viewer's attention. In a tour-de-force performance, Fairbanks satirizes contemporary heroes of silent film in pantomime, including John Barrymore as Dr. Jekyll and John Gilbert as Robin Hood, before the camera captures him in low angle resting on the enormous art-deco piano. In a long shot of the room, with Billie facing us on the balcony, the lights dim, and she begins to dance in a striped costume that emphasizes her dramatic performance. As if unwilling to leave the pyrotechnics of this performance, the director cuts to fireworks outside, and the characters, in darkness, are revealed only with each explosion in the sky. Finally, in this phantasmagoric sequence, gondolas appear on the lake, with gondoliers singing to lovers entranced by the romantic possibilities of this moonlit evening.

Clearly, the love/morality fable becomes lost amid the art decoration filmed with technical wizardry: high arched doors, a beautiful secluded cabin in the country with the very latest in interior design and fine art, and a storm outside, photographed cleverly with a close-up of car tires mired in mud, indicating that the man and woman will have to spend the night—virtuously—together. As the film progresses, the director seeks every opportunity to fill the frame with new and impressive designs: an extra-long shot emphasizing the cubist geometry of a room, massive fireplaces (long before *Citizen Kane*'s), and, perhaps most striking, as Billie looks out the window, on the upper left of the frame, a painting of her new lover's home in Argentina—which she had seen in his cabin—is the focus of an ingenious iris shot. The last major sequence of the film, a wedding, is a virtual panoply of magnificence in a long shot: arches, balcony, clothing, choir—and we notice that the decor and furnishings have become more expressionistic as the film has progressed. The final montage of musical instruments recalls the beginning of the film as the narrative comes full circle, with Billie finding true adult love in a world whose possibilitics for romance and glamour clearly do not end with marriage.

Director Dorothy Arzner's *Wild Party* was both Paramount Pictures' and Clara Bow's first talking picture. Four years later, the star was to make her last film, and it is clear from this movie why she had lost her appeal. First, she is obviously older, and the coy antics no longer seem natural. The studio did not give her sufficient voice and diction training, and her plebeian roots are all too obvious. In addition, this is a decidedly unglamorous film, with none of the technical innovation apparent in the films we have discussed. In Crawford's first sound film, *Our Blushing Brides*, however, the director, again Harry Beaumont, once more concentrates on filmic innovation and experimental art decoration, but the film fails to ignite. (See the pre–Busby Berkeley sequence, in a round pool with flowers in the center and women forming the geometrically arranged petals circling the pool.) The Great Depression had begun; the narrative concerns shopgirls living in plain apartments, with relief from the dreariness provided by the camera's excursions to a mansion in Oyster Bay, an extravagant performance featuring winter and summer sports (these shows would be features of the early Warner Brothers musicals in the 1930s), and a well-staged fashion show that Hollywood would later incorporate routinely into its Technicolor extravaganzas. There is one shot that is truly memorable; it focuses on a beautiful room with elegant art-deco designs, a recessed area, curved seating, and high ceilings that reveal the sumptuous decor. But recognizing that this world is no longer accessible to the young women who had identified with the daring flapper in the 1920s, the film bogs down in makeshift moralizing; it is unable to strike a balance between the possibilities of the Jazz Age and the realities of the Depression. It would be a few years before RKO would launch its own venture into a new high fashion, art-deco world, but the flapper was no longer relevant in a society facing the grim realities of unemployment and abject poverty. The flapper's spirit would be expanded in the new stars of the 1930s, women whose skill at finding a place in that world would involve more than dancing, drinking, and flirting. The new embodiment of the best qualities of the flapper would be Ginger Rogers—decidedly working class, with a toughness that only the skills of the debonair Fred Astaire might penetrate. Astaire and

Rogers inherited the art-deco settings, the music and costumes, but the morality of those earlier films would be buried beneath the dance floor. Bow was gone, Crawford moved on to a successful series of melodramas, and the flapper films became a footnote to film history. For F. Scott Fitzgerald, the flapper had long ceased to be central to his fiction, but his final years would be spent in Hollywood, where his lifelong fascination with film would find fulfillment in his last unfinished novel—for many readers, the most searing, accurate, and moving portrait of the industry that now dominates the popular culture of America and of the world.

Glossary of Film Terms

Close-up. The camera seems very close to the subject, so that when the image is projected most of the screen will be taken up with a face and its expressions or any object so filmed.

Crosscutting. Editing that alternates shots of two or more lines of action occurring in different places, usually simultaneously.

Cut. The point at which one shot ends and the next begins, usually made by splicing two pieces of film together.

Establishing shot. Often the opening shot of a sequence, showing the location of a scene or the arrangement of its characters; usually a long shot.

Frame. The individual picture on a strip of film.

High-angle long shot. A camera is placed on a crane, high above the action, at a distance from the object or objects being filmed.

Iris. A round moving mask on film stock that can close down to end a scene (iris-out) or open from darkness into an expanding circle within which is the image.

Long shot. The camera seems to be at a distance from the subject being filmed.

Low-angle shot. A shot that looks up at the subject.

Montage sequence. The use of rapid superimpositions and dissolves in order to create a kind of kaleidoscopic effect.

Point-of-view shot. A shot that represents what a character is looking at, seen from his/her perspective and thus often increasing the viewer's emotional identification with that character.

Soft focus. In soft focus, often used for romantic effects, all objects appear blurred because none are perfectly in focus. This diffused effect is often used to photograph aging leading ladies or, as in this case, to romanticize Joan Crawford's face.

NOTES

1. For more on Fitzgerald's interest in film, see Alan Margolies, "Fitzgerald and Hollywood," in *The Cambridge Companion to F. Scott Fitzgerald*; Latham; and Dixon. For Griffith's influence on *Tender Is the Night*, see Prigozy, "From Griffith's Girls to 'Daddy's Girl': The Masks of Innocence in *Tender Is the Night*."

2. "Head and Shoulders" was sold to MGM for $2,250; "The Offshore Pirate" brought $2,025 from the same company. Fox bought "Myra Meets His Family" for $900, along with an option for future work for $2,700. Fitzgerald had sold *This Side of Paradise* to Famous Players for $10,000 in 1923, but it was never made. Other works sold to studios include stories "The Camel's Back" (Warner Brothers, $1,000, 1923) and "The Pusher-in-the Face" (1926, price unknown, filmed in 1928 by Paramount), and the novel *The Beautiful and Damned* (Warner Brothers, $2,250, 1922).

3. The term *flapper* appears as early as Owen Johnson's 1914 novel, *The Salamander*. An offhand comment in Fitzgerald's *Notebooks* gives some sense of the character's demise in popular culture: "The flapper never really disappeared in the twenties—she merely dropped her name, put on rubber heels and worked in the dark" (204). For background on youth and womanhood in the 1920s, see Kirk Curnutt, "F. Scott Fitzgerald, Age Consciousness, and the Rise of American Youth Culture," and Rena Sanderson, "Women in Fitzgerald's Fiction," both in *The Cambridge Companion to F. Scott Fitzgerald*.

4. Colleen Moore, not Clara Bow, starred in *Flaming Youth*. Fitzgerald has said that she was the "spark that lit up *Flaming Youth*" and that "Colleen Moore was the torch." See Moore's *Silent Star*, 141.

5. Zelda Fitzgerald's interview in 1925 for *McCall's* on the subject of flappers, "What Became of the Flappers?" was published in tandem with her husband's assessment of the young men of the period, the "sheiks." See Zelda Fitzgerald, *Collected Writings*, 397; and Bruccoli and Bryer 202.

6. The film adaptations of Fitzgerald's three stories under discussion are not available for viewing and are presumed lost or destroyed.

7. In addition to the 1920 adaptation, an effective television play, "Under the Biltmore Clock," was released in 1984, featuring Sean Young as Myra.

8. See Sanderson and Fryer for further discussion of this point.

9. Fitzgerald's agent, Harold Ober, reported, "He says he got into a row with Constance Talmadge for whom the story was written and he think[s] this is the reason they didn't want to do it." See *As Ever, Scott Fitz*—— 95–96.

10 Latham's *Crazy Sundays* includes a thematic reading of *Lipstick* but does not analyze its filmic qualities. Nor does Latham mention the pre–Busby Berkeley aspect of the party scene discussed below. See 55–59.

11. For a full discussion of Fitzgerald's work on the film, see Schulberg 103–59.

12. See Everson's chapter 12 and especially Cohen's chapter 5 for analyses of the development of the stars and their styles.

13. The movie industry at this time was big business—the fourth-ranked in the nation, with an investment of $1.5 billion and producing 90 percent of the world's films (Higashi iii).

14. "It" is defined in the film as "self-confidence and indifference as to whether you are pleasing or not—and something in you that gives the impression that you are not all cold. That's 'It!' If you have It you will win the girl you love."

WORKS CITED

Bordwell, David, and Kristin Thompson. Eds. *Film Art: An Introduction*. 6th ed. New York: McGraw Hill, 2001.

Bruccoli, Matthew J., and Jackson R. Bryer. Eds. *F. Scott Fitzgerald in His Own Time: A Miscellany*. Kent, Ohio: Kent State University Press, 1971.

Cohen, Paula Marantz. *Silent Film and the Triumph of the American Myth*. New York: Oxford University Press, 2001.

Curnutt, Kirk. "F. Scott Fitzgerald, Age Consciousness, and the Rise of American Youth Culture." In *The Cambridge Companion to*

F. Scott Fitzgerald. Ed. Ruth Prigozy. New York: Cambridge University Press, 2002. 28–47.

Dixon, Wheeler Winston. *The Cinematic Vision of F. Scott Fitzgerald*. Ann Arbor, Mich.: UMI Research Press, 1986.

Everson, William K. *American Silent Film*. 1978. New York: DaCapo, 1998.

Fitzgerald, F. Scott. *As Ever, ScottFitz——*. Ed. Matthew J. Bruccoli and Jennifer M. Atkinson. Philadelphia: Lippincott, 1972.

———. *The Basil and Josephine Stories*. Ed. Jackson R. Bryer and John Kuehl. New York: Scribner's, 1973.

———. *The Beautiful and Damned*. New York: Scribner's, 1922.

———. *Before Gatsby: The First Twenty-Six Stories*. Ed. Matthew J. Bruccoli. Columbia: University of South Carolina Press, 2001.

———. *The Crack-Up*. Ed. Edmund Wilson. New York: New Directions, 1945.

———. *Flappers and Philosophers*. 1920. Ed. James L. W. West III. New York: Cambridge University Press, 2000.

———. *F. Scott Fitzgerald: A Life in Letters*. Ed. Matthew J. Bruccoli and Judith S. Baughman. New York: Scribner's, 1994.

———. *The Great Gatsby*. 1925. Ed. Ruth Prigozy. Oxford: Oxford University Press, 1998.

———. *The Love of the Last Tycoon: A Western*. 1941. Ed. Matthew J. Bruccoli. New York: Cambridge University Press, 1993.

———. "*Lipstick*." *Fitzgerald/Hemingway Annual* 10 (1978): 3–35.

———. "My 10 Favorite Plays." *New York Sun* (Sept. 10, 1934): 19; *Fitzgerald/Hemingway Annual* 10 (1978): 61–63.

———. *The Notebooks of F. Scott Fitzgerald*. Ed. Matthew J. Bruccoli. New York: Harcourt Brace Jovanovich/Bruccoli Clark, 1978.

———. *The Price Was High: The Last Uncollected Stories of F. Scott Fitzgerald*. Ed. Matthew J. Bruccoli. New York: Harcourt Brace Jovanovich/Bruccoli Clark, 1979.

———. *The Short Stories of F. Scott Fitzgerald*. Ed. Mattthew J. Bruccoli. New York: Scribner's, 1989.

———. *This Side of Paradise*. 1920. Ed. Ruth Prigozy. New York: Pocket Books, 1995.

Fitzgerald, Zelda. *The Collected Writings*. Ed. Matthew J. Bruccoli. New York: Scribner's, 1991.

Fryer, Sarah Beebe. *Fitzgerald's New Women: Harbingers of Change.* Ann Arbor, Mich.: UMI Research Press, 1988.

Higashi, Sumiko. *Virgins, Vamps, and Flappers: The American Silent Movie Heroine.* St. Albans, Vt.: Eden Press Women's Publications, 1978.

Jacobs, Lewis. *The Rise of the American Film: A Critical History.* New York: New York Teachers College Press, 1968.

Latham, Aaron. *Crazy Sundays: F. Scott Fitzgerald in Hollywood.* New York: Viking, 1971.

Lindsay, Vachel. *The Art of the Moving Picture.* 1915. New York: Liveright, 1970.

Margolies, Alan. "Fitzgerald and Hollywood." In *The Cambridge Companion to F. Scott Fitzgerald.* Ed. Ruth Prigozy. New York: Cambridge University Press, 2002. 189–208.

Moore, Colleen. *Silent Star.* Garden City, N.Y.: Doubleday, 1968.

Mowry, George E. Ed. *The Twenties: Fords, Flappers, and Fanatics.* Englewood Cliffs, N.J.: Prentice Hall, 1963.

Newquist, Roy. *Conversations with Joan Crawford.* Secaucus, N.J.: Citadel, 1980.

Pratt, George. *Spellbound in Darkness: A History of the Silent Film.* Greenwich, Conn.: New York Graphics Society, 1973.

Prigozy, Ruth. "From Griffith's Girls to '*Daddy's Girl*': The Masks of Innocence in *Tender Is the Night.*" *Twentieth-Century Literature* 26 (Summer 1980): 189–221.

Sanderson, Rena. "Women in Fitzgerald's Fiction." In *The Cambridge Companion to F. Scott Fitzgerald.* Ed. Ruth Prigozy. New York: Cambridge University Press, 2002. 143–64.

Schulberg, Budd. *Writers in America: The Four Seasons of Success.* New York: Stein and Day, 1983.

Stenn, David. *Clara Bow: Runnin' Wild.* New York: Cooper Square Press, 2000.

Fitzgerald and War

James H. Meredith

Ah, love, let us be true
To one another! For the world, which seems
So various, so beautiful, so new,
Hath really neither joy, nor love, nor light,
Nor certitude, nor peace, nor help for pain;
And we here as on a darkling plain
Swept with confused alarms of struggle and flight,
Where ignorant armies clash by night.
—Matthew Arnold, "Dover Beach"

War is an essential element of F. Scott Fitzgerald's work. While Fitzgerald's fiction, like Arnold's "Dover Beach," is primarily focused on love, war's "confused alarms of struggle" are never far removed. Throughout his adult life, Fitzgerald deeply regretted that he never clashed in combat among "ignorant armies" because like the majority of unwitting young men of his generation, he believed that war was a necessary test of manhood. Of even greater importance to him, heroic death would have been a matter of aristocratic virtue, a recognition that he had achieved the social prominence he always craved.

As he did with most issues in his life, Fitzgerald personalized this martial urge to the extreme and imagined that he would die a hero's death. In a November 14, 1917, letter, he writes to his mother about his commission in the U.S. Army and his pending assignment to Fort Leavenworth: "I'll be there three months and would have six additional months training in France before I was ordered with my regiment to the trenches." Fitzgerald, ever the Romantic, seems eager to see action. Yet he is realistic enough to be sensitive to the army's social distinctions: "I am a second [l]ieutenant in the *regular* infantry and *not* a reserve officer—I rank with a West Point graduate." Not satisfied yet in frightening his mother to death, Fitzgerald finishes his letter with this: "If you want to pray, pray for my soul and not that I won['']t get killed—the last doesn't seem to matter particularly and if you are a good Catholic the first ought to. To a profound pessimist about life, being in danger is not depressing. I have never been more cheerful" (*Life in Letters* 13–14).

What would Fitzgerald have encountered had he managed to get into the combat zone? Meirion and Susie Harries, in *The Last Days of Innocence: America at War, 1917–1918*, point out that "twenty-one days was the life expectancy of British subalterns, and the [U.S.] War Department estimated that there would be a '*wastage*' [emphasis mine] of two thousand officers a month when combat began in earnest" (103). Such were the actuarial realities of the Great War, but Fitzgerald was saved from such grim arithmetic by the November 11, 1918, Armistice, which was declared before he even embarked for Europe. Commissioned as a second lieutenant in 1917 (eventually earning promotion to the rank of first lieutenant at Camp Sheridan, near Montgomery, Alabama), he spent World War I stateside at various infantry camps in Kentucky, Georgia, Alabama, and New York instead of in trenches on the Western Front (Bruccoli 97).

Although there is a comparative shortage of scholarship about Fitzgerald and war, his fiction is nevertheless full of references to this topic. In "Fitzgerald and the War Novel," Hilton Anderson documents Fitzgerald's construction of his war fiction aesthetic, noting that "letters written throughout his life abound with references to war novels, histories, and biographies of war leaders" (150). Anderson further observes that it was the "realistic approach to war that so interested Scott Fitzgerald, and it was its violent death and bloodshed that fascinated him" (152). In an otherwise informative summary of Fitzgerald's interest in war, Anderson is somewhat misleading in this particular assertion. A more precise description of this point would be that while death and dying may have been a personal interest for him, as reflected in his letters and book reviews, Fitzgerald's literary references to war do not emphasize the naturalistic brutality or the bitter irony of war that other writers were publishing at the time, especially those who had observed combat, such as Ernest Hemingway, John Dos Passos, and E. E. Cummings (all of whom, it should be remembered, worked as ambulance drivers for various relief agencies) or their British counterparts, Siegfried Sassoon, Robert Graves, and Richard Aldington (who *were* actually soldiers). These writers, in works like *A Farewell to Arms*, *1919*, *The Enormous Room*, *Memoirs of an Infantry Officer*, *Goodbye to All That*, and *Death of a Hero*, all dismissed the Romantic notion of war as an honorable sacrifice, and their primary method was to expose readers to its dehumanizing horror. By contrast, the noncombatant Fitzgerald was careful not to overwork the war aspect in his fiction. Fitzgerald's discussion of war eschews the grit and gore, which makes his depiction of it a more everyday aspect of society rather than a naturalistic one, particularly in his fiction focusing on post–World War I life. Whereas the works of these other writers revel in the sensory immediacy of a participant's experience, Fitzgerald's does not. War itself is not the central feature in Fitzgerald's fiction, but is rather another part of the social fabric of the modern world, an essential factor that a serious writer had to confront whether he had participated in combat or not. As such, Fitzgerald's work concentrates on the bitter peace rather than the bloody war.

Observing Fitzgerald's use of war in his fiction clarifies his multifaceted sensibility and demonstrates that he was a writer of many parts: social historian, Romantic, naturalist, realist, symbolist, allegorist, modernist, and stylist. In general, Fitzgerald's writing about war follows three distinct approaches, representing the trauma of three different conflicts: the American Civil War, World War I, and medieval combat. Fitzgerald used World War I to leverage realism against his instinctual Romanticism and to articulate the tragic role of the Romantic in the modern world. The American Civil War inspired a brief foray into historical fiction at a low point in his career that led to an interestingly idiosyncratic application of modernist irony to that historic conflict. Finally, medieval allegory allowed him to communicate his vision of the dark future augured by the fascist threat of the 1930s. Thus, war became a method for Fitzgerald to express his inimitable vision of the past, present, and future, particularly concerning how conflict alters society. A wounded patron of the battlefield such as Hemingway might scoff at Fitzgerald's pragmatic use of war, yet stories such as "The Night before Chancellorsville," "The Ice Palace," and "May Day," novels such as *The Great Gatsby* and *Tender Is the Night*, and writing projects such as his 1934–1935 Philippe series reflect a persistent desire to reconcile war with the modern condition.

The best criticism about the influence of war on Fitzgerald's fiction comes from Milton Stern in *Tender Is the Night: The Broken Universe*. As Stern observes, Fitzgerald concurred with 1920s commentators who claimed that the Great War marked a decisive break from the continuity of American (and Western) history:

> In that breaking point Fitzgerald saw profoundly into a tragic inversion. Before World War I, there was the young America. The *young* America, paradoxically, was the old America, back there in the past when the American world was young. The post-war *new* America, however, was no longer the redeemer nation, but was very much part of the old, international, corrupt actuality of history that had eventually burst forth in the sickness of World War I. The new generation that emerged from the war became in Fitzgerald's vision metaphoric material for everything that always had been selfishly irresponsible and greedily self-gratifying in the same old, tired world—and in American life. (6)

While Stern and other critics such as Todd Stebbins have written about war in Fitzgerald's work, their criticism has primarily focused on *Tender Is the Night*, especially the famous scene located in between Beaumont Hamel and Thiepval in France—on the ruins of the Somme battlefield—in which Dick Diver delivers his monologue about the terrible cost of World War I on Western civilization. That scene (and novel) is certainly the most significant statement about war in Fitzgerald's work and is deserving of the scrutiny it has received. *Tender Is the Night* is ripe with Romantic idealism about war, even in the acceptance of the very loss of those ideals. Stebbins argues in particular that all of the major themes of that novel are "ultimately connected to the war theme" (3) and that "war serves as backdrop and primary metaphor for deterioration, the material from which the novel is quilted" (14). Stebbins also observes that "war most directly touches the people of the novel" (14), particularly Diver, who is characterized by "images of blood and battle" that "follow [him] through the novel and document his fall" (20). Underscoring this point, J. Gerald Kennedy, in his brilliant *Imagining Paris: Exile, Writing, and American Identity*, describes how the Great War serves as both catalyst and metaphor for the unreality of modern life: "With the exception of a battlefield visit which colors the events of the Paris section, the war emerges almost entirely through oblique, fugitive references. . . . Through such brief and seemingly incidental touches, Fitzgerald establishes the idea that although Dick did not see action at the front, he—like others of his generation—had been traumatized by the horrific carnage" (201).

This essay extends Kennedy's observation to examine not only *Tender Is the Night* but a broader cross-section of Fitzgerald's fiction as well. Throughout Fitzgerald's work, there are countless "fugitive" allusions to war that all add up to a larger statement about the impact of war not only on his generation but on a whole nation of people—past, present, and future. Fitzgerald's fiction demonstrates that wars do not end when the peace treaty is signed but continue on into the troubling aftermath.

World War I: Romance and Realism

As a general rule, U.S. presidents who have been victorious in war serve as emblems of that victory. However, one exception to this rule is Woodrow Wilson, who has become linked more with the failed peace that followed World War I than anything else. Wilson's idealistic Fourteen Points and his vision of a League of Nations not only never came to fruition, but the strenuous effort that he expended in trying to establish these initiatives destroyed him. It would not be a far stretch to have included Woodrow Wilson on the memorial at Princeton University honoring its alumni who died in the war effort.

Although at the time Wilson had successfully led America to the greatest military buildup in its history, he soon became the quixotic hero of a peace that was as mismanaged as the war had been. As Robert H. Zieger notes, "Wilson saw in the Great War the death throes of the old order. Out of its horror, and destruction must come a new, cooperative world order. Guided by God, America and America alone could lead the way to its creation and thereby redeem the Old World and, indeed, humanity itself." Zieger then contrasts Wilson's vision of this American imperative with the bruised idealism Fitzgerald evokes in the final paragraphs of *The Great Gatsby*:

> In the words of Wilson's fellow Princetonian and Great War–era novelist, F. Scott Fitzgerald, in the "Fresh, green breast of the new world, [man stood] face to face for the last time in history with something commensurate to his capacity for wonder." For Fitzgerald, the dream of a new state and a special redemption was just that, a dream, doomed to tragic failure. But for Wilson, it was the essence of America, its raison d'être, more alive and more needed in the wake of the Great War than ever before. (153–54)

For his part, Fitzgerald's discovery that the American Dream was only "a dream" took several years of personal nightmares. When he did awake, it was to the reality that the redemptive dream could also be an illusion—even a shared national delusion. Although it would certainly be a further stretch, one could make an argument to include F. Scott Fitzgerald on that Princeton monument as well. Although he died twenty-two years after the Armistice, he was, like Wilson, also a casualty of a painful peace. Unable to die a hero's death in battle like his literary hero Rupert Brooke, Fitzgerald seemed determined to die a martyr's death in a peace that seemed to have been more disturbing for him than the war had been. In Fitzgerald's life, the fog of alcohol, infidelity, corruption, and depression—the cost of personal indiscretions—proved peacetime corollaries of what nineteenth-century military theorist Carl von Clausewitz called the "fog of war," the abundant and debilitating confusion that "can prevent the enemy from being seen in time, a gun from firing when it should, a report from reaching the commanding officer" (120). In Fitzgerald's case, the fog of moral uncertainty that his generation attributed to the Great War proved a paradoxical influence upon his career, for it was both an inspiration and an impediment to his literary development.

Biographer Michael Reynolds has successfully argued that Theodore Roosevelt was a role model for Hemingway, and it is not difficult to argue that Woodrow Wilson served to similarly influence Fitzgerald. Wilson at least puts a political face on the inner despair that Fitzgerald was trying to depict in his fiction. In far less cynical times than today, both of these presidents were important symbols for two distinct views of America. Along with Roosevelt, Wilson was the other major political figure who influenced American society in the age in which U.S. presidents were becoming the photographic representatives of their times. Moreover, Wilson, as an occasional southerner, also shared Fitzgerald's conflicted relationship with the heritage of the Civil War. In his biography of Wilson, Louis Auchincloss observes that there was "more than a touch of sentimentality in his nostalgic attraction to the elegance and gracious living of the antebellum planters and their gallant fighting for a lost cause" (5)—a sentence that could easily have been lifted out of any Fitzgerald biography. More than any other public figure in the 1920s, the stroke-ravaged Wilson represented the fissure between the old and new ages that came from World War I.

As with most things dealing with Fitzgerald, this linkage with Wilson is conflicted and contradictory. As Ronald Berman points out in *"The Great Gatsby" and Fitzgerald's World of Ideas*, Fitzgerald's notion of the past was not always reverential, as he eschewed certain "virtues" of the old order that he felt Wilson represented. Berman cites Fitzgerald's *The Crack-Up*:

> When Fitzgerald analyzed the first years of the decade, he invoked Woodrow Wilson as a symbol of the last agonies of "the Victorian era": "the old American groaned in his sleep as he waited to be poisoned by his wife, upon the advice of the female Rasputin who then made the ultimate decision in our national affairs." It was more ferocious than we expect from a nonpolitical man. It has within it the reserves of an idea that chaos is better than senility. (86)

In this passage, Fitzgerald disparages the broken-down Wilson, commenting as a writer consigned to living and working in such a chaotic time in history led by such an obviously weakened man. The reason for the ferocity of Fitzgerald's comment is more personal than political. For one thing, Fitzgerald's personal identification with Wilson had probably once been far too close for comfort: the former Princeton president (who was an honorary member of Fitzgerald's University Cottage Club), with his idealistic, Romantic, and aristocratic vision of the world—a vision the writer haltingly shared—had led Western civilization into a broken peace and had representatively surrendered to the forces of collusion and compromise around him. Fitzgerald surely must have felt that Wilson was not the kind of man who could dominate his world.

As Matthew J. Bruccoli's detailed biography documents, Fitzgerald did not excel in the military (93–101). Although scholars have largely scoffed at Fitzgerald's desultory military record, it was an experience he was nevertheless highly motivated to undertake. The Princeton that Fitzgerald attended, of course, probably identified with the war more than any other college in America. Even before America joined the fray, Princeton men were enthusiastic about the war. John Prentiss Poe, Jr. (class of 1895) was killed in France on September 25, 1915. His father was a cousin of Edgar Allan Poe, and his brother, Edgar Allan Poe II, would become attorney general of Maryland and, later, a legal adviser to Fitzgerald. As a freshman, John Poe had been a football standout at Princeton, but, like Fitzgerald, he had to withdraw from school because of poor academic performance. Also like Fitzgerald, he was readmitted but did not finish his degree. When the war exploded in Europe, Poe joined the British army, first as a member of the Royal Garrison Artillery and later as a soldier in the infamous First Black Watch. The John Prentiss Poe Football Cup is still awarded to the member of the Princeton varsity football team "who has best exemplified courage, modesty, perseverance, and good sportsmanship," personal values of the Old World (*A Princeton Companion*). There is no question that the youthful battlefield death of this former football star would have emotionally registered with Fitzgerald and would have reverberated all across the university campus because, as Ruth Prigozy notes, "football was the most important activity" at Princeton (26), and John Prentiss Poe was Princeton's greatest gridiron hero. Moreover, the fact that Poe was from Maryland (as was the paternal side of Fitzgerald's family) would have only intensified his identification with the martyred sports hero, who represented everything that Fitzgerald wanted to be.

Poe's death and the discovery of Rupert Brooke's poetry—poetry that would articulate Fitzgerald's feeling about the nobility of dying young on the battlefield—came within a year of each other. The constant reminders of the impending war that would challenge the courage of America's youth fueled Fitzgerald's sentiments about martyrdom. Preparations for war could literally be seen and heard all over bucolic Princeton. For example, prosperous Princeton alumni donated four airplanes and financed mechanics, instructors, and buildings to start a flying school for Princeton undergraduates. Before the school folded when the university dropped its support, thirty-five young men had been trained there, including three future aces: Lansing Holden, George Vaughn, and Elliot White Springs. Given this preparatory environment, it is easy now to understand how Fitzgerald felt compelled to join the army at the same time that he felt anxious that his death would be the end result of his enlistment.[1] Deep down, he wanted to be like Poe and Brooke—a martyred hero. In "Who's Who—and Why," an autobiographical essay that appeared in the *Saturday Evening Post* in 1920, Fitzgerald explains that he was not alone in feeling this:

> By autumn I was in an infantry officers' training camp at Fort Leavenworth, with poetry in the discard and a brand-new ambition—I was writing an immortal novel. Every evening, concealing my pad behind Small Problems for Infantry, I wrote paragraph after paragraph on a somewhat edited history of me and my imagination. . . . I had only three months to live—in those days all infantry officers thought they had only three months to live—and I had left no mark on the world. But such consuming ambition was not to be thwarted by a mere war. (*Afternoon of an Author* 85)

In an unpublished preface to *This Side of Paradise*, the novel that eventually emerged from his "consuming ambition," Fitzgerald elaborates upon his motivation: "Two years ago, when I was a very young man indeed, I had an unmistakable urge to write a book. It was to be a picaresque novel, original in form and alternating melancholy, naturalistic egotism with a picture of the generation then hastening to war" (393). As these references indicate, Fitzgerald's literary aspirations were inexorably entwined with the fate likely awaiting him had his unit made it abroad.

No one has stated a connection between Fitzgerald and World War I better than Zelda Fitzgerald, the person who knew him best. In a tribute to her husband after his death (unpublished until 1974), she writes:

> During the last world war, many cosmic destinies were strung together on the tone of tragic gallantry and courage to the purpose of binding within tradition the dramatic and pictorial tempos to which the age had fallen heir. . . . When nobody could think up any more mathematical formulas for destruction and further ways for forwarding the plot, the war was declared to be a political inconvenience, and ended. Through the disorientations resultant from many distrusted and uncondoned experiences the soldiers looked toward home as the right of a long and hard-earned holiday. People that had been spared active participation in the gala debacle converted them-

> selves into a grand pleasure chorus as effectively as possible and dedicated the decade to reconstituting the shattered illusions of those who had served in France with, perhaps, more verve and courage than judgment. . . . The prophet destined to elucidate and catalogue these pregnant and precarious circumstances was F. Scott Fitzgerald. (707–8)

Despite her periodic lapses into mental illness and her propensity for overwrought prose, Zelda clearly understood the symbiosis between World War I and the core of her husband's work. Throughout his career, Fitzgerald never wavered from his view that World War I represented a dramatic break from the past. That break in turn is an essential element in his fiction about the modern world.

While Fitzgerald did not write about combat conditions, he did write about the war's historical effect on the individual, particularly the circumstances of those participants who either were members of the American patrician class or who aspired to be. For example, in "The Rich Boy" (1926), Anson Hunter, the epitome of the social elite, joins the U.S. Navy as an aviator. During training in Pensacola, Florida, he meets both the story's narrator and Paula Legendre, the women he will love throughout his life but never marry. Had it not been for the war, these three people would never have met each other, and the circumstances in the story would have never occurred. While this assertion may sound obvious, Fitzgerald is nevertheless insisting that the war was both Anson's fate (by introducing him to the love of his life) and his failure (in addition to Anson's drinking, his time abroad in combat contributes to the couple's eventual split). The conventional narrative formulas of the day dictated that Anson's service should either result in a martyr's death or in his heroism winning his devoted lover's hand in marriage. Either way, his time in war would be an initiation experience that demonstrated the innate aristocracy of his character. Yet Anson passes through his military duties as aloofly as he passes through life; shot down over the North Sea just one month into his tour, he awaits the Armistice fighting pneumonia, not the "Boche." In the end, the war seems to have little effect on Anson—it is not even mentioned after part 4 of the story's eight sections. It is thus merely one in a long line of initiation experiences that, as with work and romance, *fail* to initiate him into a mature appreciation of life. As such, the superiority Anson exudes is not that of the epitome—the traditional war hero whose elite refinement is at once source and symptom of his valor—but of Fitzgerald's much more flawed rich, the ones who "possess and enjoy early . . . mak[ing] them soft where we are hard, and cynical where we are trustful" (*Short Stories* 318).

In the now-standard anthology of Fitzgerald's short fiction—*The Short Stories of F. Scott Fitzgerald* (1989)—eighteen of the forty-three selections mention World War I specifically, while many others describe a postwar wasteland. The purpose of the war in them is both historical and sociological, factors that significantly add to their realism. For example, in "Head and Shoulders," the precocious protagonist, Horace Tarbox, is too young to be in the army. Tarbox is a self-absorbed boy wonder who may be first in his class at Princeton academically but who is dead last in his awareness of the war. His ignorance about the war—about the dominant historical event of that time—becomes an object of satire:

> While George M. Cohan was composing "Over There," Horace was leading the sophomore class by several lengths and digging out theses on "The Syllogism as an Obsolete Scholastic Form," and during the battle of Château-Thierry he was sitting at his desk deciding whether or not to wait until his seventeenth birthday before beginning his series of essays on "The Pragmatic Bias of the New Realists."
>
> After a while some newsboy told him that the war was over, and he was glad, because it meant that Peat Brothers, publishers, would get out their new edition of "Spinoza's Improvement of the Understanding." Wars were all very well in their way, made young men self-reliant or something, but Horace felt that he could never forgive the President for allowing a brass band to play under his window on the night of the false armistice, causing him to leave three important sentences out of his thesis on "German Idealism." (*Short Stories* 4)

The academic-minded Tarbox is totally unaware of the tragedy going on around him. To put this in perspective, while members of the home front like Tarbox were going about their daily lives, soldiers on the Western Front were becoming war-damaged veterans—if they survived at all. Fitzgerald would later convey this theme more tragically in *The Great Gatsby*. Jay Gatsby, a fictional member of the real U.S. Seventh Infantry Regiment, would have been fighting outside of Château-Thierry at the very same time Tarbox was safe at home contemplating the new realists and German idealism, ignorant of the war's effect on soldiers in the field.

Elsewhere, Fitzgerald's references to the war do not so much satirize this kind of home-front obliviousness as they demonstrate how deeply the American consciousness—almost against its will—was saturated by an awareness of war. In "Bernice Bobs Her Hair," the otherwise obtuse Bernice blurts out the line "Hello, Shell Shock," which is terminology that had not been in existence prior to the war but by the 1920s was commonplace enough to almost be banal (*Short Stories* 39). In "The Ice Palace," the haunting graves of the Confederate dead are a constant reminder of the more recent World War I dead, uniting readers from both the North and the South. And then there is Curtis Carlyle's fabricated war experience in "The Offshore Pirate":

> Then the war came. He went to Plattsburg, and even there his profession followed him. A brigadier-general called him up to headquarters and told him he could serve the country better as a band leader—so he spent the war entertaining celebrities behind the line with a headquarters band. It was not so bad—except that when the infantry came limping back from the trenches he wanted to be one of them. The sweat and mud they wore seemed only one of those ineffable symbols of aristocracy that were forever eluding him. (*Short Stories* 80)

Although Carlyle invents this story as part of his ruse to trick Ardita Farnam into a romance, it impresses her precisely because war experience imbued a man with the ineffable aura of aristocracy, even if he didn't have any money. In particular, Fitzgerald's own regret at what he lost by missing combat comes through in this passage, especially as a reminder of his own lack of social status, his lost chance at being the hero because he "didn't get over."[2]

In "May Day," by contrast, which grandly celebrates the end of the war and the return of the victorious, there is an almost mocking quality about the emotional condition of the veterans:

> There had been a war fought and won and the great city of the conquering people was crossed with triumphal arches and vivid with thrown flowers of white, red, and rose. All through the long spring days the returning soldiers marched up the chief highway behind the strump of drums and the joyous, resonant wind of the brasses, while merchants and clerks left their bickerings and figurings and, crowding to the windows, turned their white-bunched faces gravely upon the passing battalions. (*Short Stories* 97)

One detail in what Bruccoli calls this "quasi-Biblical preamble" (164) is particularly noteworthy here. The merchant's faces that "gravely" gaze upon the triumphant soldiers not only express their disappointment at not having participated in the war but also foretell the bitter peace that looms. Having survived the war, the "returning soldiers" are about to enter their own times of "bickerings and figurings," including a riot that almost immediately ensues when the marching veterans confront socialists protesting their victory celebrations. For good reason, "May Day" has the reputation as Fitzgerald's most successful experiment in naturalism. (His attempts at it in *The Beautiful and Damned* are inconsistent.) The story shows how the energies that went into winning the war, once unleashed at home, create upheaval. A striking irony of the novelette is that, despite the supposed calm brought about by the Armistice, the postwar environment is every bit as dangerous to the soldiers as the front. Nearly every veteran involved in the plot ends up wounded or defeated in ways that flout the promise of peace: Carrol Key falls to his death from a window; his buddy Gus Rose is arrested for breaking another man's leg; Phillip Dean (along with his fraternity pal Peter Himmel) degenerates into a drunken lout; and, most shockingly, Gordon Sterrett puts a bullet in his head rather than be blackmailed into an undesirable marriage. Far from ensuring order, the war has merely brought its chaos to the home front.

The short story with the clearest elaboration of the war's social impact is "The Last of the Belles," which was first published in 1929 and later anthologized in the appropriately entitled *Taps at Reveille*. Set in Tarleton, Georgia, the story explores the reminiscences of the narrator, Andy, as he looks back fifteen years to his experiences in a wartime army training camp. Despite the overarching theme of youthful romance, "Belles" is laced with the grim realities of war. As Andy realizes, love was a game he played to the hilt with the debutante Ailie Calhoun and his aristocratic rival for her, Bill Knowles. Yet it is the death of Lieutenant Horace Canby in a training accident that brings into focus the true reason that these memories continue to haunt Andy: "I had disliked Canby, but his terrible, pointless death was more real to me than the day's toll of thousands in France" (*Short Stories* 453). On one level, Canby's death was simply more real, more meaningful, because he knew Canby. However, the true significance lies deeper. Canby, who is lower down on the social scale than Andy and Knowles, had previously "made a nuisance of himself" in his "impersonal" courtship of Ailie (452). He had told her that "if she married Knowles he was going to climb up six thousand feet in his aeroplane, shut off the motor and let go" (452). His subsequent accidental death makes this threat an existential experience for Andy. Philosophically speaking, Fitzgerald asks, how could any pointless death be real, be significant, except in the oxymoronic world of meaningful negation that was the war era? Canby at least says that he is willing to die for love, although his plane crash is probably accidental, the result of a complicated airplane in the hands of a too-inexperienced pilot. This was, after all, a training environment; Canby and the others not only had a lot to learn about love, life, and, yes, death— they also had a lot to learn about the modern war machines, which should never be considered toys. Canby's death initiates Andy into the existential randomness of death, which is only a more intensified and immediate manifestation of the loss that dominates life. It would have made more sense had Canby purposefully crashed his airplane; however, the lesson that Andy learns about modern war is that it is more pointless than that. Importantly, even in 1929 Fitzgerald would not have to explain to his readers the pointlessness of death. By that time it had been front-page news for more than a decade.

Canby's death is thus made more "real" to the narrator not only because of its philosophical "pointlessness" but also because of an interesting aspect of military and social history. Of all the branches of military service, World War I aviation was the one in which the vestiges of chivalric tradition were most resilient (although this late in the war that was changing, too, as noted by the actions of Canby). As an earlier draft of this story indicates, Fitzgerald wanted to emphasize from the very first that one of the outcomes of the large mobilization of soldiers—which would primarily be composed of the lower to middle classes—was that the infantry was the first to lose the aristocratic traditions that had at one time loaned Romantic value to war (29a). These increasingly nonaristocratic officers changed the whole meaning of modern military service, and one result was thus to emphasize the concept of meaningless death. These new soldiers did not understand the nature of chivalry, which had once brought Romantic meaning to violent death.

Another result of this alteration in the social order was to change the meaning of love, which is ultimately more important to Andy's (and Fitzgerald's) sensibilities than war had been. Although Canby unwittingly participates in the chivalrous courtly love tradition, he does so ignorant of the proprieties because he is not a member of the aristocratic caste. Harvard men Andy and Knowles are, and therefore they understand that love is an impersonal game played by insincere suitors. Ailie's other suitor, Lieutenant Earl Schoen, belongs to an even lower level of the caste system. Andy comments about this social difference by discussing the military camp that Schoen comes from: "The fourth camp wasn't like the first three—the candidates were from the ranks; even from the drafted divisions. They had queer names without vowels in them, and save for a few young militiamen, you couldn't take it for granted that they came out of any background at all" (454). While Schoen may not be a product of aristocratic breeding, he does possess a tough masculinity *and* a sincerity that eventually attracts Ailie to him, which radically changes the rules of the game forever. The unspoken truth here is that love and war just do not mean what they previously did.

The pointlessness of modern war and romance is manifested in other areas of the story as well. Similar to Fitzgerald's own experience, the narrator in "The Last of the Belles" also fails to "get over" to France, and this affects his attitude about life after the war. In the brief time that it takes for Andy to be demobilized, he observes the toll the war has taken on Tarleton society:

> And now the young men of Tarleton began drifting back from the ends of the earth—some with Canadian uniforms, some with crutches or empty sleeves. A returned battalion of the National Guard paraded through the streets with open ranks for their dead, and then stepped down out of romance forever and sold things over the counter of local stores. Only a few uniforms mingled with the dinner coats at the country club dance. (458)

In one paragraph, Fitzgerald encapsulates the complex process of soldiers returning home to a peace that would never be as exciting, as Romantic, but at the same time as pointless as the war had been. Moreover, the war had also forced the change of deeply rooted social distinctions, such as courtship rituals. In the end, the narrator discovers that since the time he was a soldier, he, too, has "stepped down out of romance forever" (458). Although he never faced combat, the war brought him to another world that changed his outlook. For better or for worse, he—and a whole nation—would never be the same, and for better or for worse, the consequences of war would always be on his mind.

War was even on Fitzgerald's mind in 1936 when he published "Afternoon of an Author," one of his best later short stories. If this story is any indication, Fitzgerald's thoughts about war seem to have always been just below the surface of his consciousness:

> He went into the kitchen and said good-by[*sic*] to the maid as if he were going to Little America. Once in the war he had commandeered an engine on sheer bluff and had driven it from New York to Washington to keep from being A.W.O.L. Now he stood carefully on the street corner waiting for the light to change, while young people hurried past him with a fine disregard for traffic. On the bus corner under the trees it was green and cool and he thought of Stonewall Jackson's last words: "Let us cross over the river and rest under the shade of the trees." Those Civil War leaders seemed to have realized very suddenly how tired they were—Lee shriveling into another man, Grant with his desperate memoir writing at the end. (*Short Stories* 736)

These thoughts are not about the valorous war experiences of Lee and Grant, as one would expect, but about the entropic end of their lives, which suggests that the dissipated author is struggling to find suitable closure to his own career and life. Fitzgerald's identification with these distinguished soldiers is interesting given his own less than memorable military service. The point seems to be that his life has been a form of combat during a peace that has made him a casualty, much like Lee and Grant, who had to suffer through an ignominious peace before they died, and unlike Jackson, who died in war. According to Fitzgerald's thinking, peace was a harder imposition upon Lee and Grant than war had ever been.

Although Fitzgerald's short fiction conveys World War I as fugitive glimpses of realism, demonstrating his belief that the war was a break from the past, his novels provide a fuller picture. No Fitzgerald novel better conveys the sociological role World War I played in the break from the past than *The Great Gatsby*. Sidney H. Bremer offers a succinct assessment of the theme's import in the novel:

> Fitzgerald explicitly identified the war as a dividing point and elaborated his sense of disjunction in terms of contrasting urban images in *The Great Gatsby*. The past that Jay Gatsby "can't repeat" is literally his wartime past of whirlwind courtship. And it is the war—though only vaguely, romanti-

> cally experienced—that marks Nick Carraway's alienation from the family-based urban community of his childhood. After the war, Nick feels the traditional, moral orderliness and communal cohesion of the old mid-western cities recede to "the ragged edge of the universe," while the up-to-date, albeit "distorted" excitement of New York swirls at the world's "war center." The gap between old and new cities, which [Edith] Wharton embodies in the chronology divisions of her novel [*The Age of Innocence*], Fitzgerald represents in the geographical sections that demarcate his fictional landscape, in *The Great Gatsby* as in his other fictions. (278)

Besides these sociological aspects, the importance of the war in *The Great Gatsby* is conveyed on an individual basis as well. For example, Gatsby first recognizes Nick Carraway as a veteran who, like him, served in the Third Division, Nick as a member of the Ninth Machine-Gun Battalion, Gatsby in the Seventh Infantry. As Nick notes, the war inspires an instant rapport: "We talked for a moment about some wet, grey little villages in France" (52). That these two men talk about the places they both saw establishes their mutual credibility and underscores Fitzgerald's eye for realistic detail and narrative development. It therefore falls to fellow veteran Nick to write this novel about Gatsby the war hero, including a verbatim report of Gatsby's own description of how he "tried very hard to die" in the Argonne Forest:

> I took two machine-gun detachments so far forward that there was a half-mile gap on either side of us where the infantry couldn't advance. We stayed there two days and two nights, a hundred and thirty men with sixteen Lewis guns, and when the infantry came up at last they found the insignia of three German divisions among the piles of dead. I was promoted to be a major and every Allied government gave me a decoration—even Montenegro, little Montenegro down on the Adriatic Sea! (70)

Gatsby, of course, is a fairly transparent con man, but, strikingly, Nick never seems to doubt this story. Part of the reason may be that such tales of amazing individual heroism were quite commonplace. Gatsby's experiences, in fact, parallel those of the famous Sergeant Alvin York. David D. Lee, in *Sergeant York: An American Hero*, summarizes the hero's much-publicized feats, including at least one interesting detail shared by the fictional Gatsby:

> York marched out of the Argonne Forest and into the annals of American legend. In the midst of the greatest battle the U.S. Army had ever fought, a backwoods corporal from Pall Mall, Tennessee, had accomplished one of the most spectacular feats of individual heroism in the nation's history. Having acted virtually alone, he was credited with killing 25 Germans and capturing 132, and with putting thirty-five Machine guns out of action while armed only with a rifle and a pistol. He was promoted to sergeant and showered with so many medals that York said he would have to wear two coats if he wanted to wear them all at the same time. . . . The United States gave him the Distinguished Service Cross immediately and a few months later, after a thorough investigation of the incident bestowed on him the Medal of Honor. Even tiny Montenegro, which York had probably never heard of, gave him a medal. (39)

The heroic exploits of York were first made known to the American public in an April 26, 1919, *Saturday Evening Post* article. Fitzgerald was obviously familiar with the soldier's legend—he is mentioned by name in "Dalyrimple Goes Wrong," a 1920 story. The *Post* article on York may have even influenced his depiction of Gatsby as a war hero. At the very least, Fitzgerald would not have had to educate his readers about the plausibility of Gatsby's combat experience. Abundant accounts of battlefield heroics had already done so.

From a military historian's perspective, it is significant that Fitzgerald chose to have his hero fight in the Argonne Forest, for this phase in the larger Meuse-Argonne offensive (September–November 1918) was particularly conducive to the type of small-unit fighting that allowed for heroic feats such as Gatsby's and York's. As Zieger notes, American troops had to replace "mass frontal assaults," which accomplished little more than depleting infantry ranks, with "flanking movements and coordinated small-unit assaults against machine gun nests and heavily fortified German positions":

> One by one, German machine guns were knocked out, pillboxes seized, strongholds eliminated. Even so, the German defenses, bristling with artillery and machine guns, blunted the American advance. These fresh assaults, like their earlier counterparts, came to a fitful halt short of their objectives, their gains measured in yards. Each day's battle claimed an average of more than 550 American dead. (101)

Although this new strategy did little to cut casualties, it made the survivors' heroism seem all the more singular and extraordinary.

Another significant point that Gatsby makes in recounting his war experience is the date that he left the Seventh Infantry Regiment, June 1918, which would have also put him in the battle for Belleau Wood, which ended on June 26, 1918, when American forces finally secured that forest outside of France's Château-Thierry. The battle for Belleau Wood was the first engagement in which the American doughboys proved to be a determined fighting force, but the victory came at a significant cost. During the three weeks of fighting around that French forest preserve, the Americans experienced more than 4,000 casualties (Zieger 97). Fitzgerald's friend Thomas Boyd, author of *Through the Wheat* and reporter for the *Minneapolis Star* and the *St. Paul Daily News*, was actually engaged in this battle. Boyd had been a member of the Fourth Marine Brigade, a fact that may have gained Fitzgerald some inside information on soldiers' experiences in this campaign. Although there is no textual evidence to confirm it, the fact that Gatsby left his unit at this particular time could indicate that he had been wounded in that battle and later transferred into another unit as a replacement soldier. Gatsby would have fought in the Argonne with this new unit and not with the Seventh Infantry.

Again, it seems significant that in a story whose protagonist is surrounded by preposterous speculation that Fitzgerald should choose to construct such a plausible combat record. While many both in and outside of the book have questioned Gatsby's military exploits, Nick does not. In chapter 8, in which he narrates the second recitation of Gatsby's war record, Nick also makes no attempt to contradict or clarify Gatsby's war experience. Certainly by the time he would have written Gatsby's story, he would have investigated these claims independently since he claims to be a scrupulous pursuer of the truth. Nick narrates: "He did extraordinarily well in the war. He was a captain before he went to the front and following the Argonne battles he got his majority and the command of the divisional machine guns. After the Armistice he tried frantically to get home but some complication or misunderstanding sent him to Oxford instead" (158).

Interestingly, even that Gatsby was sent to Oxford would have checked out (had Nick actually been checking) because there was an extensive program to send promising Americans to European educational institutions. One purpose of this initiative was to improve these soldiers—to prepare them for their civilian lives back home during the peace. The program also came about for the simple reason that the American Expeditionary Forces did not know what to do with all of these soldiers overseas after the Armistice, and university campuses offered luxurious accommodations compared to the war front to which they were accustomed.[3] It is important to note that these soldiers were *ordered* to attend school; the military would have determined that Gatsby was qualified for this type of service and sent him there, thereby frustrating his anxious desire to return stateside and reclaim Daisy. These military facts are a history lesson today, but in Fitzgerald's time, they would have been current events and, therefore, relatively common knowledge, which loaned Gatsby's claims credibility.

How do the facts that Gatsby is a bona-fide war hero and Nick a fellow veteran contribute to a reading of the novel? First of all, they not only make Gatsby a sympathetic character; more important, they make him sympathetic to Nick. This sympathy explains the formation of the strong but otherwise inexplicable bond between these two veterans, which does not exist between them and Tom Buchanan, who seems not to have served in the military during the war at all. Gatsby's desire to win back Daisy may also be motivated by a need to heal his combat traumas: she becomes for him the necessary reward to live for now that he has escaped death in the war. It is an understandable and noteworthy goal considering the horrific experience he has gone through and the lack of anything else he has to strive for. Gatsby's goal of recapturing Daisy's affections after the war separates them thus becomes more existential rather than blindly romantic or naively idealistic. Having faced death in battle, he has to find something to live for in peace.

Fitzgerald also hints that Nick may be suffering his own post-traumatic difficulties. As a member of the Ninth Machine-Gun Battalion, Carraway would have probably seen the same action that Gatsby had experienced: "I graduated from New Haven in 1915, just a quarter of a century after my father, and a little later I participated in that delayed Teutonic migration known as the Great War," he writes. "I enjoyed the counterraid so thoroughly that I came back restless. Instead of being the warm center of the world the middle-west now seemed like the ragged edge of the universe—so I decided to go east and learn the bond business" (7). The "counterraid" was a small-unit engagement fought in no-man's land, primarily with the intention to harass, to gather intelligence, or to kill the enemy in the lulls between larger combat offensives. Later in the opening chapter, Nick seems to be having a problem with the peacetime world:

> When I came back from the East last autumn I felt that I wanted the world to be in uniform and at a sort of moral attention forever; I wanted no more riotous excursions with privileged glimpses into the human heart. Only Gatsby, the man who gives his name to this book, was exempt from my reaction—Gatsby who represented everything for which I have an unaffected scorn. (6)

Gatsby escapes Nick's negative reaction to the world because Nick, too, understands the moral difficulty Gatsby experiences in peace, which proves to be more difficult than the war had been. Nick had been a fellow soldier, after all. It is, therefore, an irony probably not missed by Nick that Gatsby, having escaped combat alive, is violently killed at home in his own swimming pool.

All of this should be a reminder that not only was World War I the first global war; it also initiated the first global peace in which everyone experienced the war's aftermath, even in privileged West Egg, New York. *The Great Gatsby* is a much different novel if it is read as a veteran's story à la John Dos Passos's *Three Soldiers* or Ernest Hemingway's "Soldiers Home," both fictions about postwar disillusionment and finding one's way in a world dramatically changed by a war that few properly understood. Jay Gatsby and Nick Carraway are veterans of the same division who saw serious action at the front and who also found peace troubling. There is no doubt that Gatsby is the most important war hero in the Fitzgerald canon, and this fact significantly determines his fate.

Although Fitzgerald was interested in the effects of war on the individual psyche, he was also sensitive to its impact on the global stage, at first in America and then later in Europe after he expatriated there in the mid–1920s. By the time that he wrote *Tender Is the Night* a decade later, Fitzgerald had become more interested in portraying how the war affected not just society in the United States but the larger Western culture as well. As Milton R. Stern observes, "World War I changed the human universe, quite literally. The Western world, especially, was never the same again. . . . In its aftermath of enveloping cynicism and profoundly anarchic disillusion, it gave enormous impetus to everything anti-establishmentarian, socially and politically, and to everything existential, personally and culturally" ("American History" 116). Maybe it was the ambiguous nature of the Armistice or the cynical Treaty of Versailles that laid the foundation for the calamitous peace, but whatever the cause, the effect was still the same: wrenching social change and trauma. Needless to say, the two decades after the war were a difficult period in which to live, particularly for someone as sensitive to the desire for historical continuity and tradition as Fitzgerald was.

Fitzgerald's ideas about war greatly matured and developed in complexity as he aged. The best evidence for this maturation is in the famous chapter 13 in Book 1 of *Tender Is the Night*, in which

Dick Diver and his entourage are touring the Somme battlefield. Dick ruminates:

> This western-front business couldn't be done again, not for a long time. The young men think they could do it but they couldn't. They could fight the first Marne again but not this. This took religion and years of plenty and tremendous sureties and the exact relation that existed between the classes. . . . All my beautiful lovely safe world blew itself up here with a great gust of high explosive love. (67–68)

Fitzgerald's perspective here reflects years of reading and reflection on the historical calamity that was the Great War. Fitzgerald now understands and regrets the great historical, deterministic forces that act upon nations and propel them to war—impersonal forces—but what Diver mourns in particular is *the loss of the meaning of loss*, which means that the war made the comprehension of loss a statistical casualty. This attitude reflects what has become a commonplace since the early twentieth century: the idea that one death is a tragedy, but a million deaths are merely a statistic. The losses of the Great War were just too huge, too cataclysmic, too mechanized for the individual not only to comprehend but also to feel within his soul— particularly for one prone to Romantic rumination.

Tender Is the Night explores this loss in an episode immediately following Dick's battlefield speech. The scene features a young female expatriate from Knoxville, Tennessee, who is trying to find her brother's grave among so many on the battlefield. The War Department cannot even give her the right number to find him, which means in essence that his grave is lost. Although his death is a tragedy to the girl, it is a statistic to everyone else. However, faced with the reality of so many graves herself, she succumbs to the psychology of the statistic. It is just too easy for Dick and his friends to convince her to place her wreath on a random grave instead of continuing to search for her brother's. Afterward, the group repairs for drinks in Amiens, where the "Tennessee girl forgot her sorrow and enjoyed herself, even began flirtations of tropical eye-rollings and pawing, with Dick and

Abe" (69). In the face of such impersonalized loss, the expatriate inclination toward dissipation possesses a certain logic, for the war exacted such staggeringly incomprehensible costs that escapism seems the lone possible response.

In many ways, this whole chapter bears similarities to William Wordsworth's "Lines Composed a Few Miles above Tintern Abbey on Revisiting the Banks of the Wye during a Tour, July 13, 1798," which suggests how the war transformed the Romantic sensibility. What the comparison suggests is that both scenes are about the artist reading the landscape; the differences between the passages, however, illustrate the contrasting epistemologies between the late eighteenth and early twentieth centuries. Although he is a psychologist instead of a poet, Diver is truly a Romantic in the Wordsworthian sense of that term, particularly in the way he personifies what he sees and thinks—in his personification (or personalization) of time and history itself. But while Wordsworth's and Diver's literary processes and sensibilities are similarly Romantic, their histories, as *Tender Is the Night* confirms, are radically different. Wordsworth writes:

While here I stand, not only with the sense
Of present pleasure, but with pleasing thoughts
That in this moment there is life and food
For future years. And so I dare to hope,
Though changed, no doubt, from what I was when first
I came among these hills (118)

The poet looks back upon the past and feels "pleasing thoughts" about the future—despite the differences he senses in his five-year absence from that particular spot on the Wye River. On the other hand, Diver mourns the loss of the past and a feeling of connectedness to it that he knows Romantics like Wordsworth had felt. Diver looks back five years to life before the war blew up his "beautiful lovely safe world," and he sees an unfathomable gap—an unconnected chasm. Wordsworth sees Tintern Abbey's ruins being overcome by nature as a reassurance that the future will be better than the past and that the old ways will pass into the flowing continuum of his memory. He knows "that Nature never did betray" him (119). Christopher Salvesen has written that "for Wordsworth, the deepest experience of nature, of landscape, was always unified—the experience was a sensuous and a spiritual totality, of past forms remembered, working with present forms, these not so much seen as 'heard and felt'" (69). Yet Diver is standing exactly in the middle of one gigantic rupture in that unity, and he must acknowledge that the future will have no resemblance to the present because from where he stands the past has already been dislocated. Whereas the old formula of time and place had been a relatively simple equation for Wordsworth, for a modernist like Diver it has been transmogrified into a calculus almost beyond comprehension.

A primary commonality that Diver shares with Wordsworth is the process of discovery of their world, a literary liturgy of time and place and observation that makes both of them high priests of Romanticism. That said, Wordsworth is in the proper time for a man of his sensibilities; however, Diver is not. All of this is not to say that "Tintern Abbey" influenced Fitzgerald directly in writing Diver's speech. Rather, Wordsworth's poem illustrates both that Diver, and by extension Fitzgerald, was a frustrated Romantic and that the war was both cause and effect of his situation. The war forced the modern sensibility onto Diver, whether he liked it or not. Therefore, like Wordsworth in "Tintern Abbey," Diver reads the landscape, personifies the ruins and scene, and then turns these elements into a homily about the self and history. Geoff Dyer explains this process somewhat differently:

> Wordsworth established an imaginative template with the stories of silent suffering read in the ruins of "Michael" or "The Ruined Cottage." So pervasive was the cult of ruination that a ruin became a place where[a] certain set of responses lay perfectly intact. The Great War ruined the idea of ruins. Instead of the slow patient work of ruination observed by Shelly's[*sic*] "Ozymandias," artillery brought about instant obliteration. Things survived only by accident or chance—like the cavalry at Ypres—or mistake. Destruction was the standard and the norm. Cottages and villages did not crumble and decay—they were swept away. (20)

The war also ruined the Romantic idea of ruins because even the most gifted artists found the loss difficult to articulate. It is significant that Diver tours this particular battlefield, for not only was it the site of one of the most devastating engagements ever, but it was also one of the first of the World War I battlefields to become a historical site. The ruins of the battlefield are still distinctly evident today. Earl Haig, the British commanding general during the battle, dedicated the Beaumont Hamel Memorial Park on June 7, 1925, which only slightly predates the chronological moment in *Tender* in which Diver eulogizes the old past. Bruccoli notes that Fitzgerald actually visited this battlefield during the fall of 1925 (284). The exact location at which Diver stands when he delivers his remarks is essential because he is at an intersection of two important sites of mourning for the World War I dead. Moreover, Diver's comments are prescient in that they foretell the monument that architect Sir Edwin Lutyens would later create with his *Monument to the Missing of the Battle of the Somme at Thievpal*, which was unveiled by the prince of Wales on July 31, 1932, several years after Fitzgerald's visit and just two years before the novel's publication. Jay Winter writes in *Sites of Memory, Sites of Mourning*:

> Lutyens again chose geometry to express the inexpressible nature of war and its human costs. He took the forms of the triumphal arch, and multiplied it. Four such arches describe the base of the memorial; their height is two and[a] half their width, and they are superseded by a series of larger arches placed at right angles from the base. The ratio of the dimensions of the larger to the smaller arches is also precisely 2.5 to 1. The progression extends upward, from smaller arch, and therefore still larger arch in the center of the monument, to nothing at all. We arrive at the vanishing point well above the ground, just as was the case with the Cenotaph [Lutyens's British war monument in London's Whitehall]. Just as in the case of the Cenotaph, Lutyens brilliantly managed to create an embodiment of nothingness, an abstract space unique among memorials of the Great War. (105)

"An embodiment of nothingness" is suggestive of what Diver is expressing in his speech, underscoring a collective desire for artists to express the seemingly inexplicable sense of loss. Diver's comments thus have less to do with the war itself than with the great emotional shock wave that was spreading across Europe. As Winter explains, "In the years following the war, in the face of the army of the dead, the effort to commemorate went beyond the conventional shibboleths of patriotism. Yes, these millions died for their country, but to say so was merely to begin, not to conclude, the search for the 'meaning' of the unprecedented slaughter of the Great War" (2). While Diver had been in uniform during the war, he did not experience combat conditions; therefore, his perspective on the commemoration of the loss has the poignancy both of someone close to the scene and also someone without the trauma of the trenches. For example, while Abe North "had seen battle service and he had not," Diver is better able to see the historical consequences of the war. In North's case, the war itself has traumatized him to the point that he can only see the dead. Like Egyptian hieroglyphics without the Rosetta Stone, North cannot read the landscape and know what it means beyond his personal pain. On the other hand, Diver's personal trauma comes after the Armistice, during the broken peace, so he is better able to see the larger implications of the war, although he is nevertheless powerless to transcend them.

Such was the fate of the Romantic in the modern, war-ravaged world: how to shore up idealism and belief in the human capacity to make experience meaningful through imaginative interventions when those tools themselves seemed superannuated by the Great War. To his credit, Fitzgerald never succumbed to the stoic nihilism that typifies the war writings of Hemingway, Dos Passos, and Cummings. Although his depiction of the aftermath of the war does include an occasional accent of satire, Fitzgerald's dominant literary instinct was to elegize. To mourn and lament for him were means of coping with the loss that colored the postwar mood; these acts in essence allowed him to accept the new reality of devastation and rupture without giving in to pessimism. It should be noted, however, that this response holds true only for the Great War, which so deeply affected the character of Fitzgerald's generation. When Fitzgerald looked further back to the Civil War, his reaction took a very different turn that was in part inspired by a desire to bring an element of modernity to the literary genre of historical fiction.

The Civil War: "The Night before Chancellorsville" and Historical Fiction

On the night before the climactic battle of Chancellorsville, May 1, 1863, Confederate generals Robert E. Lee and Thomas "Stonewall" Jackson sat "themselves on a fallen log in a little clearing in the woods" (Sears 224) at the intersection of Plank and Catherine Furnace roads, two miles southwest of the battle's epicenter—at the chancellor's brick tavern and home—and hatched a scheme that would turn into one of the greatest battlefield victories in history and a model for future military strategists (McGowan 392). The next day, Jackson would attack the unprotected right wing of the Union army and send the blue-clad soldiers into a rout, the worst defeat in U.S. Army history, confirming Lee's and Jackson's places in the history books. It was a scheme these two men planned and executed out of desperation, outnumbered two to one by a foe who was only a stone's throw away; they were facing their worst hour. On that same evening, Private Henry Fleming—had he been a real, flesh-and-blood soldier in the Union army and not the fictional protagonist of Stephen Crane's *The Red Badge of Courage* (1895)—would have been bivouacked just a few miles north of these two men, totally unaware of the chaos he would be caught up in and the role he would play in American fiction because of it. Fleming, too, was about to face his greatest test. Besides the likes of Lee and Jackson and Fleming, Chancellorsville is also a place made conspicuous by Union general "Fighting Joe" Hooker, his name popularly but errantly synonymous with those who practice prostitution, his reputation sullied by accusations of drunkenness on duty during the battle. And on that day in 1863, "Fighting Joe" also proved to be an inept fighter.

For all of these reasons and more, Chancellorsville was an area rich with literary potential for a writer like Fitzgerald, who bore a lifelong interest in the Civil War largely inherited from his father, Edward Fitzgerald, "who as a boy [had] guided Confederate spies" in Maryland (Bruccoli 12). After the relative commercial failure of *Tender Is the Night* in 1934, Fitzgerald briefly turned to historical fiction in "an attempt to find new [and profitable] material, for he had pretty much exhausted the *Post* vein of gold" (Bruccoli 459)—that is, the stories of young love that had for so long supported him. Thus, while "The Night before Chancellorsville" may not necessarily rate as one of his best short stories, it does represent an important career excursus, for it suggests the extremes to which Fitzgerald was compelled to travel to overcome the professional desperation he felt in the mid–1930s.[4] More important, the story is intriguing for its peculiarly comedic treatment of its subject matter, which is atypical not only of Fitzgerald but of the vast majority of Civil War fiction of his time. Ultimately, "The Night before Chancellorsville" reveals its author applying a heavy coat of modernist irony to the Civil War in order to strip away the patina of chivalric romance found in most literary representations of it, including Margaret Mitchell's soon-to-be-quintessential *Gone with the Wind*, published one year after this story in 1936.

Given the hauntingly elegiac tone of such Great War–infused works as "The Last of the Belles," *Tender Is the Night*, and others examined above, Fitzgerald's narrative strategy is curious indeed. Instead of paying homage to the potential solemnity of the night before the battle of Chancellorsville by writing a serious story, he commemorates it humorously. The story's plot concerns two prostitutes, Nora and Nell, on their way "to work" with the Union troops in Virginia. The women are in desperate straits because many of their best customers are away at the front; they must therefore take a dilapidated train to the Union Army of the Potomac bivouacked on the banks of the Rappahannock in northern Virginia. The scenario demonstrates Fitzgerald's keen regard for historical accuracy. At the time at which the story takes place, the Union army had been in winter camp for quite some time, and Hooker, its newly appointed commander, had recently made some changes in the army's organization. *Harper's* reported in 1866 on the innovations that would have necessitated Nora and Nell's journey:

> Hooker set himself strenuously at work to improve the condition of the army. At the very outset he broke up the grand divisions, and restored its former organization into corps, each being placed under the command of a general in whom he had confidence. Then the great evil of desertions was to be encountered. The loose system of furloughs was thoroughly revised. Hitherto the corps commanders had granted leaves of absence at discretion. By the new regulations no leave of absence could be granted except from head-quarters to officers of high rank. In no regiment could more than one field officer or two line officers be absent at the same time. Not more than two privates out of a hundred in any regiment could be absent on furlough at the same time, and no man could receive a furlough unless he had a good record for attention to his duties. . . . Express trains were examined, and all citizens' clothing found therein was burned. (Guernsey and Alden 484)

Because Union soldiers were no longer permitted to leave their camp as freely as they had previously, there were not enough customers on the streets of Philadelphia to allow Nora and Nell to subsist. As Nell says, "Philly is as dead as Baltimore and we've got to eat this summer" (211). Because prostitutes had to go to the army to find work, the number of working women in and around the Union camps increased, which is probably why Hooker's name became associated with this particular trade (although it should be noted that he did not personally participate in it).

The story dramatizes the inability of noncombatants to appreciate not only the consequences of battle but the historical import of the events around them. In recounting her journey with Nell, Nora reveals herself to be exceptionally disengaged. She begins her monologue by dismissing the courage of Union soldiers who, amid their retreat, failed to ensure her comfort: "I tell you I didn't have any notion what I was getting into or I wouldn't of gone down there. They can have their army—it seems to me they were all a bunch of yella-bellies" (211). As the story proves, Nora *never* gains any notion of what she was "getting into," for the battle at Chancellorsville for her is merely one long inconvenience. She complains about the lack of food, the noise of the cannon fire, even the dishevelment of the Union officers. "After *this* ride I don't care who wins," she declares at one point (213). Not surprisingly, she proves indifferent to the suffering of the wounded soldiers on the train. She fails to notice one man has lost an eye, and she does not blink when Nell holds her nose in disgust at the odor of death. "If the trip down was slow the trip back was terrible," she reports. "The wounded began groaning and we could hear in our car, so nobody couldn't get a decent sleep. We stopped everywhere." Even after the train completes its retreat to Washington, Nora betrays nary a whit of understanding about what has happened: "There was a lot of people in the station and they were all anxious about what had happened to the army, but I said You can search me. All I wanted was my little old room and my little old bed. I never been treated like that in my life." The story ends with Nora expressing outrage at one final slight: "In the papers the next day they never said anything about how our train got attacked, or about us girls at all! Can you beat that!" (215). In the end, Nora fails to realize that she has borne witness to an important historical event because she is too busy wondering why nobody paid attention *to her*.

Such blatant disregard for the historical significance of this battle reveals Nora to be an unreliable narrator; speaking in a fashion seemingly satirized by Fitzgerald in his 1920s fiction, she might as well be a mindless flapper from one of Gatsby's parties. Her selfishness and solipsism may be intended to reflect the post-battle attitude of most northern citizens toward the Union army at the time of the battle—an army that had fled the Chancellorsville battlefield. Equally significant, it reflects the post–World War I attitude of indifference toward military concerns, but not in a way that Fitzgerald's contemporary readers might have expected. Most World War I veterans were dismissive of civilians who had not fought in the war, especially those who ignored the desperate plight of those damaged by armed conflict. Even if Fitzgerald did not experience combat, his work nevertheless sympathizes with the veterans' point of view by satirizing the gross obliviousness of noncombatants—one thinks again of Horace Tarbox in "Head and Shoulders"—to the psychological ravages of military engagement. In this respect, "The Night before Chancellorsville" attempts something similar to Richard Aldington's treatment of the wartime home front in *Death of a Hero* (1929), in which a community cannot begin to fathom the possibility that one of its sons might commit suicide to escape the misery of combat. Most Civil War fiction about noncombatants, whether *Gone with the Wind*, Faulkner's *The Unvanquished* (1938), or Margaret Walker's *Jubilee* (1966), dramatizes characters' initiation into the reality that war's consequences are not confined to the battlefield. What makes "The Night before Chancellorsville" such an unusual addition to the genre is the absence of any such epiphany or revelation. From start to stop, Nora remains clueless, her complete lack of insight an ironic means of conveying the story's point. The approach is also the reason the story is such an anomaly among Fitzgerald's fiction: the ironic-comic mode is not only a modernist style employed commonly in World War I novels and stories by Fitzgerald's peers—it is the very style Fitzgerald *declines* to use in his treatments of the Great War's aftereffects. If Fitzgerald was compelled to mourn the historical rupture that was World War I rather than treat it absurdly, here historical distance seems to grant him the emotional objectivity to satirize his character's lack of war awareness.

One way to appreciate Fitzgerald's experimental approach in "The Night before Chancellorsville" is to examine its somewhat surprising inclusion in Shelby Foote's anthology of Civil War fiction, *Chickamauga and Other Civil War Stories* (1993). Here, the story's take on historical fiction comes into relief in a way not readily apparent when it originally appeared in the fashion-preoccupied pages of *Esquire* in February 1935, nor in *Taps at Reveille*, in which Fitzgerald chose to republish it immediately preceding the somber "The Last of the Belles," thus creating a jarring juxtaposition. In his introduction, Foote comments on the state of historical fiction:

> In this country, historical fiction has in general been left to second-raters and hired brains, and this is particularly true of those who have chosen the Civil War as a major subject. Aside from Crane, our best fiction writers have given it mere incidental attention or none at all. Hemingway is a case in point; so is Henry James. This is regrettable on several counts, especially to those who would understand our nation by learning just what happened during that blood-drenched era—good and bad things, both in abundance—to make us what we are. Facts we have had and are having in ever greater numbers, perhaps a glut, through the years leading up to and away from the Sumter centennial, when biographies, overall explications, and brochures came pouring in a torrent from the presses and binderies. Yet there is a multifaceted truth outside the facts—beyond them, so to speak, or hidden inside them—and of this we have had all too little, because in this respect our novelists have let us down. (vii)

On its own merits, "The Night before Chancellorsville" strikes most critics, somewhat unfairly, as an interesting but ultimately unsuccessful experiment, for Nora's unenlightened perspective seems too narrow and the action too abbreviated to supply the historical context necessary for casual readers to properly appreciate Fitzgerald's point. In Foote's anthology, however, amid more obvious selections by Ambrose Bierce, Faulkner, Thomas Wolfe, and Eudora Welty, the story contributes to the "multifaceted truth outside the facts" by dramatizing the reality that many people are capable of remaining absolutely untouched by war, even when bullets are shattering glass all around them. Ultimately, as Alice Hall Petry has claimed, Nora's ignorance reveals Fitzgerald "facing certain realities: that we exist on a continuum of historical time which we simply cannot grasp; that the ramifications of what is happening in our immediate vicinity, historically and personally, are often unrealized simply because we lack the necessary objectivity" (182–83).

Further insight into the intention behind "The Night before

Chancellorsville" and Fitzgerald's regard for historical fiction as a medium for expressing his feelings about war may be found in his abortive plan to turn the story into a full-length movie script. A February 1, 1940, letter to MGM executive Edwin Knopf outlines a plot that combines elements of "Chancellorsville" and "The End of Hate," a story based on Edward Fitzgerald's Civil War reminiscences that Fitzgerald had been revising since 1936. (After numerous rejections, *Collier's* finally published "The End of Hate" in June 1940).[5] "I would begin my story with two girls who come South from Concord seeking the body of their brother who has been killed at Fredericksburg," Fitzgerald wrote. "They are sheltered puritanical girls used to the life of a small New England town. On the train going down they encounter a charming Union cavalry captain with whom the gayer of the two Concord girls falls in love." This overly romantic extension greatly alters the original story, potentially setting up an interesting antithesis between the purity of the Yankee girls and the impurity of Nora, whom Fitzgerald envisioned as "a semicomic character" comparable to "the tart in [John Ford's 1939 film] *Stagecoach*" (*Life in Letters* 430).

In an effort to convince Knopf of the scenario's viability, Fitzgerald then segues into an interesting analysis of war fiction and the cinema:

> There are two Civil Wars and there are two kinds of Civil War novels. So far, pictures have been made only from one of them—the romantic chivalric-Sir Walter-Scott story like *Gone with the Wind*, *The Birth of a Nation*, the books of Thomas Nelson Page and Mary Johnson. But there is also the realistic type modeled primarily on Stendhal's great picture of Waterloo in *Le Chartreuse de Parme*, Stephen Crane's *The Red Badge of Courage* and the stories of Ambrose Bierce. This way of looking at war gives great scope for comedy without bringing in Stepin Fetchitt[*sic*] and Hattie McDaniels as faithful Negro slaves, because it shows how small the individual is in the face of great events, how comparatively little he sees, and how little he can do even to save himself. The Great War has been successfully treated like this—*Journey's End* and *All Quiet*—the Civil War never. (*Life in Letters* 430–31)

Fitzgerald argues that comedy, in the classical sense, is the ultimate outcome of this second type of war fiction. It is a high comedy generated from the differences between the limited perspective of the individual and the broader perspective that history affords the audience: the individual thinks he sees one thing, but the reader, who has a more omniscient view, sees a fuller picture. Fitzgerald's criteria almost seem customized to fit the short-story version of "The Night before Chancellorsville," for Nora's inability to place her impressions within the scope of "great events" indeed reduces her to a "small" figure.

Interestingly, recent scholarship on Civil War fiction substantiates Fitzgerald's thinking about the limited perspective of the individual. In a book on the war writings of Ambrose Bierce and John W. De Forest, Michael W. Schaefer writes: "In these men's works the individual soldier sees only his own unit and perhaps one or two others in a clearing amid dense woods or an otherwise eerily empty field. He has little idea where the rest of his army is and what it is doing; all he knows of strategy and tactics is that the enemy may emerge from any direction at any moment" (xiv). Since this analysis confirms Fitzgerald's understanding of military fiction and the type of comedy or irony it can generate, it is no wonder Foote recognized "The Night before Chancellorsville" as a contribution to Civil War literature, despite the story's one obvious flaw: it lacks the panoptic contrast to Nell's limited perspective that would allow the narrative to rise to Fitzgerald's comedic expectations. By virtue of being an interior monologue (as well as a short story, or "sketch," as Fitzgerald referred to it), the story never reaches the level of high comedy he associated with *Red Badge* and *The Charterhouse of Palma*. In the end, "The Night before Chancellorsville" indicates Fitzgerald understood considerably more about war fiction than he was able to deliver.

Philippe and the Vagaries of Allegory in the Modern Age

In the same period during which he experimented with Civil War fiction to explore the individual perspective on history,

Fitzgerald was also searching for a literary form appropriate for addressing the fascist movement that by the mid–1930s was threatening to start a second world war. Fitzgerald was well aware of fascism's quick rise to prominence: he and Zelda had lived in Italy in 1924–1925, just two years after Benito Mussolini led his fascist Blackshirts to power. Throughout the last years of his life, Fitzgerald also kept abreast of the spreading wave of Mussolini-inspired totalitarianism. In February 1933, Adolf Hitler, elected chancellor only a month earlier, seized dictatorial control over the German government after the mysterious burning of the Reichstag (the German Parliament building) allowed him to increase his grip over the country. In March of that year, Dachau, the first of many concentration camps in Germany and elsewhere, was constructed near Munich. In October 1935, Mussolini's Italian army invaded Ethiopia, and in July 1936, the Spanish Civil War began, which pitted the Soviet-backed Republican forces against General Francisco Franco's army, which was sponsored by fascist Germany and Italy. Using new weapons of war, the Spanish fascists terrorized the countryside and eventually won the war for Franco in 1939. On September 29, 1938, Germany occupied the German-speaking area of Czechoslovakia after British prime minister Neville Chamberlain negotiated an appeasement treaty with Hitler. On September 1, 1939, the German Wehrmacht invaded Poland, and Britain and France declared war against the aggressor nation. World War II had begun.

It was no coincidence that, during this time, Fitzgerald grew increasingly pessimistic about the future—both his and history's. As he had throughout his literary career, Fitzgerald personalized the historical events of his day. The best evidence for this is in his correspondence with Zelda, for the couple frequently dramatized their emotional highs and lows through political/historical corollaries, including fascism. A good example of this tendency is in an October 1934 letter from Zelda while she was in the Sheppard and Enoch Pratt Hospital in Baltimore:

> Darling: Life is difficult. There are so many problems. 1) The problem of how to stay here and 2) The problem of how to get out. And I want so desperately to go to Guatemala still

> and ride a bicycle to the end of a long white road. The road is lined with lebanon cedars and poplars and ancient splendors crumble down the parched bleached hills and natives sleep in the shade beside a high grey wall. Whereas here Grace Moore sings prettily over the radio and obscure kings get themselves killed by what I am convinced are Mussolini[']s henchmen so that Lowell Thomas will not disappoint the old ladies—It is very depressing. (*Correspondence* 388)

Another Zelda letter includes a line imploring her husband: "Please pay no attention to any Splenglarian[*sic*] collapses or other portentous disasters should any take place between now and the time for your visit" (*Correspondence* 390). Her reference to Oswald Spengler, the author of *The Decline of the West* (1918–1922), suggests that she and Scott were discussing how current events indicated that Western civilization was headed toward a second Dark Ages. The mention of this popular (if not fashionable) historical tome is no accident, for Fitzgerald often cited Spengler as an intellectual influence, even claiming to have read the philosopher's work as he was toiling over *The Great Gatsby* in 1924–1925. (Inasmuch as an English translation of *Decline* was not available until 1926, this seems unlikely.) Bruccoli summarizes Fitzgerald's attraction to Spenglerian philosophy: "Because Fitzgerald was excited by large ideas about the movement of civilizations and felt insecure about his own education, he regarded *The Decline of the West* as a summation of intellectual history." As Bruccoli goes on to note, *Decline* attracted many modernists in part because Spengler's notion of cyclical history explained the erosion of order and stability of which warfare in the twentieth century was symptomatic: "[The book] presented an organic view of Western history, contending that there has been a pattern of cultural movements that repeat the same cycle of development and decay—with the twentieth century in the phase of decay" (240).

Because Fitzgerald attached so much intellectual currency to Spengler, he was understandably troubled when commentators began to view the German philosopher's theories as justification for the Nazi brand of fascism. In a June 6, 1940, letter to Maxwell

Perkins, Fitzgerald thanks his editor for sending him a copy of J. F. C. Fuller's *Decisive Battles: Their Influence upon History and Civilization*, a recent entry in the Scribner's catalog. According to Fitzgerald, Fuller's battlefield analyses carried a "curious philosophic note" that he found vexing:

> The note was reminiscent, exultant and dumb, but not until I found the name Spengler did [Fuller's] psychology become clear to me. Up to then I had thought: "What a wide range for a military man!" Then the truth became plain. Poor old Spengler has begotten Nazis that would make him turn over in his grave, and Fuller makes his own distortion. Spengler believed that the Western world was dead, and he believed nothing else but that—though he had certain ideas of a possible Slavic rebirth. This did *not* include Germany, which he linked with the rest of western Europe as in decline. And that the fine flower of it all was to be the battle of Vittorio Veneto and the rise of Mussolini—well, Spengler's turn in his grave must have been like that of an airplane propeller. (*Life in Letters* 289–90)

As this passage suggests, Fitzgerald viewed the rise of fascism as a sign of Western civilization's fall, *not*, as fascist sympathizers insisted, as evidence of the first stage of its cyclical rebirth.

Indeed, by 1940 Fitzgerald had already given a great deal of thought to the human qualities, both intellectual and artistic, needed to combat the forces of decay to bring about renewal. For a model of a new emergent culture, he looked deep into history to the medieval age, specifically to the Dark Ages of the ninth century. Kim Moreland, in her excellent book *The Medievalist Impulse in American Literature*, explains why: "Just as it had for Twain and [Henry] Adams, the medieval setting provided Fitzgerald with a 'feeling of escape from the modern world.' . . . He felt that he was escaping the breakdown of civilization, whose premonitory symptoms were manifested in world war, economic depression, and the immorality of the young." But whereas other modernists, Adams in particular, chose the "High Middle Ages of the twelfth and thirteenth centuries" as their preferred historical milieu, Fitzgerald peered even further into the past to the time immediately preceding the age of courtly ideals. As Moreland writes, "[He] was most interested not in a culture's apex but in a new culture's development and consolidation upon a preceding civilization's disintegration" (132). Thus, having had the full possibilities of a Romantic outlook closed off to him by the catastrophe of World War I, Fitzgerald turned to the medieval world, which offered him both form and content for a new back-to-the-future world view.

Fitzgerald's medieval turn took shape as what Bruccoli describes as a historical novel "in the form of a series of connected stories which he could then revise into a book," which he planned at different points to entitle either *The Castle* or *Philippe, Count of Darkness* (*Price* 513). The series centered upon a hero named Philippe, Count of Villefranche (located in France's Loire Valley, near Tours), who returns from exile to reclaim the land from Viking invaders. Although he planned a total of eight Philippe stories, Fitzgerald completed only four: "In the Darkest Hour," "The Count of Darkness," "The Kingdom in the Dark," and "Gods of Darkness." Of these, only three were actually published in Fitzgerald's lifetime, appearing in *Redbook* between October 1934 and August 1935. (The magazine declined to print "Gods of Darkness" until November 1941, nearly a year after Fitzgerald's death.) For obvious reasons, the stories did not inspire editorial enthusiasm; Fitzgerald's agent, Harold Ober, found them a difficult sell because magazine editors were convinced that the public was programmed to read stories about contemporary life by Fitzgerald, not historical fiction set in the early Middle Ages. Nor have these pieces attracted much critical interest—when discussed at all, they tend to be dismissed as artistic embarrassments. Scott Donaldson's comments are typical: "Fitzgerald knew a good deal about French history, and did considerable research for 'Philippe.' But the results were less than satisfactory. In the first place, the dialogue was written in an unintentionally comic patois mixing medieval formality with modern slang. The four installments . . . read as poorly as anything Fitzgerald wrote" (181).

Despite their lack of artistic merit, the Philippe stories remain interesting for both their vision of history as cyclical and the literary method by which Fitzgerald draws parallels between medieval and modern times. Bruccoli identifies this method in his assessment of the stories' failings: "It is remotely possible that the Philippe stories were intended as political allegory, that Fitzgerald was suggesting comparisons between the Middle Ages and the Depression; but the point is lost" (457). In describing the stories as allegorical, Bruccoli does not mean that there is within them an overt system of parallels that connects their literal and figurative levels of meaning, as the strictest sense of that literary term would imply (which may be why, for Bruccoli, the point is unclear). In other words, characters in Philippe are not named Fortitude or Patience, and the action is not set in the Valley of Despair or some such transparently unrealistic locale. Rather, the series is allegorical in the sense that Philippe is meant to embody the characteristics of the *modern* man who could shape the direction of contemporary history and rescue it from its present period of darkness and chaos. Similarly, the Viking hordes that the young count battles can be said to represent the type of organized, roving thuggery that Hitler and Mussolini encouraged. Amid the violence and terror such forces perpetuate, Fitzgerald insists, only a leader with epic strength, will, and foresight can impose order upon confusion. The parallel between the medieval Dark Ages and those of the 1930s is clearest in a passage from "In the Darkest Hour":

> There are epochs when certain things sing in the air, and certain strong courageous men hear them intuitively long before the rest. This was an epoch of disturbance and change; all over Europe men were thinking exactly like Philippe, taking direction from the arrows of history that seemed to float dimly overhead. Each of those men thought himself to be alone, but really each was an instrument of response to a great human need. (Price 522–23)

Interestingly, Fitzgerald's admittedly vague use of allegory here is not without precedent. Indeed, it reflects a literary direction commonly chosen by frustrated Romantics. In his essay "Allegory and Irony in Baudelaire," Paul de Man describes why the author of *Fleur du mal* was attracted to this technique:

> To see the material and the spiritual world connected by a system of correspondences can reduce nature to a set of signs that refer, allegorically, to a unity of a greater order, the senses being as it were, the key to this allegorical deciphering. Among Baudelaire's numerous sources for this conception many are of romantic origin; through Poe, Mrs. Crowe, and de Quincey, his description of the universe "as a storehouse of images and signs to which the imagination gives a place and a relative value" is related to Coleridge, [who was] himself directly derived from Schelling. This assertion is a commonplace of romantic idealism, much more frequent, however, as a general assertion of faith than as a poetic practice. (106)

As de Man suggests, allegory tends to be a method to which Romantics revert when seeking to confirm the presence of some overarching system of "greater order" than the current, war-torn convolutions of history allow one to perceive. In other words, the correspondences that allegory posits provide for that synoptic perspective on history that "The Night before Chancellorsville" (and historical fiction in general) would fail to achieve. By developing the Philippe stories as an extended allegory, Fitzgerald was indicating that historical fiction alone could not express his vision of history as cyclical, for it required no "assertion of faith," no investment of imaginative equity in that elusive pattern that explaines the continuous rise and fall of civilizations. In essence, allegory offered Fitzgerald a more abstract set of metaphors by which he could reconcile his Romantic sensitivity with the worsening contemporary world. It should be noted that in medieval poetry, allegories of war generally represent spiritual conflict or the battle for the soul (Hermann 2). Fitzgerald's use of allegory, therefore, would have been a perfect fit for his own vision of modern man fighting for the soul of civilization.

One final question about the Philippe series remains: what specific political ideology did Fitzgerald believe would deliver the modern world from its present ebb? Much has been made of Fitzgerald's claim that "just as Stendahl's[*sic*] portrait of a Byronic man made *Le Rouge et Noir* ['] so couldn't *my* portrait of Ernest as Phillipe [*sic*] make the real modern man" (*Notebooks* 159). As Bruccoli suggests, Fitzgerald's former friend Hemingway—by the mid–1930s they were little more than casual acquaintances—supposedly combined the physical, intellectual, and artistic verve that Philippe was meant to project: "Fitzgerald was impressed by Hemingway's talent and awed by his inflated reputation as a war hero and athlete. Fitzgerald's regret at having missed battle was exacerbated by what he believed was Hemingway's record as a combat veteran. His response to Hemingway was not unusual: early and late Hemingway had the ability to charm and dominate" (264). Fitzgerald admired if not envied Hemingway's charisma—a dangerous component of character in an age when Mussolini, Hitler, and Franco had marshaled armed forces out of the cults of personality they created for themselves. But whereas these dictators exuded a one-dimensional brutality, Hemingway was what in *The Crack-Up* Fitzgerald described as the "entire man in the Goethe-Byron-Shaw tradition" (84), someone for whom the literary and military (at least in Fitzgerald's admiring conception of him) were not separate spheres of endeavor.

All of which is to say that, as a model of the manhood needed to bring about a new age, Hemingway is a red herring. Readers seeking some residual resemblance between him and Philippe are likely to be disappointed; the count of Villefranche simply does not comport himself in any manner that immediately recalls the author of *The Sun Also Rises* and *A Farewell to Arms*. The real solution to the threat of fascism, Fitzgerald implies, is a resurgence of aristocratic nobility, for over the course of the four completed stories Philippe establishes himself as a benevolent feudal lord, "a precursor," as Moreland notes, "of the chivalric knight of the High Middle Ages who will have the comparative luxury of acting in accordance with an elaborately defined code of martial behavior" (135).

This code is nowhere more evident than in Philippe's behavior on the battlefield, for the young count distinguishes himself in warfare not only with inestimable courage but with keen obedience to the rules of engagement. "In the Darkest Hour," for instance, describes how Philippe must organize the peasantry to reclaim his father's land from the Viking marauders, whose villainy is conveyed through the repeated use of verbs such as "roving," "raging," and "ravaging." In contrast to these invaders, Philippe teaches his motley band of "farmers, lay brothers, [and] monastery serfs" the strategies by which to comport oneself nobly in battle: "He told them briefly the technique of the charge, the adjustment to the speed of the different animals, the weight of the shock, the ride through, the wheel-around, and return through the enemy to form for a second charge." As Fitzgerald insists, these lessons are indicative of Philippe's prescience, for they will become the essence of High Middle Ages ideals of soldierly valor: "Philippe's idea was a prefiguration of an age already beginning, when mounted men would take over the shaping of feudal Europe. His chief advantage . . . was just this" (*Price* 524). Philippe's morality is further demonstrated when, after his men rout the Vikings, he stops some of the peasants from exacting revenge on the prisoners they take captive (*Price* 526). Finally, he upholds the honor of the vanquished dead, taking "care that the bodies of [the Viking chieftain] Robert and his son [Goldgreaves] were placed atop the prospective pyre" in respect to the knightly order (*Price* 528). In concert with the knight-errant tradition, Philippe is not a perfect soldier; over the course of the completed stories, he makes mistakes and occasionally succumbs to hubris and vanity in ways necessary for him to better appreciate the importance of codes of military conduct. What makes his education process most interesting, however, is how he must intuit these codes, for he is effectively responsible for establishing them. As Philippe declares in "The Count of Darkness": "There *are* no habits—I *make* the habits!" (21).

Unfortunately for Fitzgerald, by 1940 the idea that nobles posed any sort of viable opposition to fascism was so anachronistic as to be laughable. The Philippe stories demonstrate the degree to which Fitzgerald continued to cling to pre–Great War notions of aristocratic preeminence even as lords across Europe were pressing parliamentary representatives to appease Hitler and Mussolini in hopes of retaining vestiges of their baronial privilege. The failure of any aristocratic resolve to confront the rise of fascism may offer a historical explanation for why, when faced in late 1939 with committing either to the completion of *Philippe* (as Maxwell Perkins was encouraging him to do) or beginning a contemporary novel about Hollywood, *The Last Tycoon*, Fitzgerald chose the latter option (Bruccoli 546). No matter how committed a Spengler devotee he remained, allegory proved too ineffectual a tool for reassuring himself that the looming world war would be just one more hour of darkness in history's ongoing convolutions. In this regard, the Philippe stories are more important for what was attempted in them (and why) rather than for what they achieved.

According to Fitzgerald's mistress, Sheilah Graham, the impending Second World War was on Fitzgerald's mind on December 21, 1940, the day of his death. Reading newspaper accounts of the German-Italian pact, he voiced his belief that America would inevitably find itself drawn into the conflict, just as it had two decades earlier. More surprisingly, he announced a desire to travel to Europe to work as a war correspondent as soon as he completed *The Last Tycoon*. "Ernest won't have that field all to himself, then," Graham reports him saying (329). The image of the dapper author of *This Side of Paradise* hitting the beaches on D-Day or rolling into a newly liberated Paris seems almost absurdly idiosyncratic—but only if one fails to appreciate just how deeply entrenched war was in his thinking. Although there is no way of knowing for sure, the subject may even have come to mind later that afternoon as he read about his alma mater's football team in the *Princeton Alumni Weekly*, his last act before a fatal heart attack claimed him. Princeton, after all, had been home to John Prentiss Poe, that great football hero who died a martyr on a World War I battlefield. Although Fitzgerald's failure to "get over" during that war rendered him—in both his own eyes and those of his contemporaries—somewhat suspect as a commentator on the topic, his fiction is nevertheless saturated with it. Ultimately, his discussions of the matter remind us that wars involve many fronts and that the repercussions at home are every bit as compelling as those experienced in the trenches. Indeed, Fitzgerald's lack of direct exposure to combat may be said to have granted him the distance necessary to assess war from the vantage point of history. While Hemingway, Dos Passos, and others were busy demonstrating the visceral horrors of battle, Fitzgerald sought to understand the way that war defined the character of an epoch, including, most obviously, his own. In this sense, his depictions of its effects on American society and the difficulty of gaining historical understanding in the thick of its upheavals are no less valuable an addition to the literary response to war than works by writers prone to boast of having made it to the frontlines.

NOTES

1. For a description of Princeton's climate during the war, see Daniel's analyses of the university's school newspaper, *The Daily Princetonian*, in "'Blue as the Sky, Gentlemen': Fitzgerald's Princeton through *The Prince*."

2. Fitzgerald expresses this regret more somberly in a later story actually entitled "I Didn't Get Over" (1936), in which a former army captain who failed to make it to the World War I front confesses his responsibility for a training-camp accident that claimed the lives of several soldiers.

3. An item in Bulletin No. 24, Headquarters Third Division (the one to which Gatsby and Nick would have been assigned), American Expeditionary Forces, USAPO 740–26, February 1919, indicates the prominence of this program. The bulletin notes: "Soldiers ordered to English and French Universities will be carried by their respective organizations on detached service. All records pertaining to the soldier will be sent by the officer or non-commissioned officer in charge of the detachment to be turned over to the Commandant of the American School detachment of the University to which the soldier is ordered. If the organization is ordered to the United States prior to the return of the soldier to his organization the provisions of section 4, para. 2 B, G. O. 17. c.s., will apply. The travel directive in sending students to universities is necessary in the military service" (1).

4. The story was entitled "The Night before Chancellorsville" when it appeared in *Esquire* in February 1935. Interestingly, the table of contents in *Taps at Reveille* lists it as "The Night of Chancellorsville," while the title later given in the book is "The Night at Chancellorsville," indicating that Fitzgerald was never quite sure how to center the action in this story. The night *before* Chancellorsville suggests the aforementioned anticipatory solemnity of the occasion, whereas the night *of* and *at* both emphasize the action of the battle itself. However, there typically are not many wounded soldiers the night *before* a battle, which makes the number of wounded on the train in the story somewhat problematic. Complicating this issue is the fact that Chancellorsville was a multiday battle, so *of* or *at* are relatively imprecise designations. Fitzgerald apparently considered May 2, 1863—the date of Jackson's famous rout of the Union army—as the day *at* Chancellorsville. For an analysis of Fitzgerald's regard for the Civil War, see Wegener, "The 'Two, Civil Wars' of F. Scott Fitzgerald."

5. Originally entitled "Thumbs Up," "The End of Hate" tells the story of a Confederate soldier whose thumbs must be amputated after Yankees hang him by his fingers. Although the soldier loves the sister of the doctor who performs the operation, he is intent on exacting revenge on the man—until his feelings for the woman intervene. As this summary suggests, the story is an odd (and ineffective) amalgam of war realism and sentimental romance.

WORKS CITED

Anderson, Hilton. "Fitzgerald and the War Novel." *Publications of the Mississippi Philological Association* (1987): 143–53.

Auchincloss, Louis. *Woodrow Wilson*. New York: Viking, 2000.

Berman, Ronald. *"The Great Gatsby" and Fitzgerald's World of Ideas*. Tuscaloosa: University of Alabama Press, 1997.

Bremer, Sidney H. "American Dreams and American Cities in Three Post–World War I Novels." *South Atlantic Quarterly* 79 (1980): 274–85.

Bruccoli, Matthew J. *Some Sort of Epic Grandeur: The Life of F. Scott Fitzgerald*. 1981. Rev. ed. New York: Carroll and Graf, 1991.

"Bulletin No. 24." Headquarters Third Division, American Expeditionary Forces, USAPO 740–26. February 1919. 1–2.

Danièl, Anne Margaret. "'Blue as the Sky, Gentlemen': Fitzgerald's Princeton through *The Prince*." In *F. Scott Fitzgerald in the Twenty-First Century*. Ed. Jackson R. Bryer, Ruth Prigozy, and Milton R. Stern. Tuscaloosa, Ala.: University of Alabama Press, 2003. 10–37.

Donaldson, Scott. *Hemingway vs. Fitzgerald: The Rise and Fall of a Literary Friendship*. Woodstock, N.Y.: Overlook, 1999.

Dyer, Geoff. "*The Missing of the Somme*." In *The Great War Reader*. Ed. James Hannah. College Station: Texas A&M University Press, 2000. 16–21.

Fitzgerald, F. Scott. *Afternoon of an Author: A Selection of Uncollected Stories and Essays*. New York: Scribner's, 1958.

———. *Correspondence of F. Scott Fitzgerald*. Ed. Matthew J. Bruccoli and Margaret M. Duggan. New York: Random House, 1980.

———. *The Crack-Up*. Ed. Edmund Wilson. New York: New Directions, 1945.

———. *F. Scott Fitzgerald: A Life in Letters*. Ed. Matthew J. Bruccoli, with Judith S. Baughman. New York: Scribner's, 1994.

———. "Gods of Darkness." *Redbook* 78 (Nov. 1941): 30–33, 88–91.

———. *The Great Gatsby*. 1925. Ed. Matthew J. Bruccoli. New York: Cambridge University Press, 1991.

———. "The Last of the Belles." Manuscript. F. Scott Fitzgerald Archives. Firestone Library, Princeton University. Reel 3.

———. *Letters of F. Scott Fitzgerald*. Ed. Andrew Turnbull. New York: Scribner's, 1963.

———. "The Night of [before] Chancellorsville." In *Taps at Reveille*. New York: Scribner's, 1935. 211–15.

———. *The Notebooks of F. Scott Fitzgerald*. Ed. Matthew J. Bruccoli. New York: Harcourt Brace Jovanovich/Bruccoli Clark, 1978.

———. Preface to *This Side of Paradise*. 1920. Ed. James L. W. West III. New York: Cambridge University Press, 1995. 393–95.

———. *The Price Was High: The Last Uncollected Stories of F. Scott Fitzgerald*. Ed. Matthew J. Bruccoli. New York: Harcourt Brace Jovanovich/Bruccoli Clark, 1979.

———. *The Short Stories of F. Scott Fitzgerald*. Ed. Matthew J. Bruccoli. New York: Scribner's, 1989.

———. *Tender Is the Night*. New York: Scribner's, 1934.

Fitzgerald, Zelda. "Tribute to F. Scott Fitzgerald." In Bruccoli 707–10.

Foote, Shelby. Introduction to *Chickamauga and Other Civil War Stories*. Ed. Shelby Foote. New York: Delta, 1993.

Graham, Sheilah, with Gerald Frank. *Beloved Infidel*. New York: Holt, Rinehartand Winston, 1958.

Guernsey, Alfred H., and Henry M. Alden. *Harper's Pictorial History of the Civil War*. New York: Fairfax, 1866.

Harries, Meirion, and Susie Harries. *The Last Days of Innocence: America at War, 1917–1918*. New York: Random House, 1997.

Hermann, John P. *Allegories of War: Language and Violence in Old English Poetry*. Ann Arbor: University of Michigan Press, 1989.

Kennedy, J. Gerald. *Imagining Paris: Exile, Writing, and American Identity*. New Haven, Conn.: Yale University Press, 1993.

Lee, David D. *Sergeant York: An American Hero*. Lexington: University of Kentucky Press, 1985.

de Man, Paul. "Allegory and Irony in Baudelaire." In *Romanticism and Contemporary Criticism: The Gauss Seminar and Other Papers*. Ed. E. S. Burt, Kevin Newmark, and Andrzej Warminski. Baltimore, Md.: Johns Hopkins University Press, 1993. 101–22.

McGowan, Stanley S. "Battle of Chancellorsville (2–3 May 1863)." In *Encyclopedia of the American Civil War: A Political, Social, and Military History*. Ed. David Stephen Heidler and Jeanne T. Heidler. New York: Norton, 2002. 392..

Moreland, Kim. *The Medievalist Impulse in American Literature: Twain, Adams, Fitzgerald, and Hemingway*. Charlottesville: University Press of Virginia, 1996.

Petry, Alice Hall. *Fitzgerald's Craft of Short Fiction: The Collected Stories 1920–1935*. Tuscaloosa: University of Alabama Press, 1989.

Prigozy, Ruth. *Illustrated Lives: F. Scott Fitzgerald*. London: Penguin, 2001.

A Princeton Companion. http://etc.princeton.edu/cgibin/mfs/05/Companion/poe_brothers.html.

Reynolds, Michael S. *The Young Hemingway*. Cambridge, Mass.: Blackwell, 1986.

Salvesen, Christopher. *The Landscape of Memory: A Study of Wordsworth's Poetry*. Lincoln: University of Nebraska Press, 1965.

Schaefer, Michael W. *Just What War Is: The Civil War Writings of De*

Forest and Bierce. Knoxville: University of Tennessee Press, 1997.

Sears, Stephen W. *Chancellorsville*. Boston: Mariner, 1996.

Stebbins, Todd Harrison. "*Tender Is the Night*: The Last Love Battle, with a Newly Generated Concordance." Ph.D. diss., University of South Carolina, 1993.

Stern, Milton. *Tender Is the Night: The Broken Universe*. New York: Twayne, 1994.

———. "*Tender Is the Night* and American History." In *The Cambridge Companion to F. Scott Fitzgerald*. Ed. Ruth Prigozy. New York: Cambridge University Press, 2002. 95–117.

von Clausewitz, Carl. *On War*. Ed. Michael Howard and Peter Paret. Princeton, N.J.: Princeton University Press, 1976.

Wegener, Frederick. "The 'Two Civil Wars' of F. Scott Fitzgerald." In *F. Scott Fitzgerald in the Twenty-First Century*. Ed. Jackson R. Bryer, Ruth Prigozy, and Milton R. Stern. Tuscaloosa Ala.: University of Alabama Press 2003. 238–66.

Winter, Jay. *Sites of Memory, Sites of Mourning: The Great War in European Cultural History*. New York: Cambridge University Press, 1995.

Wordsworth, William. "Lines Composed a Few Miles above Tintern Abbey on Revisiting the Banks of the Wye during a Tour, July 13, 1798." In *Lyrical Ballads and Other Poems, 1797–1800*. Ed. James Butler and Karen Green. Ithaca, N.Y.: Cornell University Press, 1992. 116–20.

Zieger, Robert H. *America's Great War: World War I and the American Experience*. Lanham, Md.: Rowman and Littlefield, 2000.

ILLUSTRATED CHRONOLOGY

Fitzgerald's Life

1896: Francis Scott Key Fitzgerald is born September 24 to Edward and Mary "Mollie" Fitzgerald in St. Paul, Minnesota.

1898: The Fitzgeralds move to Buffalo, New York, after Edward Fitzgerald's furniture factory fails. Over the next ten years, the family will relocate to Syracuse (1901) and then back to Buffalo (1903) as Edward works for Proctor & Gamble.

1908: The Fitzgeralds return to St. Paul after Edward loses his job; Scott Fitzgerald enrolls in the St. Paul Academy and begins writing short stories and plays.

F. Scott Fitzgerald at two, already displaying an aristocratic flair. Courtesy Princeton University Library.

Historical Events

1895: Louis and Auguste Lumière of Lyons, France, invent the Lumière Cinematograph, the first machine to successfully project moving pictures onto a screen, paving the way for movies to become mass entertainment.

1900: Death of philosopher Friedrich Nietzsche (b. 1844), an important intellectual influence on Fitzgerald; Sigmund Freud (1856–1939) publishes *The Interpretation of Dreams*; Joseph Conrad (1857–1924) publishes *Lord Jim*; Theodore Dreiser (1871–1945) publishes *Sister Carrie.*

1901: William McKinley assassinated.

1903: *The Great Train Robbery*, the first commercially successful silent movie, premieres.

1904: Conrad publishes *Nostromo*; G. Stanley Hall's *Adolescence* popularizes the modern notion of teenagers as a distinct demographic segment of the American population.

1908: The Ford Motor Company introduces the Model T.

1909: Gertrude Stein (1874–1946) publishes *Three Lives*; the National Association for the Advancement of Colored People is founded.

Like many young men his age, Fitzgerald dreamed of becoming a college football hero. He was an undistinguished member of his prep-school squad, however, and was cut during first-week college tryouts at Princeton. Courtesy Princeton University Library.

1911: Fitzgerald transfers to the preparatory Newman School in Hackensack, New Jersey.

1913: Fitzgerald is accepted at Princeton University as a member of the class of 1917; there, he meets Edmund Wilson.

1915: Fitzgerald drops out of Princeton after a lackluster academic career; returns the following year as a member of the class of 1918 but never completes degree.

1917: Fitzgerald is commissioned as a second lieutenant in the U.S. infantry. After reporting to Fort Leavenworth, Kansas, he begins "The Romantic Egotist," a preliminary version of *This Side of Paradise.*

Psychologist G. Stanley Hall (1844–1924), author of the influential study Adolescence *(1904), was instrumental in shaping modern ideas of youth, which Fitzgerald would mine in* This Side of Paradise *and his Basil and Josephine series.*

1918: While stationed at Camp Sheridan outside Montgomery, Alabama, Fitzgerald meets Zelda Sayre (b. 1900) at a country-club dance. Although the prestigious publishing firm Charles Scribner's Sons rejects "The Romantic Egotist," editor Maxwell Perkins encourages Fitzgerald to revise and resubmit.

Fitzgerald, far right, while stationed at Camp Sheridan in Montgomery, Alabama, in 1918, when he met Zelda Sayre. "I had only three months to live," he would later claim, explaining the haste with which he wrote his first novel. "In those days all infantry officers thought they had only three months to live." Courtesy Princeton University Library.

1919: After working briefly in the advertising industry in New York, Fitzgerald begins a lucrative association with the *Saturday Evening Post,* which will publish sixty-five of his short stories in the next eighteen years.

1920: Scribner's publishes *This Side of Paradise* on March 26; the book goes on to sell upwards of 50,000 copies. Fitzgerald marries Zelda on April 3 in New York; *Flappers and Philosophers*, Fitzgerald's first short-story collection, is published in September.

Zelda Sayre dressed for a Montgomery "Folly Ball" shortly after meeting Fitzgerald at a similar event. "The war brought men to the town like swarms of benevolent locusts eating away the blight of unmarried women that had overrun the South since its economic decline" (Save Me the Waltz). *Courtesy Princeton University Library.*

1921: The Fitzgeralds travel throughout Europe; daughter Frances Scott ("Scottie") is born October 26 in St. Paul.

1922: *The Beautiful and Damned* appears in book form after serialization the previous fall and winter in *Metropolitan Magazine*; Scribner's also publishes *Tales of the Jazz Age*, Fitzgerald's second story collection.

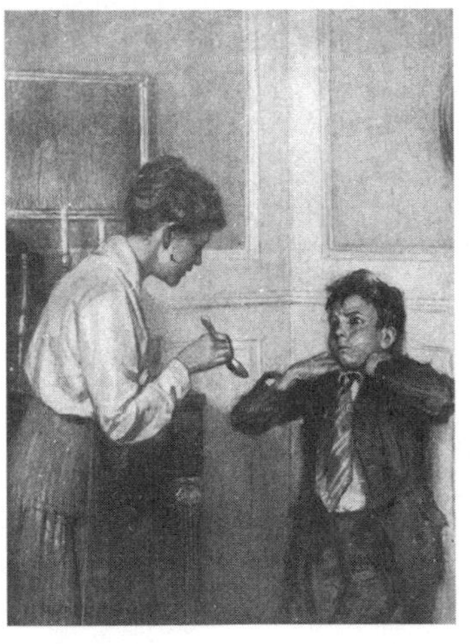

Before Fitzgerald, novels such as Booth Tarkington's Penrod and Sam *(1916) portrayed adolescents as naive, foppish "mooncalfs" (above left). The stories collected in* Flappers and Philosophers, *by contrast, emphasized their adultlike attraction to sex and sophistication, best symbolized by Bernice's bobbed hair (above right).*

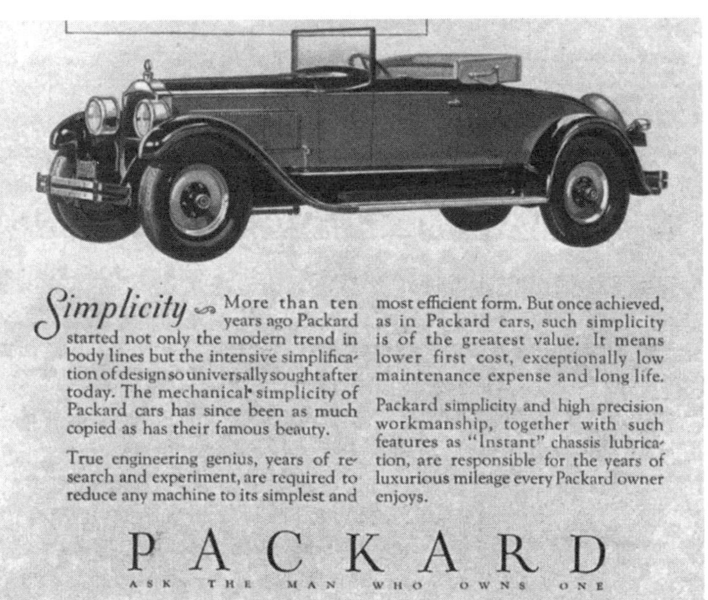

By freeing young people from parental supervision, the automobile revolutionized not only travel but sexual mores as well.

Fitzgerald as he wanted to be seen—as a serious, professional writer. Courtesy Princeton University Library.

1923: Breaking from his image as a "flapper novelist," Fitzgerald tries his hand at Broadway-style comedy. *The Vegetable* proves a critical disaster during its Atlantic City tryout, however, and never opens in New York.

1924: The Fitzgeralds embark for the French Riviera, where Fitzgerald completes *The Great Gatsby*; Zelda's romance with French aviator Edouard Jozan that summer threatens the couple's marriage.

1925: Scribner's publishes *The Great Gatsby* on April 10; six weeks later Fitzgerald meets Ernest Hemingway in Paris.

Fitzgerald's popularity coincided with the rise of the art-deco design movement. Just as his fiction projected the graceful dynamism of youth, so, too, art deco conveyed the sleek fluidity associated with early twentieth-century ideas of modernity.

1913: The Armory Show, the first exhibition of modern art in America, opens; Henry Ford creates assembly-line mode of mass production; U.S. Congress establishes personal income tax.

1914: World War I begins when a Bosnian nationalist assassinates Archduke Ferdinand of Austria; thousands are killed in first battle of the Marne and first battle of Ypres; Margaret Sanger popularizes the term "birth control"; Stein applies the innovations of cubist painter Pablo Picasso to poetry and prose in *Tender Buttons*.

Scott and Zelda Fitzgerald at the height of their fame, posed for the May 1923 cover of Hearst's International Magazine. *An accompanying caption read: "Mrs. F. Scott Fitzgerald started the flapper movement in this country. So says her husband, the best-loved author of the younger generation." Courtesy Princeton University Library.*

The Fitzgeralds with their daughter, Scottie (born 1921), on the French Riviera in the Summer of 1924, while Fitzgerald was writing The Great Gatsby. *Zelda was then embroiled in an extramarital relationship with a French aviator that threatened the couple's marriage. Courtesy Princeton University Library.*

1915: T. S. Eliot (1888–1965) publishes "The Love Song of J. Alfred Prufrock."

1917: America enters World War I; Russian Revolution ends reign of Czar Nicholas II, establishing communism as a force of global reckoning for the next seventy years.

World War I propaganda posters stressed sacrifice, conservation, and patriotism, the very mores that the Lost Generation would question in the 1920s. Courtesy Government History Collection, Provincial Museum of Alberta.

THE BOOKMAN ADVERTISER

F. Scott Fitzgerald's new novel

The large public which has followed with such close interest the career of the author of THIS SIDE OF PARADISE *will be gratified by this novel as the product of Mr. Fitzgerald's literary maturity. It is an admirably rounded piece of work, with no loss of that spontaneity which has always made Mr. Fitzgerald so delightful.*

THE GREAT GATSBY

Brilliant, ironic, a vital and glamorous narrative, underlaid by shrewd thought of an unusual quality. $2.00

Trade advertisements trumpeted The Great Gatsby *as "the product of Mr. Fitzgerald's literary maturity . . . with no loss of that spontaneity which has always made [his writing] so delightful." Although instantly recognized as its author's best work,* Gatsby *was not a commercial success.*

Although Prohibition (1919–1933) aimed to elevate American morality by making alcohol illegal, it succeeded only in creating a profitable black market for bootleggers, including Fitzgerald's Jay Gatsby. Courtesy MSCUA, University of Washington Libraries.

1918: Germany surrenders, ending World War I; Woodrow Wilson proposes League of Nations.

1919: The Paris Peace Conference leads to Treaty of Versailles; Congress passes Eighteenth Amendment to the U.S. Constitution, prohibiting alcohol sales and consumption; more than 2 million people of color on four continents claim membership in black nationalist Marcus Garvey's Universal Negro Improvement Association; Sherwood Anderson (1876–1941) publishes *Winesburg, Ohio.*

In the early 1920s Fitzgerald found himself a frequent subject of caricature. In this New York Tribune *illustration, cartoonist Gene Markey depicted him and fellow novelist John Dos Passos as impudent children.*

1920: U.S. passes Nineteenth Amendment, granting women the right to vote; Warren G. Harding elected president; American Civil Liberties Union established; Alain Locke (1886–1954) publishes *The New Negro*, inaugurating the African-American arts movement known as the Harlem Renaissance; swindler Charles Ponzi inspires the term "Ponzi scheme" after promising clients a 50 percent return on investments in a money-order scam.

Also influencing Fitzgerald in the mid–1920s were Gerald and Sara Murphy (far left, seated), the wealthy expatriate couple whose aristocratic glamour was the inspiration for Dick and Nicole Diver in Tender Is the Night. *Scott and Zelda spent much of 1926 socializing with the Murphys on the French Riviera. Courtesy John F. Kennedy Library.*

1926: Fitzgerald's third story collection, *All the Sad Young Men*, published; Fitzgeralds pass the summer on the Riviera with Hemingway and his first wife, Hadley Richardson, and Gerald and Sara Murphy, a wealthy expatriate couple who serve as the inspiration for Dick and Nicole Diver in *Tender Is the Night*.

*Although Fitzgerald's flappers were intelligent, complex women, Hollywood portrayed them as empty-headed emissaries of fun. At the height of her fame, actress Colleen Moore (*Flaming Youth*) epitomized the daffy exuberance of this cinematic character type. Courtesy Museum of Modern Art, Film Stills Archive.*

1921: Silent-film comedian Roscoe "Fatty" Arbuckle charged with manslaughter after a Hollywood starlet dies in his hotel room; the scandal moves Hollywood to adopt the Hayes Code, a rigid set of standards designed to ensure the morality of movies.

1922: James Joyce (1882–1941) publishes *Ulysses*; Eliot publishes *The Waste Land*; Benito Mussolini leads Fascist party to power in Italy.

1923: The "world's most pulchritudinous evangelist," the charismatic Aimee Semple McPherson, opens the million-dollar Angelus Temple, home to her Church of the Four-Square Gospel, in Los Angeles.

1924: After expatriating to Paris two years earlier, Ernest Hemingway (1899–1961) begins producing such classic short stories as "Indian Camp," "Soldier's Home," and "Big Two-Hearted River."

1927: After returning to America the previous December, Fitzgerald makes his first foray to Hollywood; two months later, he and Zelda settle near Wilmington, Delaware, where Zelda takes ballet lessons.

1928: Seeking an outlet for her own artistic expression, Zelda commits to a ballet regime in Paris under Lubov Egorova of the renowned Ballets Russe; Fitzgerald publishes "The Scandal Detectives," the first entry in his Basil and Josephine series.

1930: Zelda suffers first breakdown; between April 23 and June 5 she is admitted to three different psychiatric clinics in France and Switzerland.

1925: Hemingway publishes *In Our Time*; Stein publishes *The Making of Americans*; Clarence Darrow defends Tennessee schoolteacher John Scopes for teaching Charles Darwin's evolutionary theories in a case popularly known as the "Monkey Trial"; membership in the Ku Klux Klan reaches 4 million; Bruce Barton's *The Man Nobody Knows*, a runaway bestseller, celebrates Jesus Christ as a forefather of the of the American entrepreneurial spirit.

Ernest Hemingway in the late 1920s, with his second wife, Pauline Pfeiffer. Fitzgerald was instrumental in introducing Hemingway to his publisher, Scribner's, and in helping to polish Hemingway's first major novel, The Sun Also Rises *(1926). Courtesy John F. Kennedy Library.*

Seeking an artistic venue of her own as she neared thirty, Zelda returned to a childhood passion and began studying ballet. Fitzgerald would later claim that her devotion to dance exacerbated her mental illness. Courtesy Princeton University Library.

1931: In January Fitzgerald's father dies; the following month, the *Saturday Evening Post* publishes "Babylon Revisited," an indictment of the Lost Generation, which will posthumously become Fitzgerald's most widely read short story; in September Zelda is released from the Prangins Clinic in Nyon, Switzerland, after a year and a half of treatment; the couple settles briefly in Montgomery, Alabama, and Fitzgerald travels to Hollywood in search of financial security.

1926: Hemingway publishes *The Sun Also Rises;* Sinclair Lewis (1885–1951) declines Pulitzer Prize for *Arrowsmith*; first liquid-propelled rocket launched in United States; H. L. Mencken's *American Mercury* banned in Boston for publishing an article about a prostitute entertaining clients in Catholic cemeteries.

1927: Charles Lindbergh completes first solo transatlantic flight in the *Spirit of St. Louis*; despite protests by leading literary and cultural figures, Italian anarchists Nicola Sacco and Bartolomeo Vanzetti are executed in Massachusetts; Shanghai Massacre of 6,000 communists by Chiang Kai-shek inaugurates theChinese Civil War, which will last until 1949.

1928: Huey Long's election to the governorship of Louisiana launches a politics; populist wave in American Babe Ruth bats an unprecedented .625 as his New York Yankees sweep baseball's World Series.

Fitzgerald feared that Zelda's novel, Save Me the Waltz, *would trump his long-delayed* Tender Is the Night. *Although* Scribner's Magazine, *the house organ of Fitzgerald's publisher, serialized his book in 1934, neither novel was a commercial success. Courtesy Scott and Zelda Fitzgerald Museum, Montgomery, Alabama.*

1932: After a second breakdown, Zelda enters a psychiatric clinic in Baltimore; while there she writes her novel, *Save Me the Waltz,* which appears in October; struggling to complete *Tender Is the Night*, Fitzgerald is outraged at what he regards as the poaching of his literary material.

1933: Zelda's play, *Scandalabra*, opens to withering reviews in Baltimore.

1934: Almost nine years to the day after *The Great Gatsby* appeared, *Tender Is the Night* is finally published on April 12; ongoing psychiatric problems force Zelda to be hospitalized again.

1929: St. Valentine's Day Massacre in Chicago orchestrated by gangster Al Capone; Great Depression begins when U.S. stock market crashes; William Faulkner (1897–1962) publishes *The Sound and the Fury*; Hemingway publishes *A Farewell to Arms*.

1930: Advertising agent Earnest Elmo Caulkins publishes *Modern Publicity*, which promotes planned obsolescence as a means of guaranteeing growth of American consumerism; John Dos Passos (1896–1970) publishes *42nd Parallel*; Faulkner publishes *As I Lay Dying*; Sinclair Lewis wins first U.S. Nobel Prize in literature.

1935: Scribner's publishes *Taps at Reveille*, Fitzgerald's fourth and last story collection in his lifetime; while staying in a North Carolina hotel, he begins writing the essays collectively known as *The Crack-Up*; *Esquire* publishes them the following spring.

1936: Fitzgerald's depression heightens in the fall when his mother dies; in September, around his fortieth birthday, he is the subject of an unflattering *New York Post* article that portrays him as a washed-up alcoholic.

1937: Fitzgerald ventures once more to Hollywood to work as a screenwriter; in July he meets his eventual mistress, Sheilah Graham.

1932: Dos Passos publishes *Nineteen-Nineteen*; Faulkner publishes *Light in August*; kidnapping and murder of Lindbergh's son; Mahatma Gandhi begins nonviolent campaigns for poor.

1933: Stein publishes *The Autobiography of Alice B. Toklas;* Adolf Hitler leads Nazi party to power in Germany; United States passes Twenty-First Amendment, repealing Prohibition.

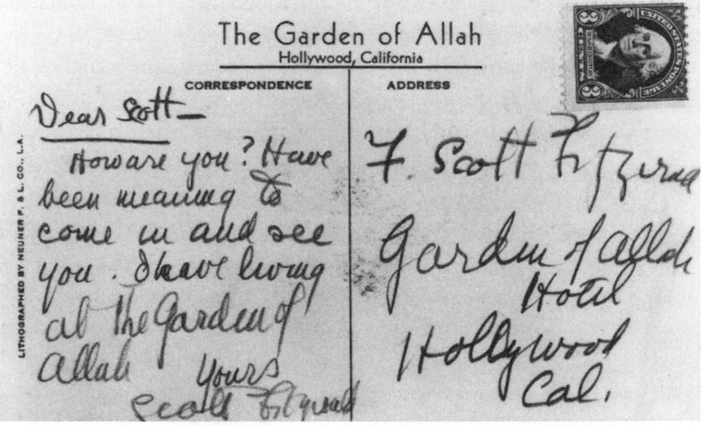

Depressed and lonely while toiling in Hollywood, Fitzgerald sent himself this postcard. Courtesy Princeton University Library.

Zelda included this sketch of Scott in a 1938 letter begging him to take her traveling. "I will cook," the note reads, "and maybe discover gold if you will take me to Guatemala—or are you too busy?" Courtesy Princeton University Library.

1938: After toiling in screenwriting for a year and a half with little success, Fitzgerald learns that his contract with Metro-Goldwyn-Mayer will not be renewed; he accepts freelance opportunities with other motion picture studios such as Paramount, Universal, and Twentieth Century Fox.

1940: After four years in a North Carolina sanitarium, Zelda returns to Montgomery to live with her mother; Fitzgerald enjoys steady progress on his fifth novel, *The Last Tycoon* (also known as *The Love of the Last Tycoon*); before completing a draft, however, Fitzgerald dies of a heart attack on December 21.

1934: The Federal Bureau of Investigation under J. Edgar Hoover captures and kills famed outlaws John Dillinger, "Pretty Boy" Floyd, Bonnie Parker, and Clyde Barrow.

1936: Spanish Civil War begins; Faulkner publishes *Absalom, Absalom!* Margaret Mitchell (1900–1949) publishes *Gone with the Wind*; Eugene O'Neill (1888–1953) wins Nobel Prize in literature.

1938: Germany invades Austria; British prime minister Nigel Chamberlain signs Munich Agreement granting Czechoslovakia to Germany in return for "peace in our time."

1939: Germany invades Poland; World War II begins; John Steinbeck (1902–1968) publishes *The Grapes of Wrath.*

1940: Roosevelt wins third presidential term; Winston Churchill succeeds Chamberlain as British prime minister; Germany invades Denmark, Norway, Holland, Belgium, and France; Hemingway publishes *For Whom the Bell Tolls*; Richard Wright (1908–1960) publishes *Native Son.*

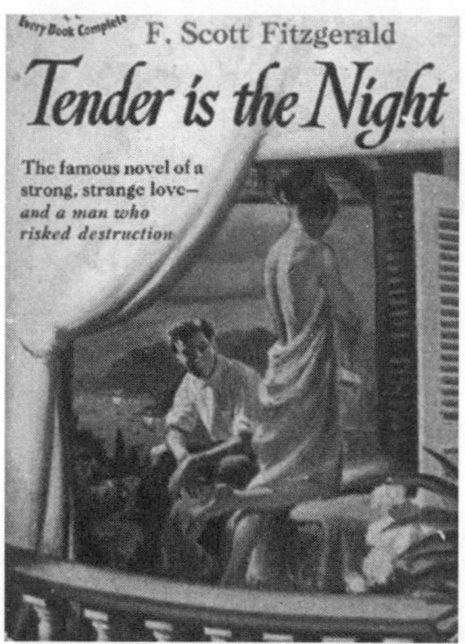

The Fitzgerald revival wasn't merely an academic phenomenon; it was also a technological one, driven in part by the emergence of the paperback industry in the late 1940s. As this 1951 cover of Tender Is the Night *suggests, paperbacks emphasized sex and salaciousness. Courtesy Scott and Zelda Fitzgerald Museum, Montgomery, Alabama.*

1941: Scribner's publishes the unfinished *Last Tycoon* manuscript, with editorial notes by Fitzgerald's former Princeton classmate Edmund Wilson.

1945: Wilson edits a collection of Fitzgerald nonfiction called *The Crack-Up*. Included are several important critical essays later credited with inaugurating the Fitzgerald revival.

1941: Germany invades Russia in defiance of Hitler-Stalin pact; "The Final Solution," the Nazi plan for extermination of European Jews begins; Japanese bombing of Pearl Harbor compels U.S. into World War II; James Agee publishes *Now Let Us Praise Famous Men*, with photographs by Walker Evans; Albert Camus publishes *The Stranger*; deaths of James Joyce, Sherwood Anderson, and Virginia Woolf.

1943: Mussolini deposed in Italy, which declares war on Germany; Jews in the Warsaw, Poland, ghetto stage unsuccessful uprising against Nazis; Ayn Rand publishes *The Fountainhead*.

1944: Allied forces storm the beaches of Nazi-occupied France on D-Day; Saul Bellow publishes *Dangling Man*.

1945: Allies declare victory in World War II; Hitler commits suicide; the United Nations is founded; U.S. drops the atomic bomb on Hiroshima and Nagasaki, forcing Japanese surrender.

1946: Robert Penn Warren publishes *All the King's Men*.

The Fitzgeralds' gravesite in Rockville, Maryland, features an inscription from Gatsby. *They were not buried together until 1975.*

1948: Zelda dies in a sanitarium fire in Asheville, North Carolina, on March 10.

1948: More than 135 million paperback books are published in U.S., radically changing the publishing industry; Ezra Pound publishes *The Pisan Cantos*.

Bibliographical Essay

The Contours of Fitzgerald's Second Act

Albert J. DeFazio III

Casting a long eye over Fitzgerald's bibliographical footprint reveals that the man who was dubious about second acts has earned encores for more than sixty years. In the 1920s, F. Scott Fitzgerald was at the zenith of his literary popularity, and he and his beautiful and unconventional wife, Zelda, were celebrities. By his death in 1940 and hers in 1948, the Fitzgeralds had cracked up. Fitzgerald died an unemployed screenwriter in Hollywood, and his literary acclaim had reached its nadir; Zelda suffered her first mental breakdown in 1930 and spent the rest of her life as a resident or outpatient of sanitariums.

Today Scott Fitzgerald is recognized as being among the most important American authors of the twentieth century. His death, like his life, was greeted with mixed reviews, but thoughtful overviews by colleagues and the warm reception of the posthumously published *The Last Tycoon* in 1941 suggested that Fitzgerald's critical fortunes merited reexamination. The appearance in 1945 of Edmund Wilson's edition of *The Crack-Up* and Dorothy Parker's *The Portable F. Scott Fitzgerald* provided occasion for important and favorable reassessments, raising the curtain on Fitzgerald's "second act." Since that time his reputation has been borne forward, ceaselessly propelled by the twin forces of his artistic genius and persistent scholarly attention.

Fitzgerald's own genius is, of course, the primary reason for continued interest in him and his art, but his bibliographical record clearly indicates that scholars methodically nurtured his revival, treating his life and work almost as if they were on an archaeological dig. The editions by Wilson and Parker in 1945 were treasures that teased the public from its indifference. In the 1950s the resurgence of interest in Fitzgerald's life and art was confirmed by the appearance of the first biography, collection of criticism, full-length study, and comprehensive edition of his short stories. Memoirs appeared, too, joined by new collections, reprints, and substantial articles and book chapters that contemplated *The Great Gatsby*, predominantly, as well as Fitzgerald's social criticism of America's culture and its dreams. Decade's end saw the founding of the *Fitzgerald Newsletter* (1958–1968), which included notes, articles, and a checklist of the increasing supply of materials by or about Fitzgerald.

In the 1960s scholars excavated a lower layer, bringing out collections of short stories, apprenticeship fiction, three volumes of reprinted *Gatsby* criticism, and another devoted to *Tender Is the Night*, marking a widening of interest within the field. More substantial memoirs appeared, joining the first selection of letters and enhancing the public's grasp of Fitzgerald's biography. Bibliographical work commenced with a thorough volume on Fitzgerald's critical reputation by Jackson R. Bryer, who also provided a pair of essays that reviewed research and scholarship. *American Literary Scholarship*'s annual bibliographical essays began in 1963 and continue to canvass the trends in scholarship. This decade's end witnessed the *Fitzgerald Newsletter*'s blossoming into the *Fitzgerald/Hemingway Annual* (1969–1979), a hefty compendium of critical and textual studies that provided an extensive checklist, testifying to the ever-increasing relevance of its subjects.

Bibliographical and textual studies were the signal contributions of the 1970s. Matthew J. Bruccoli's descriptive bibliography (1972, followed by a supplement in 1980 and a revised edition in 1987) initiated what can be described as the democratization of Fitzgerald studies. The archive was gradually and carefully published: a facsimile, concordance, and apparatus for *Gatsby*; dozens of previously uncollected magazine stories; editions of

Fitzgerald's screenplay, plays, notebooks, ledger, and scrapbooks; and volumes of his correspondence with his editor and agent. Joining valuable collections of reprinted criticism were ten critical books, the best of which considered his American identity. One focused exclusively on the short stories; another on Fitzgerald's Catholic sensibility; and a third on *Tender Is the Night*. Zelda received her first substantial book-length biography, and the portrait of her as a liberated woman and creative genius contributed to the ongoing debate about whether one Fitzgerald was responsible for ruining the other.

By the 1980s the primary bibliography was revised by Bruccoli, and Bryer's supplement (1984) to his annotated study of Fitzgerald's critical reputation more than doubled the number of entries in the 1967 volume. Interest in Fitzgerald abroad was significant enough to warrant an analysis and annotated bibliography of Fitzgerald's foreign critical reception. Scholarly work in the archive yielded the largest collections of short stories and correspondence we have yet had, as well as a volume of poetry and studies of the making of *This Side of Paradise* and *Tender Is the Night*. The proliferation of critical articles continued. Three collections of original essays appeared: the first covered the short stories; another addressed Fitzgerald's entire canon; and the last was devoted to *Gatsby*. Of the four biographies, the superior one was Bruccoli's, which brought to light a wealth of data unearthed since the publication of the first biography in 1951. The best of the eight full-length studies focused on Fitzgerald's skills as a social observer, on his female characters, and on close readings of the short fiction.

The 1992 founding of the F. Scott Fitzgerald Society, host thus far to six international conferences, as well as the 1996 centenary celebrations and their attendant publications, contributed to a decade that remains unsurpassed for its contributions to Fitzgerald studies. The archive yielded eighteen volumes of facsimiles (manuscripts, typescripts, stories, essays, and a play), which made clear that Fitzgerald was a careful reviser. The rigorously edited Cambridge Editions of the Works of F. Scott Fitzgerald commenced with *Gatsby* (1991) and has grown to include *The Love of the Last Tycoon* (1993), *This Side of Paradise* (1995), *Flappers and Philosophers*

(2000), and *Trimalchio* (2000). In addition, the archive expanded when the Thomas Cooper Library at the University of South Carolina obtained the Bruccolis' enormous collection of Fitzgerald materials. A pair of encyclopedic reference works provided thousands of biographical and bibliographical entries, corraling many of the facts that had been herded in preceding decades.

Both biographical and critical works became more specialized in the 1990s. Two assessments of Fitzgerald's relationship with Hemingway appeared (one was revised); Fitzgerald's granddaughter and Sheilah Graham's son contributed lengthy treatments of their parents. Most of the seventeen book-length critical studies focused on single works; however, one general study analyzing material written prior to the "opulent synthesis," *Gatsby*, appeared, and another pursued its cultural context. *Tender Is the Night* claimed both a critical examination and a companion, rife with annotations, and *This Side of Paradise* earned serious treatment as a *Bildungsroman*. Three valuable books on the short stories were joined by anthologies of original essays on the neglected short fiction and on the "French connections" of Fitzgerald and Hemingway. A four-volume collection of criticism containing 226 selections is surely the most comprehensive text available, but its cost and small print run make it hard to obtain. While one collection of reprinted essays was dedicated to the short stories, the other five addressed *Gatsby*. The most notable collection surveyed the novel's critical reception through the 1990s, canvassing and excerpting the scholarship in an extended bibliographical essay.

So far, in the first decade of the twenty-first century, we have enjoyed the ongoing publication of the Cambridge Editions as well as specialized collections of the short fiction, including a generously illustrated and thoroughly annotated edition of Fitzgerald's first twenty-six stories. *Gatsby* remains the most written-about work, garnering a documentary volume, replete with information about the sources, composition, and reception of the novel, a pair of reader's guides with resources for close reading and discussion, and a refreshingly new collection of essays examining the intellectual history of the 1920s. The most impressive anthology of the decade so far, *The Cambridge Com-*

panion (2002), addresses most of the canon and pertinent themes, including the cultures of youth and celebrity, history, women, nonfiction, and Hollywood. It also features Jackson R. Bryer's "The Critical Reception of F. Scott Fitzgerald," as thorough a review as we are likely to need for some time. The Fitzgeralds' tumultuous marriage attracted biographical treatment, and their epistolary relationship blossoms in *Dear Scott/Dearest Zelda*, a carefully edited and well-annotated edition of their extant correspondence with engaging interstitial chapters that bridge the gaps in their exchanges. Fitzgerald's life is the subject of Ruth Prigozy's gorgeously illustrated, compact biography. The current cache of articles suggests that the past is prelude: *Gatsby*, *Tender Is the Night*, and the short stories garner the most interest. Comparative and influence studies remain popular, and thematic works focus on Fitzgerald's treatment of wealth and Jews.

The following bibliography indicates that the dig continues, as does Fitzgerald's remarkable second act. It is arranged with standard subheadings and includes primary and secondary sections for Zelda Fitzgerald. Readers in search of the most comprehensive bibliographies, to which this one is indebted, are directed to Matthew J. Bruccoli's *F. Scott Fitzgerald: A Descriptive Bibliography* (revised and augmented edition; Pittsburgh, Pa.: University of Pittsburgh Press, 1987) and to Jackson R. Bryer's *The Critical Reputation of F. Scott Fitzgerald: A Bibliographical Study* (Hamden, Conn.: Archon, 1967) and *The Critical Reputation of F. Scott Fitzgerald: A Bibliographical Study, Supplement 1 Through 1981* (Hamden, Conn.: Archon, 1984). Annual checklists have appeared in the *F. Scott Fitzgerald Society Newsletter* (1991–2001) and in the *F. Scott Fitzgerald Review* (2003–). *American Literary Scholarship: An Annual, 1963–* (Durham, N.C.: Duke University Press, 1965–) publishes "Fitzgerald and Hemingway," a bibliographical essay accounting for the year's work.

SELECTED BIBLIOGRAPHY

Works by F. Scott Fitzgerald (in Chronological Order)

This Side of Paradise. New York: Scribner's, 1920. Ed. James L. W. West III. New York: Cambridge University Press, 1995.

Flappers and Philosophers. New York: Scribner's, 1920. Ed. James L. W. West III. New York: Cambridge University Press, 2000.

The Beautiful and Damned. New York: Scribner's, 1922. Ed. Alan Margolies. Oxford: Oxford University Press, 1998.

Tales of the Jazz Age. New York: Scribner's, 1922.

The Vegetable; or, From President to Postman. New York: Scribner's, 1923. New York: Scribner's, 1976.

The Cruise of the Rolling Junk. 1924. Bloomfield Hills, Mich.: Bruccoli Clark, 1976.

The Great Gatsby. New York: Scribner's, 1925. Ed. Matthew J. Bruccoli. New York: Cambridge University Press, 1991. Ed. Ruth Prigozy. Oxford: Oxford University Press, 1998.

All the Sad Young Men. New York: Scribner's, 1926.

Tender Is the Night. New York: Scribner's, 1934. Rev. ed., New York: Scribner's, 1951. New York: Scribner's, 1995. Ed. Matthew J. Bruccoli. Everyman Centennial Edition. London: Dent, 1996.

Taps at Reveille. New York: Scribner's, 1935.

"An Author's Mother." *Esquire* 6 (Sept. 1936): 36.

The Last Tycoon: An Unfinished Novel Together with "The Great Gatsby" and Selected Stories. Ed. Edmund Wilson. New York: Scribner's, 1941. Ed. Matthew J. Bruccoli. New York: Cambridge University Press, 1993 (as *The Love of the Last Tycoon: A Western*).

The Crack-Up. Ed. Edmund Wilson. New York: New Directions, 1945.

The Portable F. Scott Fitzgerald. Selected by Dorothy Parker. New York: Viking, 1945.

"Last Kiss." *Collier's* 123 (Apr. 16, 1949): 16–17, 34, 38, 41, 43–44.

The Stories of F. Scott Fitzgerald. New York: Scribner's, 1951.

Three Novels of F. Scott Fitzgerald. New York: Scribner's, 1953.

"Imagination and a Few Mothers." *"Ladies' Home Journal" Treasury*. Ed. John Mason Brown. New York: Simon and Schuster, 1956. 180–81.

Afternoon of an Author: A Selection of Uncollected Stories and Essays. Ed. Arthur Mizener. Princeton, N.J.: Princeton University Press, 1957. New York: Scribner's, 1958.

The Bodley Head Scott Fitzgerald. 6 vols. London: Bodley Head, 1958–1963.

Six Tales of the Jazz Age and Other Stories. New York: Scribner's, 1960.

The Pat Hobby Stories. New York: Scribner's, 1962.

The Fitzgerald Reader. Selected by Arthur Mizener. New York: Scribner's, 1963.

The Apprentice Fiction of F. Scott Fitzgerald: 1909–1917. Ed. John Kuehl. New Brunswick, N.J.: Rutgers University Press, 1965.

Thoughtbook of Francis Scott Key Fitzgerald. Princeton, N.J.: Princeton University Press, 1965.

"My Generation." *Esquire* 70 (Oct. 1968): 119–21.

"Dearly Beloved." *Fitzgerald/Hemingway Annual* 1 (1969): 1–3.

"Letter to Ernest Hemingway." *Fitzgerald/Hemingway Annual* 2 (1970): 10–13.

"'Sleep of a University': An Unrecorded Fitzgerald Poem." *Fitzgerald/Hemingway Annual* 2 (1970): 14–15.

F. Scott Fitzgerald in His Own Time: A Miscellany. Ed. Matthew J. Bruccoli and Jackson R. Bryer. Kent, Ohio: Kent State University Press, 1971.

"Oh, Sister, Can You Spare Your Heart." *Fitzgerald/Hemingway Annual* 4 (1972): 114–15.

"Preface to *This Side of Paradise*." *Fitzgerald/Hemingway Annual* 4 (1972): 1–2.

The Basil and Josephine Stories. Ed. Jackson R. Bryer and John Kuehl. New York: Scribner's, 1973.

F. Scott Fitzgerald's Ledger: A Facsimile. Washington, D.C.: NCR/Microcard Editions, 1973.

Bits of Paradise: 21 Uncollected Stories by F. Scott and Zelda Fitzgerald. Selected by Scottie Fitzgerald and Matthew J. Bruccoli. London: Bodley Head, 1973. New York: Scribner's, 1974.

"'Ballet Shoes': A Movie Synopsis." *Fitzgerald/Hemingway Annual* 8 (1976): 3–7.

"F. Scott Fitzgerald's Memo in the Typescript of *A Farewell to Arms*." *Fitzgerald/Hemingway Annual* 8 (1976): 146–52.

"The Defeat of Art." *Fitzgerald/Hemingway Annual* 9 (1977): 11–12

"The Feather Fan." *Fitzgerald/Hemingway Annual* 9 (1977): 3–5.

"*Lipstick*." *Fitzgerald/Hemingway Annual* 10 (1978): 3–35.

F. Scott Fitzgerald's Screenplay for "Three Comrades" by Erich Maria Remarque. Ed. Matthew J. Bruccoli. Carbondale: Southern Illinois University Press, 1978.

The Notebooks of F. Scott Fitzgerald. Ed. Matthew J. Bruccoli. New York: Harcourt Brace Jovanovich/Bruccoli Clark, 1978.

F. Scott Fitzgerald's St. Paul Plays: 1911–1914. Ed. Alan Margolies. Princeton, N.J.: Princeton University Library, 1978.

The Price Was High: The Last Uncollected Stories of F. Scott Fitzgerald. Ed. Matthew J. Bruccoli. New York: Harcourt Brace Jovanovich/Bruccoli Clark, 1979.

Poems: 1911–1940. Ed. Matthew J. Bruccoli. Bloomfield Hills, Mich. and Columbia, S.C.: Bruccoli Clark, 1981.

The Short Stories of F. Scott Fitzgerald: A New Collection. Ed. Matthew J. Bruccoli. New York: Scribner's, 1989.

F. Scott Fitzgerald: Manuscripts. 18 vols. Ed. Matthew J. Bruccoli. New York: Garland, 1990–1991.

Babylon Revisited: The Screenplay. New York: Carroll and Graf, 1993.

Fitzgerald, F. Scott, D. D. Griffin, A. L. Booth, and P. B. Dickey. *Fie! Fie! Fi-Fi! A Facsimile of the 1914 Acting Script and the Musical Score*. Columbia: University of South Carolina Press for the Thomas Cooper Library, 1996.

F. Scott Fitzgerald: The Princeton Years: Selected Writings, 1914–1920. Ed. Chip Deffaa. Fort Bragg, Calif.: Cypress House, 1996.

F. Scott Fitzgerald on Authorship. Ed. Matthew J. Bruccoli with Judith S. Baughman. Columbia: University of South Carolina Press, 1996.

"Trimalchio" by F. Scott Fitzgerald: A Facsimile Edition of the Original Galley Proofs for "The Great Gatsby." Afterword by Matthew J. Bruccoli. Columbia: University of South Carolina Press, 2000.

Trimalchio: An Early Version of "The Great Gatsby." Ed. James L. W. West III. New York: Cambridge University Press, 2000.

Before Gatsby: The First Twenty-Six Stories. Ed. Matthew J. Bruccoli with Judith S. Baughman. Columbia: University of South Carolina Press, 2001.

Conversations with F. Scott Fitzgerald. Ed. Matthew J. Bruccoli and Judith S. Baughman. Jackson, Miss.: University Press of Mississippi, 2003.

Works by Zelda Sayre Fitzgerald (in Chronological Order)

Save Me the Waltz. New York: Scribner's, 1932. London: Grey Walls, 1953.

Bits of Paradise: 21 Uncollected Stories by F. Scott and Zelda Fitzgerald. Selected by Scottie Fitzgerald and Matthew J. Bruccoli. London: Bodley Head, 1973. New York: Scribner's, 1974.

Scandalabra. Bloomfield Hills, Mich., and Columbia, S.C.: Bruccoli Clark, 1980.

Zelda Fitzgerald: The Collected Writings. Ed. Matthew J. Bruccoli. New York: Scribner's, 1991.

Letters

As Ever, Scott Fitz——: Letters between F. Scott Fitzgerald and His Literary Agent, Harold Ober, 1919–1940. Ed. Matthew J. Bruccoli and Jennifer M. Atkinson. Philadelphia, Pa.: Lippincott, 1972.

Correspondence of F. Scott Fitzgerald. Ed. Matthew J. Bruccoli and Margaret M. Duggan, with Susan Walker. New York: Random House, 1980.

Dear Scott/Dear Max: The Fitzgerald-Perkins Correspondence. Ed. John Kuehl and Jackson R. Bryer. New York: Scribner's, 1971; London: Cassell, 1973.

Dear Scott/Dearest Zelda: The Love Letters of Scott and Zelda Fitzgerald. Ed. Jackson R. Bryer and Cathy W. Barks. New York: St. Martin's, 2002.

F. Scott Fitzgerald: Letters to His Daughter. Ed. Andrew Turnbull. New York: Scribner's, 1965.

F. Scott Fitzgerald: A Life in Letters. Ed. Matthew Bruccoli, with Judith S. Baughman. New York: Scribner's, 1994.

Letters of F. Scott Fitzgerald. Ed. Andrew Turnbull. New York: Scribner's, 1963.

Biographical Works

Aaron, Daniel. "The Legend of the Golden Couple." *Virginia Quarterly Review* 48 (1972): 157–60.

Banning, Margaret Culkin. "Scott Fitzgerald in Tryon, North Carolina." *Fitzgerald/Hemingway Annual* 5 (1973): 151–54.

Blackshear, Helen F. "Mama Sayre, Scott Fitzgerald's Mother-in-Law." *Georgia Review* 19 (Winter 1965): 465–70.

Bruccoli, Matthew J. *Fitzgerald and Hemingway: A Dangerous Friendship.* New York: Carroll and Graf, 1994.

———. *Scott and Ernest: The Authority of Failure and the Authority of Success*. New York: Random House, 1978.

———. *Some Sort of Epic Grandeur: The Life of F. Scott Fitzgerald*. New York: Harcourt Brace Jovanovich, 1981. Rev. ed., New York: Carroll and Graf, 1991. 2nd Rev. ed., Columbia: University of South Carolina Press, 2002.

Bruccoli, Matthew J., Scottie Fitzgerald Smith, and Joan P. Kerr. Eds. *The Romantic Egoists: A Pictorial Autobiography from the Scrapbooks and Albums of Scott and Zelda Fitzgerald*. New York: Scribner's, 1974; rpt. Columbia: University of South Carolina Press, 2003.

Buttitta, Tony. *After the Good Gay Times: Asheville—Summer of '35—A Season with F. Scott Fitzgerald*. New York: Viking, 1974.

Callaghan, Morley. *That Summer in Paris*. New York: Coward-McCann, 1963.

Donaldson, Scott. *Fool for Love: F. Scott Fitzgerald*. New York: Congdon and Weed, 1983.

———. *Hemingway vs. Fitzgerald: The Rise and Fall of a Literary Friendship*. Woodstock, N.Y.: Overlook, 1999.

Fain, J. T. "Recollections of F. Scott Fitzgerald." *Fitzgerald/Hemingway Annual* 7 (1975): 133–39.

Graham, Sheilah. *College of One*. New York: Viking, 1967.

———. *The Real F. Scott Fitzgerald: Thirty-Five Years Later*. New York: Grosset and Dunlap, 1976.

———. *The Rest of the Story*. New York: Coward-McCann, 1964.

Graham, Sheilah, and Gerald Frank. *Beloved Infidel*. New York: Holt, Rinehart and Winston, 1958.

Hearne, Laura Guthrie. "A Summer with F. Scott Fitzgerald." *Esquire* 62 (Dec. 1964): 160–65, 232, 236, 237, 240, 242, 246, 250, 252, 254–58, 260.

Hemingway, Ernest. *A Moveable Feast*. New York: Scribner's, 1964.

Johnson, Christine. "Daughter and Father: An Interview with Mrs. Frances Scott Fitzgerald Smith, Washington, D.C., August 29, 1973." *Etudes Anglaises* 29 (Jan.–Mar. 1976): 72–75.

Koblas, John J. *F. Scott Fitzgerald in Minnesota: His Homes and Haunts*. St. Paul: Minnesota Historical Society Press, 1978.

Lanahan, Eleanor. *Scottie, the Daughter of . . . : The Life of Frances Scott Fitzgerald Lanahan Smith*. New York: HarperCollins, 1995.

Lanahan, Eleanor. Ed. *Zelda: An Illustrated Life: The Private World of Zelda Fitzgerald*. New York: Abrams, 1996.

Latham, J. Aaron. *Crazy Sundays: F. Scott Fitzgerald in Hollywood*. New York: Viking, 1971.

Leslie, Shane. "Some Memories of F. Scott Fitzgerald." *Times Literary Supplement* (London) (Oct. 31, 1958): 632.

LeVot, André. *F. Scott Fitzgerald*. Paris: Julliard, 1979. Garden City, N.Y.: Doubleday, 1983. London: Allen Lane, 1984.

Loeb, Harold, Morrill Cody, Florence Gillman, and André Chamson. "Fitzgerald and Hemingway in Paris." *Fitzgerald/Hemingway Annual* 5 (1973): 33–76.

MacKie, Elizabeth Beckwith. "My Friend Scott Fitzgerald." *Fitzgerald/Hemingway Annual* 2 (1970): 16–27.

McMaster, John D. "As I Remember Scott (Memoir)." *Confrontation* 7 (Fall 1973): 3–11.

Mayfield, Sara. *Exiles from Paradise: Zelda and Scott Fitzgerald*. New York: Delacorte, 1971.

Mellow, James R. *Invented Lives: F. Scott and Zelda Fitzgerald*. Boston: Houghton Mifflin, 1984.

Meyers, Jeffrey. *Scott Fitzgerald*. New York: HarperCollins, 1994. New York: Cooper Square Press, 2000.

Milford, Nancy. *Zelda: A Biography*. New York: Harper and Row, 1970.

Mizener, Arthur. "Arthur Mizener on F. Scott Fitzgerald." In *Talks with Authors*. Ed. Charles F. Madden. Carbondale: Southern Illinois University Press, 1968. 23–38.

———. *The Far Side of Paradise*. Boston: Houghton Mifflin, 1951. Rev. ed., New York: Vintage, 1959.

———. *Scott Fitzgerald and His World*. New York: Putnam's, 1972.

Nathan, George Jean. "Memories of Fitzgerald, Lewis and Dreiser: The Golden Boys of the Twenties." *Esquire* 50 (Oct. 1958): 148–49.

Page, David, and John Boblas. *F. Scott Fitzgerald in Minnesota: Toward the Summit*. St. Cloud, Minn.: North Star, 1996.

Powell, Anthony. "Hollywood Canteen: A Memoir of Scott Fitzgerald in 1937." *Fitzgerald/Hemingway Annual* 3 (1971): 71–80.

Prigozy, Ruth. *F. Scott Fitzgerald*. Woodstock, N.Y.: Overlook, 2001.

Ring, Frances Kroll. *Against the Current: As I Remember F. Scott Fitzgerald*. San Francisco, Calif.:Ellis/Creative Arts, 1985.

———. "Footnotes on Fitzgerald." *Esquire* 52 (Dec. 1959): 149–50.

———. "The Resurrection of F. Scott Fitzgerald." *F. Scott Fitzgerald Society Newsletter* (Oct. 1995): 1–4.

Schulberg, Budd. "Old Scott: The Mask, the Myth, and the Man." *Esquire* 55 (Jan. 1961): 97–101.

Smith, Scottie Fitzgerald. "Notes about My Now-Famous Father." *Family Circle* 84 (May 1974): 118–20.

Stewart, Donald Ogden. "Recollections of F. Scott Fitzgerald and Hemingway." *Fitzgerald/Hemingway Annual* 3 (1971): 177–88.

Taylor, Kendall. *Sometimes Madness Is Wisdom: Zelda and Scott Fitzgerald: A Marriage*. New York: Ballantine, 2001.

Tompkins, Calvin. *Living Well Is the Best Revenge*. New York: Viking, 1971.

Turnbull, Andrew. "Further Notes on Fitzgerald at La Paix." *New Yorker* 32 (Nov. 17, 1956): 153–65.

———. *Scott Fitzgerald*. New York: Scribner's, 1962. London: Bodley Head, 1962.

———. "Scott Fitzgerald at La Paix." *New Yorker* 32 (Apr. 17, 1956): 98–109.

Westbrook, Robert. *Intimate Lies: F. Scott Fitzgerald and Sheilah Graham*. New York: HarperCollins, 1995.

Selected Critical Studies

Allen, Joan. *Candles and Carnival Lights: The Catholic Sensibility of F. Scott Fitzgerald*. New York: New York University Press, 1978.

Anderson, Hilton. "*Daisy Miller* and 'The Hotel Child': A Jamesian Influence on F. Scott Fitzgerald." *Studies in American Fiction* 17 (Autumn 1989): 213–18.

Arnold, Edwin T. "The Motion Picture as Metaphor in the Works of F. Scott Fitzgerald." *Fitzgerald/Hemingway Annual* 9 (1977): 43–60.

Astro, Richard. "*Vandover and the Brute* and *The Beautiful and Damned*: A Search for Thematic and Stylistic Reinterpretations." *Modern Fiction Studies* 14 (Winter 1968–1969): 397–413.

Atkinson, Jennifer McCabe. "Lost and Unpublished Stories by F. Scott Fitzgerald." *Fitzgerald/Hemingway Annual* 2 (1971): 32–63.

Babb, Howard S. "*The Great Gatsby* and the Grotesque." *Criticism* 5 (Fall 1963): 336–48.

Baldwin, Marc. "F. Scott Fitzgerald's 'One Trip Abroad': A Metafantasy of the Divided Self." *Journal of the Fantastic in the Arts* 4.3 (1991): 69–78.

Barbour, Brian M. "*The Great Gatsby* and the American Past." *Southern Review*, n.s. 9 (Spring 1973): 288–99.

Barrett, Laura. "'Material without Being Real': Photography and the End of Reality in *The Great Gatsby*." *Studies in the Novel* 30 (Winter 1998): 540–57.

Baughman, Judith S., with Matthew J. Bruccoli. *Literary Masters: F. Scott Fitzgerald*. Detroit, Mich.: Gale, 2000.

Bender, Bert. "'His Mind Aglow': The Biological Undercurrent in Fitzgerald's *Gatsby* and Other Works." *Journal of American Studies* 32 (Dec. 1998): 399–420.

Berman, Ronald. *Fitzgerald, Hemingway, and the Twenties*. Tuscaloosa: University of Alabama Press, 2001.

———. *Fitzgerald-Wilson-Hemingway: Language and Idea*. Tuscaloosa: University of Alabama Press, 2003.

———. *"The Great Gatsby" and Fitzgerald's World of Ideas*. Tuscaloosa: University of Alabama Press, 1997.

———. *"The Great Gatsby" and Modern Times*. Urbana: University of Illinois Press, 1994.

Berryman, John. "F. Scott Fitzgerald." *Kenyon Review* 8 (Winter 1946): 103–12.

Bewley, Marius. "Scott Fitzgerald's Criticism of America." *Sewanee Review* 62 (Spring 1954): 223–46.

Bicknell, John W. "The Waste Land of F. Scott Fitzgerald." *Virginia Quarterly Review* 30 (Autumn 1954): 556–72.

Bigsby, C. W. E. "The Two Identities of F. Scott Fitzgerald." In *The American Novel and the Nineteen Twenties*. Ed. Malcolm Bradbury and David Palmer. London: Arnold, 1971. 129–49.

Bloom, James D. "Out of Minnesota: Mythography and Generational Poetics in the Writings of Bob Dylan and F. Scott Fitzgerald." *American Studies* 40 (Spring 1999): 5–21.

Breitwieser, Mitchell. "*The Great Gatsby*: Grief, Jazz, and the Eye-Witness." *Arizona Quarterly* 47 (Autumn 1991): 17–70.

———. "Jazz Fractures: F. Scott Fitzgerald and Epochal Representation." *American Literary History* 12.3 (2000): 359–81.

Brondell, William J. "Structural Metaphors in Fitzgerald's Short Fiction." *Kansas Quarterly* 14 (Spring 1982): 95–112.

Bruccoli, Matthew J. "Bibliographical Notes on F. Scott Fitzgerald's *The Beautiful and Damned.*" *Studies in Bibliography* 13 (1960): 258–61.

———. "A Collation of F. Scott Fitzgerald's *This Side of Paradise.*" *Studies in Bibliography* 9 (1957): 263–65.

———. *The Composition of "Tender Is the Night": A Study of the Manuscripts.* Pittsburgh, Pa.: University of Pittsburgh Press, 1963.

———. "Getting It Right: The Publishing Process and the Correction of Factual Errors—with Reference to *The Great Gatsby*" *Library Chronicle of the University of Texas* 21.3–4 (1991): 40–59.

———. *The Last of the Novelists: F. Scott Fitzgerald and "The Last Tycoon."* Carbondale and Edwardsville: Southern Illinois University Press, 1977.

———. "Material for a Centenary Edition of *Tender Is the Night.*" *Studies in Bibliography* 17 (1964): 177–93.

———. "'A Might Collation': Animadversions on the Text of F. Scott Fitzgerald." In *Editing Twentieth-Century Texts.* Ed. Francis G. Halpenny. Toronto: University of Toronto Press, 1972. 28–50.

———. "Where They Belong: The Acquisition of the F. Scott Fitzgerald Papers." *Princeton University Library Chronicle* 50 (1988): 30–37.

Bruccoli, Matthew J., with Judith S. Baughman. *Reader's Companion to F. Scott Fitzgerald's "Tender Is the Night."* Columbia: University of South Carolina Press, 1996.

———. Ed. *Apparatus for F. Scott Fitzgerald's "The Great Gatsby"* [*Under the Red, White, and Blue*]. Columbia: University of South Carolina Press, 1974.

———. *F. Scott Fitzgerald's "The Great Gatsby": A Documentary Volume.* In *Dictionary of Literary Biography.* Vol. 219. Ed. Matthew J. Bruccoli. Detroit, Mich.: Bruccoli Clark Layman/Gale Research, 2000.

Bryer, Jackson R. *Fifteen Modern American Authors: A Survey of Research and Criticism.* Durham, N.C.: Duke University Press, 1969.

———. "Four Decades of Fitzgerald Studies: The Best and the Brightest." *Twentieth-Century Literature* 26 (1980): 247–67.

———. *Sixteen Modern American Authors: A Review of Research and Criticism.* Durham, N.C.: Duke University Press, 1974.

———. *Sixteen Modern American Authors*. Vol. 2: *A Survey of Research and Criticism since 1972*. Durham, N.C.: Duke University Press, 1990.

———. "'Torches of Fury': The Correspondence of F. Scott and Zelda Fitzgerald." In *American Literary Dimensions: Poems and Essays in Honor of Melvin J. Friedman*. Ed. Ben Siegel and Jay L. Hailo. Newark: University of Delaware Press, 1999. 65–80.

Bufkin, E. C. "A Pattern of Parallels and Doubles: The Function of Myrtle in *The Great Gatsby*." *Modern Fiction Studies* 15 (Winter 1969–1970): 517–24.

Burhans, Clinton S., Jr. "'Magnificently Attuned to Life': The Value of 'Winter Dreams.'" *Studies in Short Fiction* 6 (Summer 1969): 401–12.

———. "Structure and Theme in *This Side of Paradise*." *Journal of English and Germanic Philology* 68 (Oct. 1969): 605–24.

Burnam, Tom. "The Eyes of Dr. Eckleburg: A Re-examination of *The Great Gatsby*." *College English* 14 (Oct. 1952): 7–12.

Burroughs, Catherine B. "Of 'Sheer Being': Fitzgerald's Aesthetic Typology and the Burden of Transcription." *Modern Language Studies* 22 (Winter 1992): 102–109.

Burton, Mary E. "The Counter-Transference of Dr. Diver." *ELH* 38 (Sept. 1971): 459–71.

Callahan, John F. "F. Scott Fitzgerald's Evolving American Dream: The 'Pursuit of Happiness' in *Gatsby*, *Tender Is the Night*, and *The Last Tycoon*." *Twentieth-Century Literature* 42 (Fall 1996): 374–95.

———. *The Illusions of a Nation: Myth and History in the Novels of F. Scott Fitzgerald*. Urbana: University of Illinois Press, 1972.

Cardwell, Guy A. "The Lyric World of Scott Fitzgerald." *Virginia Quarterly Review* 38 (Spring 1962): 299–323.

Carr, Nancy, et al. Eds. *Reader's Guide to "The Great Gatsby."* Chicago, Ill.: Great Books Foundation, 2001.

Casty, Alan. "'I and It' in the Stories of F. Scott Fitzgerald." *Studies in Short Fiction* 9 (Winter 1972): 47–58.

Cartwright, Kent. "Nick Carraway as an Unreliable Narrator." *Papers on Language and Literature* 20 (Spring 1984): 218–32.

Cashill, Jack. "The Keeper of the Faith: Mogul as Hero in *The Last Tycoon*." *Revue Française d'Etudes Americaines* 19 (Feb. 1984): 33–38.

Cass, Colin S. "Fitzgerald's Second Thoughts about 'May Day': A Collation and Study." *Fitzgerald/Hemingway Annual* 2 (1970): 69–95.

Chambers, John B. *The Novels of F. Scott Fitzgerald*. London: Macmillan. New York: St Martin's, 1989.

Chan, K. K. Leonard. "Molecular Story Structures: Lao She's *Rickshaw* and F. Scott Fitzgerald's *The Great Gatsby*." *Style* 25 (Summer 1991): 240–50.

Charvat, William. *The Profession of Authorship in America, 1800–1870*. Ed. Matthew J. Bruccoli. Columbus: Ohio State University Press, 1968.

Chase, Richard. *The American Novel and Its Tradition*. Garden City, N.Y.: Doubleday, 1957.

Cohen, Milton A. "Fitzgerald's Third Regret: Intellectual Pretense and the Ghost of Edmund Wilson." *Texas Studies in Literature and Language* 33 (Spring 1991): 64–88.

Coleman, Dan. "Tuning in to Conversation in the Novel: *Gatsby* and the Dynamics of Dialogue." *Style* 34.1 (Spring 2000): 52–77.

———. "'A World Complete in Itself': *Gatsby*'s Elegiac Narration." *Journal of Narrative Technique* 27 (Spring 1997): 207–33.

Coleman, Tom C., III. "Nicole Warren Diver and Scott Fitzgerald: The Girl and the Egotist." *Studies in the Novel* 3 (Spring 1971): 34–43.

Cowley, Malcolm. *Exiles Return: A Literary Odyssey of the 1920s*. 1934. New York: Penguin, 1976.

———. "Fitzgerald: The Double Man." *Saturday Review of Literature* 34 (Feb. 24, 1951): 9–10, 42–44.

———. "The Fitzgerald Revival, 1941–53." *Fitzgerald/Hemingway Annual* 6 (1974): 11–13.

———. "Fitzgerald's *Tender*: The Story of a Novel." *New Republic* 125 (Aug. 20, 1951): 18–20. Reprinted as introduction to *Tender Is the Night*. Rev. ed. New York: Scribner's, 1951. ix–xviii.

———. "F. Scott Fitzgerald: The Romance of Money." *Western Review* 17 (Summer 1953): 245–55.

———. "The Scott Fitzgerald Story." *New Republic* 124 (Feb. 12, 1951): 17–20.

———. *A Second Flowering: Works and Days of the Lost Generation*. New York: Viking, 1973.

———. *Think Back on Us: A Contemporary Chronicle of the 1930s*. Carbondale: Southern Illinois University Press, 1967.

———. "Third Act and Epilogue." *New Yorker* 21 (June 30, 1945): 53–58.

Cross, K. G. W. *F. Scott Fitzgerald*. Edinburgh: Oliver and Boyd, 1964. New York: Grove, 1964.

Curnutt, Kirk. "Making a 'Clean Break': Confession, Celebrity Journalism, Image Management and F. Scott Fitzgerald's *The Crack-Up*." *Genre* 32 (Winter 1999): 297–328.

Curry, Ralph, and Janet Lewis. "Stephen Leacock: An Early Influence on F. Scott Fitzgerald." *Canadian Review of American Studies* 7 (Spring 1976): 5–14.

Curry, Stephen, and Peter L. Hays. "Fitzgerald's *Vanity Fair*." *Fitzgerald/Hemingway Annual* 9 (1977): 63–75.

Dahlie, Hallvard. "Alienation and Disintegration in *Tender Is the Night*." *Humanities Association Bulletin* 22 (Fall 1971): 3–8.

Daniels, Thomas E. "Pat Hobby: Anti-Hero." *Fitzgerald/Hemingway Annual* 5 (1973): 131–39.

———. "The Texts of 'Winter Dreams.'" *Fitzgerald/Hemingway Annual* 9 (1977): 77–100.

———. "Toward a Definitive Edition of F. Scott Fitzgerald's Short Stories." *Publications of the Bibliographical Society of America* 71 (Third Quarter 1977): 295–310.

Decker, Jeffrey Louis. "*Gatsby*'s Pristine Dream: The Diminishment of the Self-Made Man in the Tribal Twenties." *Novel* 28 (Fall 1994): 52–71.

Dessner, Lawrence Jay. "Photography and *The Great Gatsby*." *Essays in Literature* 6 (Spring 1979): 79–90.

DiBattista, Maria. "The Aesthetic of Forbearance: Fitzgerald's *Tender Is the Night*." *Novel* 11 (Fall 1977): 26–39.

Dickstein, Morris. "The Authority of Failure." *American Scholar* 69 (Spring 2000): 69–81.

———. "Fitzgerald's Second Act." *South Atlantic Quarterly* 90 (Summer 1991): 555–78.

Dixon, Wheeler Winston. *The Cinematic Vision of F. Scott Fitzgerald*. Ann Arbor, Mich.: UMI Research Press, 1986.

Donaldson, Scott. "The Crisis of Fitzgerald's *Crack-Up*." *Twentieth-Century Literature* 26 (Summer 1980): 171–88.

———. "F. Scott Fitzgerald's Romance with the South." *Southern Literary Journal* 5 (Spring 1973): 3–17.

———. "'No, I Am Not Prince Charming': Fairy Tales in *Tender Is the Night.*" *Fitzgerald/Hemingway Annual* 5 (1973): 105–12.

———. "The Political Development of F. Scott Fitzgerald." *Prospects* 6 (1981): 313–55.

———. "Possessions in *The Great Gatsby.*" *Southern Review* 37.2 (2001): 187–210.

———. "A Short History of *Tender Is the Night.*" In *Writing the American Classics*. Ed. James Barbour and Tom Quirk. Chapel Hill: University of North Carolina Press, 1990. 177–208.

Drake, Constance. "Josephine and Emotional Bankruptcy." *Fitzgerald/Hemingway Annual* 1 (1969): 5–13.

Dudley, Juanita Williams. "Dr. Diver, Vivisectionist." *College Literature* 2 (Spring 1975): 128–34.

Dyer, Geoff. "Fitzgerald's Afterglow." *American Scholar* 70.2 (2001): 136–41.

Ebel, Kenneth. "The Craft of Revision: *The Great Gatsby.*" *American Literature* 36 (Nov. 1964): 315–26.

———. F. Scott Fitzgerald. New York: Twayne, 1963. Rev. ed., New York: Twayne, 1977.

———. "*The Great Gatsby.*" *College Literature* 1 (Winter 1974): 34–47.

Elias, Amy J. "The Composition and Revision of Fitzgerald's *The Beautiful and Damned.*" *Princeton University Library Chronicle* 51 (Spring 1990): 245–66.

Ellis, James. "Fitzgerald's Fragmented Hero: Dick Diver." *University Review* 32 (Oct. 1965): 43–49.

Elmore, A[lbert] E. "Color and Cosmos in *The Great Gatsby.*" *Sewanee Review* 78 (Summer 1970): 427–43.

———. "*The Great Gatsby* as Well-Wrought Urn." In *Modern American Fiction: Form and Function*. Ed. Thomas Daniel Young. Baton Rouge: Louisiana State University Press, 1989. 57–92.

———. "Nick Carraway's Self-Introduction." *Fitzgerald/Hemingway Annual* 3 (1971): 130–47.

Emmitt, Robert J. "Love, Death and Resurrection in *The Great Gatsby.*" In *Aeolian Harps: Essays in Literature in Honor of Maurice Browning Cramer*. Ed. Donna G. Fricke. Bowling Green, Ohio: Bowling Green University Press, 1976. 273–89.

Epstein, Joseph. "F. Scott Fitzgerald's Third Act." *Commentary* 98 (Nov. 1994): 52–57.

Evans, Oliver H. "'A Sort of Moral Attention': The Narrator of *The Great Gatsby*." *Fitzgerald/Hemingway Annual* 3 (1971): 117–29.

Fahey, William A. *F. Scott Fitzgerald and the American Dream*. New York: Crowell, 1973.

Fedo, David. "Women in the Fiction of F. Scott Fitzgerald." *Ball State University Forum* 21 (Spring 1980): 26–33.

Ferguson, Robert A. "The Grotesque in the Novels of F. Scott Fitzgerald." *South Atlantic Quarterly* 78 (Autumn 1979): 460–77.

Fetterley, Judith. "Who Killed Dick Diver? The Sexual Politics of *Tender Is the Night*." *Mosaic* 17 (Winter 1984): 111–28.

Flahiff, F[rederick] T. "*The Great Gatsby*: Scott Fitzgerald's Chaucerian Rag." In *Figures in a Ground: Canadian Essays on Modern Literature Collected in Honor of Sheila Watson*. Ed. Diane Bessai and David Jackel. Saskatoon: Western Producer Prairie, 1978. 87–98.

Forrey, Robert. "Negroes in the Fiction of F. Scott Fitzgerald." *Phylon* 28 (Third Quarter 1967): 293–98.

Foster, Richard. "Time's Exile: Dick Diver and the Heroic Idea." *Mosaic* 8 (Spring 1975): 89–108.

Frohock, W. M. "Morals, Manners, and Scott Fitzgerald." *Southwest Review* 40 (Summer 1955): 220–28.

Fryer, Sarah Beebe. *Fitzgerald's New Women: Harbingers of Change*. Ann Arbor, Mich.: UMI Research Press, 1988.

Fussell, Edwin S. "Fitzgerald's Brave New World." *ELH* 19 (Dec. 1952): 291–306.

Gale, Robert L. *An F. Scott Fitzgerald Encyclopedia*. Westport, Conn.: Greenwood, 1998.

———. "Names in F. Scott Fitzgerald." *Journal of Modern Literature* 24.1 (2000): 177–80.

Gallo, Rose Adrienne. *F. Scott Fitzgerald*. New York: Ungar, 1978.

Gammons, P. Keith. "The South of the Mind: The Changing Myth of the Lost Cause in the Life and Work of F. Scott Fitzgerald." *Southern Quarterly* 36.4 (1998): 106–12.

Gervais, Ronald J. "'Sleepy Hollow's Gone': Pastoral Myth and Artifice in Fitzgerald's *The Beautiful and Damned*." *Ball State University Forum* 22 (Summer 1981): 75–79.

———. "The Snow of Twenty-nine: 'Babylon Revisited' as *ubi sunt* Lament." *College Literature* 7 (Winter 1980): 47–52.

———. "The Socialist and the Silk Stockings: Fitzgerald's Double Allegiance." *Mosaic* 15 (June 1982): 79–92.

Gibbens, Elizabeth Pennington. *The Baby Vamp and the Decline of the West: Biographical and Cultural Issues in F. Scott Fitzgerald's Portrayals of Women*. Ann Arbor, Mich.: UMI Research Press, 1994.

Giles, Paul. *American Catholic Arts and Fictions*. New York: Cambridge University Press, 1992.

Giltrow, Janet, and David Stouck. "Style as Politics in *The Great Gatsby*." *Studies in the Novel* 29 (Winter 1997): 476–90.

Gindin, James. "Gods and Fathers in F. Scott Fitzgerald's Novels." *Modern Language Quarterly* 30 (Mar. 1969): 64–85.

Godden, Richard. "Money Makes Manners Make Man Make Woman: *Tender Is the Night*, a Familiar Romance?" *Literature and History* 12 (Spring 1986): 16–37.

Goldhurst, William. *F. Scott Fitzgerald and His Contemporaries*. Cleveland, Ohio: World, 1963.

Goldman, Arnold. "F. Scott Fitzgerald: The 'Personal Stuff.'" In *American Studies: Essays in Honor of Marcus Cunliffe*. Ed. Brian Holden Reid, John White, and Arthur M. Schlesinger, Jr. New York: St. Martin's, 1991. 210–30.

Gollin, Rita K. "The Automobiles of *The Great Gatsby*." *Studies in the Twentieth Century* 6 (Fall 1970): 63–83.

———. "Modes of Travel in *Tender Is the Night*." *Studies in the Twentieth Century* 8 (Fall 1971): 103–14.

Good, Dorothy Ballweg. "'A Romance and a Reading List': The Literary References in *This Side of Paradise*." *Fitzgerald/Hemingway Annual* 8 (1976): 35–64.

Greenwald, Fay T. "Fitzgerald's Female Narrators." *Mid-Hudson Language Studies* 2 (1979): 116–33.

Grenberg, Bruce L. "Fitzgerald's 'Figured Curtain': Personality and History in *Tender Is the Night*." *Fitzgerald/Hemingway Annual* 10 (1978): 105–36.

Gross, Barry. "The Dark Side of Twenty-five: Fitzgerald and *The Beautiful and Damned*." *Bucknell Review* 16 (Dec. 1968): 40–52.

———. "Fitzgerald in the Fifties." *Studies in the Novel* 5 (Fall 1973): 324–35.

———. "Fitzgerald's Midwest: 'Something Gorgeous Somewhere'—Somewhere Else." *Midamerica* 6 (1979): 111–16.

———. "Jay Gatsby and Myrtle Wilson: A Kinship." *Tennessee Studies in Literature* 8 (1963): 57–60.

———. "Success and Failure in *The Last Tycoon*." *University Review* 31 (June 1965): 273–76.

———. "*This Side of Paradise*: The Dominating Intention." *Studies in the Novel* 1 (Spring 1969): 51–59.

———. "Would 25-Cent Press Keep *Gatsby* in the Public Eye—or Is the Book Unpopular?" In *Seasoned Authors for a New Season: The Search for Standards in Popular Writing*. Ed. Louis Filler. Bowling Green, Ohio: Bowling Green University Press, 1980. 51–57.

Gross, Dalton, and Maryjean Gross. *Understanding "The Great Gatsby": A Student Casebook to Issues, Sources, and Historical Documents*. Westport, Conn.: Greenwood, 1998.

Gross, Seymour L. "Fitzgerald's 'Babylon Revisited.'" *College English* 25 (Nov. 1963): 128–35.

Gross, Theodore L. "F. Scott Fitzgerald: The Hero in Retrospect." *South Atlantic Quarterly* 67 (Winter 1968): 64–77.

Grube, John. "*Tender Is the Night*: Keats and Scott Fitzgerald." *Dalhousie Review* 44 (Winter 1964–1965): 433–51.

Gunn, Giles. "F. Scott Fitzgerald, *Gatsby*, and the Imagination of Wonder." *Journal of the American Academy of Religion* 41 (June 1973): 171–83.

Haegert, John. "Repression and Counter-Memory in *Tender Is The Night*." *Essays in Literature* 21 (Spring 1994): 97–115.

Hagemann, E. R. "Should Scott Fitzgerald Be Absolved for the Sins of 'Absolution?'" *Journal of Modern Literature* 12 (Mar. 1985): 169–74.

Hall, William F. "Dialogue and Theme in *Tender Is the Night*." *Modern Language Notes* 76 (Nov. 1961): 616–22.

Hanzo, Thomas A. "The Theme and the Narrator of *The Great Gatsby*." *Modern Fiction Studies* 2 (Winter 1956–57): 183–90.

Harding, D. W. "Scott Fitzgerald." *Scrutiny* 18 (Winter 1951–1952): 166–74.

Hart, Jeffrey. "Anything Can Happen: Magical Transformation in *The Great Gatsby*." *South Central Review* 25 (Spring 1993): 37–50.

Hart, John E. "Fitzgerald's *The Last Tycoon*: A Search for Identity." *Modern Fiction Studies* 7 (Spring 1961): 63–70.

Harvey, W. J. "Theme and Texture in *The Great Gatsby*." *English Studies* 38 (Feb. 1957): 12–20.

Hays, Peter L. "*Gatsby*, Myth, Fairy Tale, and Legend." *Southern Folklore Quarterly* 41 (1977): 213–23.

Haywood, Lynn. "Historical Notes for *This Side of Paradise*." *Resources for American Literary Study* 10 (Autumn 1980): 191–208.

Hearn, Charles R. "F. Scott Fitzgerald and the Popular Magazine Formula Story of the Twenties." *Journal of American Culture* 18 (Fall 1995): 33–40.

Hendriksen, Jack. *"This Side of Paradise" as a Bildungsroman*. New York: Lang, 1993.

Higgins, Brian, and Hershel Parker. "Sober Second Thoughts: The 'Author's Final Version' of *Tender Is the Night*." *Proof* 4 (1975): 111–34.

Higgins, John A. *F. Scott Fitzgerald: A Study of the Stories*. Jamaica, N.Y.: St. John's University Press, 1971.

Hindus, Milton. "F. Scott Fitzgerald and Literary Anti-Semitism." *Commentary* 3 (June 1947): 508–16.

———. *F. Scott Fitzgerald: An Introduction and Interpretation*. New York: Holt, Rinehart and Winston, 1968.

———. "The Mysterious Eyes of Doctor T. J. Eckleburg." *Boston University Studies in English* 3 (Spring 1957): 22–31.

Hochman, Barbara. "Disembodied Voices and Narrating Bodies in *The Great Gatsby*." *Style* 28 (Spring 1994): 95–118.

Hoffman, Frederick J. Ed. *"The Great Gatsby": A Study*. New York: Scribner's, 1962.

Hoffman, Madelyn. "*This Side of Paradise*: A Study of Pathological Narcissism." *Literature and Psychology* 28.3–4 (1978): 178–85.

Hoffman, Nancy Y. "*The Great Gatsby*: *Troilus and Cressida* Revisited?" *Fitzgerald/Hemingway Annual* 3 (1971): 148–58.

Hook, Andrew. *F. Scott Fitzgerald*. London: Arnold, 1992.

Hughes, G. I. "Sub Specie Doctor T. J. Eckleburg: Man and God in *The Great Gatsby*." *English Studies in Africa* 15 (Sept. 1972): 81–92.

Hunt, Jan, and John M. Suarez. "The Evasion of Adult Love in Fitzgerald's Fiction." *Centennial Review* 17 (Spring 1973): 152–69.

Huonder, Eugen. *The Functional Significance of Setting in the Novels of Francis Scott Fitzgerald*. Bern, Switzerland: Lang, 1974.

Irwin, John T. "Compensating Visions: *The Great Gatsby*." *Southwest Review* 77 (Autumn 1992): 536–45.

———. "Is Fitzgerald a Southern Writer?" *Raritan* 16 (Winter 1997): 1–23.

Ishikawa, Akiko. "From 'Winter Dreams' to *The Great Gatsby*." *Persica* (Jan. 1978): 79–92.

Jacobs, Deborah F. "Feminist Criticism / Cultural Studies / Modernist Texts: A Manifesto for the '90s." In *Rereading Modernism: New Directions in Feminist Criticism*. Ed. Lisa Rado. New York: Garland, 1994. 273–95.

Johnson, Christine. "*The Great Gatsby*: The Final Vision." *Fitzgerald/Hemingway Annual* 8 (1976): 108–15.

Johnson, Kenneth. "Fitzgerald's 'Crazy Sunday': Cinderella in Hollywood." *Literature/Film Quarterly* 6 (Summer 1978): 214–21.

Joy, Neill R. "*The Last Tycoon* and Max Eastman: Fitzgerald's Complete Political Primer." *Prospects* 12 (1987): 365–92.

Kahn, Sy. "*This Side of Paradise*: The Pageantry of Disillusion." *Midwest Quarterly* 7 (Winter 1966): 177–94.

Kallich, Martin. "F. Scott Fitzgerald: Money or Morals." *University of Kansas City Review* 15 (Summer 1949): 271–80.

Kane, Patricia. "F. Scott Fitzgerald's St. Paul: A Writer's Use of Material." *Minnesota History* 45 (Winter 1976): 141–48.

Kennedy, J. Gerald. "Modernism as Exile: Fitzgerald, Barnes, and the Unreal City." In *Imagining Paris: Exile, Writing, and American Identity*. New Haven, Conn.: Yale University Press, 1993. 185–242.

Kerr, Frances. "Feeling 'Half-Feminine': Modernism and the Politics of Emotion in *The Great Gatsby*." *American Literature* 68 (June 1996): 405–31.

Kirkby, Joan. "Spengler and Apocalyptic Typology in F. Scott Fitzgerald's *Tender Is the Night*." *Southern Review* (Australia) 12 (Nov. 1979): 246–61.

Knodt, Kenneth S. "The Gathering Darkness: A Study of the Effects of Technology in *The Great Gatsby*." *Fitzgerald/Hemingway Annual* 8 (1976): 130–38.

Kopf, Josephine Z. "Meyer Wolfsheim [*sic*] and Robert Cohn: A

Study of Jewish Type and Stereotype." *Tradition* 10 (Spring 1969): 93–104.

Korenman, Joan S. "'Only Her Hairdresser . . . ': Another Look at Daisy Buchanan." *American Literature* 46 (Jan. 1975): 574–78.

———. "A View from the (Queensboro) Bridge." *Fitzgerald/Hemingway Annual* 7 (1975): 93–96.

Kuehl, John. *F. Scott Fitzgerald: A Study of the Short Fiction*. Boston: Twayne, 1991.

———. "Scott Fitzgerald: Romantic and Realist." *Texas Studies in Literature and Language* 1 (Autumn 1959): 412–26.

Kuhnle, John H. "*The Great Gatsby* as Pastoral Elegy." *Fitzgerald/Hemingway Annual* 10 (1978): 141–54.

Langman, F. H. "Style and Shape in *The Great Gatsby*." *Southern Review* (Australia) 6 (Mar. 1973): 48–67.

Lathbury, Roger. *Literary Masterpieces: "The Great Gatsby."* Detroit, Mich.: Gale, 2000.

Laurucella, John A. "The Black Sox Signature: Baseball in *The Great Gatsby*." *Aethlon* 10 (Fall 1992): 83–98.

LeGates, Charlotte. "Dual-Perspective Irony and the Fitzgerald Short Story." *Iowa English Bulletin: Yearbook* 26 (1977): 18–20.

Lehan, Richard D. *F. Scott Fitzgerald and the Craft of Fiction*. Carbondale: Southern Illinois University Press, 1966.

———. "F. Scott Fitzgerald and Romantic Destiny." *Twentieth-Century Literature* 26 (Summer 1980): 137–56.

———. *"The Great Gatsby": The Limits of Wonder*. Boston: Twayne, 1990.

Lena, Alberto. "Deceitful Traces of Power: An Analysis of the Decadence of Tom Buchanan in *The Great Gatsby*." *Canadian Review of American Studies* 28.1 (1998): 19–41.

———. "The Seducer's Stratagems: *The Great Gatsby* and the Early Twenties." *Forum for Modern Language Studies* 34 (Oct. 1998): 303–13.

Lewis, Christopher D. "*Tender Is the Night* and the Critics: From 1982 to the Present." *Bulletin of Bibliography* 58.2 (2001): 109–24.

Lewis, Janet. "'The Cruise of the Rolling Junk': The Fictionalized Joys of Motoring." *Fitzgerald/Hemingway Annual* 10 (1978): 69–81.

———. "Fitzgerald's 'Philippe, Count of Darkness.'" *Fitzgerald/Hemingway Annual* 7 (1975): 7–32.

Lhamon, W. T., Jr. "The Essential Houses of *The Great Gatsby*." *Markham Review* 6 (Spring 1977): 56–60.

Lisca, Peter. "Nick Carraway and the Imagery of Disorder." *Twentieth-Century Literature* 13 (Apr. 1967): 18–28.

Lockridge, Ernest H. "F. Scott Fitzgerald's *Trompe l'Oeil* and *The Great Gatsby*'s Buried Plot." *Journal of Narrative Technique* 17 (Spring 1987): 163–83.

Long, Robert E. *The Achieving of "The Great Gatsby"*: F. Scott Fitzgerald, 1920–1925. Lewisburg, Pa.: Bucknell University Press, 1979.

———. "Fitzgerald and Hemingway on Stage." *Fitzgerald/Hemingway Annual* 1 (1969): 143–44.

———. "*The Great Gatsby* and the Tradition of Joseph Conrad: Part I." *Texas Studies in Literature and Language* 8 (Summer 1966): 257–76.

———. "*The Great Gatsby* and the Tradition of Joseph Conrad: Part II." *Texas Studies in Literature and Language* 8 (Fall 1966): 407–22.

Lowry, Malcolm. *The Cinema of Malcolm Lowry: A Scholarly Edition of Lowry's "Tender Is the Night."* Ed. Miguel Mota and Paul Tiessen. Vancouver: University of British Columbia Press, 1990.

Lowry, Malcolm, and Margerie Bonner Lowry. *Notes on a Screen Play for F. Scott Fitzgerald's "Tender Is the Night."* Bloomfield Hills, Mich. and Columbia, S.C.: Bruccoli Clark, 1976.

Lucas, John. "In Praise of Scott Fitzgerald." *Critical Quarterly* 5 (Summer 1963): 132–47.

McCall, Dan. "'The Self-Same Song That Found a Path': Keats and *The Great Gatsby*." *American Literature* 42 (Jan. 1971): 521–30.

McCay, Mary A. "Fitzgerald's Women: Beyond 'Winter Dreams.'" In *American Novelists Revisited: Essays in Feminist Criticism*. Ed. F. Fleischmann. Boston: Hall, 1982. 311–24.

McNicholas, Mary Verity. "Fitzgerald's Women in *Tender Is the Night*." *College Literature* 4 (Winter 1977): 40–70.

MacPhee, Laurence E. "*The Great Gatsby*'s 'Romance of Motoring': Nick Carraway and Jordan Baker." *Modern Fiction Studies* 18 (Summer 1972): 207–12.

Maimon, Elaine P. "F. Scott Fitzgerald's Book Sales: A Look at the Record." *Fitzgerald/Hemingway Annual* 5 (1973): 165–73.

Male, Roy R. "'Babylon Revisited': A Story of the Exile's Return." *Studies in Short Fiction* 2 (Spring 1965): 270–77.

Mallios, Peter. "Undiscovering the Country: Conrad, Fitzgerald, and Meta-National Form." *Modern Fiction Studies* 47.2 (2001): 356–90.

Mangum, Bryant. *A Fortune Yet: Money in the Art of F. Scott Fitzgerald's Short Stories*. New York: Garland, 1991.

Margolies, Alan. "F. Scott Fitzgerald and *The Wedding Night*." *Fitzgerald/Hemingway Annual* 2 (1970): 224–25.

———. "F. Scott Fitzgerald's Work in the Film Studios." *Princeton University Library Chronicle* 32 (Winter 1971): 81–110.

———. "The Maturing of F. Scott Fitzgerald." *Twentieth-Century Literature* 43 (Spring 1997): 75–93.

———. "'Particular Rhythms' and Other Influences: Hemingway and *Tender Is the Night*." In *Hemingway in Italy and Other Essays*. Ed. Robert W. Lewis. New York: Praeger, 1990. 69–75.

Marquand, John P. "Looking Backwards—I. Fitzgerald: *This Side of Paradise*." *Saturday Review of Literature* 22 (Aug. 6, 1949): 30–31.

Martin, Marjory. "Fitzgerald's Image of Woman: Anima Projections in *Tender Is the Night*." *English Studies Collections* 1 (Sept. 1976): 1–17.

Martin, Robert A. "The Hot Madness of Four O'Clock in Fitzgerald's 'Absolution' and *Gatsby*." *Studies in American Fiction* 2 (Autumn 1974): 230–38.

Martin, Robert K. "Sexual and Group Relationships in 'May Day': Fear and Longing." *Studies in Short Fiction* 15 (Winter 1978): 99–101.

Matterson, Stephen. *"The Great Gatsby."* Basingstoke, England: Macmillan, 1990.

Mazzella, Anthony J. "The Tension of Opposites in Fitzgerald's 'May Day.'" *Studies in Short Fiction* 14 (Fall 1977): 379–85.

Merrill, Robert. "*Tender Is the Night* as a Tragic Action." *Texas Studies in Literature and Language* 25 (Winter 1983): 597–615.

Michals, Walter Benn. *Our America: Nativism, Modernism, and Pluralism*. Durham, N.C.: Duke University Press, 1995.

Michelson, Bruce. "The Myth of *Gatsby*." *Modern Fiction Studies* 26 (Winter 1980–1981): 563–77.

Miller, James E., Jr. *The Fictional Technique of F. Scott Fitzgerald*. The

Hague: Martinis Nijhoff, 1957. Rev. ed., *F. Scott Fitzgerald and His Technique*. New York: New York University Press, 1964.

———. "Fitzgerald's *Gatsby*: The World as Ash Heap." In *The Twenties: Fiction, Poetry, Drama*. Ed. Warren French. Deland, Fla.: Everett/Edwards, 1975. 181–202.

Millgate, Michael. "Scott Fitzgerald as Social Novelist: Statement and Technique in *The Great Gatsby*." *Modern Language Review* 57 (July 1962): 335–39.

———. "Scott Fitzgerald as Social Novelist: Statement and Technique in *The Last Tycoon*." *English Studies* 43 (Feb. 1962): 29–34.

Minter, David. *A Cultural History of the American Novel: Henry James to William Faulkner*. Cambridge: Cambridge University Press, 1994.

Mizener, Arthur. "The Maturity of F. Scott Fitzgerald." *Sewanee Review* 67 (Autumn 1959): 658–75.

———. *Scott Fitzgerald and His World*. New York: Putnam's, 1972.

———. "Scott Fitzgerald and the 1920's." *Minnesota Review* 1 (Winter 1961): 161–74.

———. *Twelve Great American Novels*. New York: New American Library, 1967.

Monk, Craig. "The Political F. Scott Fitzgerald: Liberal Illusion and Disillusion in *This Side of Paradise* and *The Beautiful and the* [*sic*] *Damned*." *American Studies International* 33 (Oct. 1995): 60–70.

Monk, Donald. "Fitzgerald: The Tissue of Style." *Journal of American Studies* 17 (Apr. 1983): 77–94.

Monteiro, George. "Expatriate Life Away from Paris." *Antioch Review* 59.3 (2001): 587–607.

———. "Fitzgerald vs. Fitzgerald: 'An Alcoholic Case.'" *Literature and Medicine* 6 (1987): 110–16.

———. "James Gatz and John Keats." *Fitzgerald/Hemingway Annual* 4 (1972): 291–94.

———. "The Limits of Professionalism: A Sociological Approach to Faulkner, Fitzgerald, and Hemingway." *Criticism* 15 (Spring 1973): 145–55.

Moore, Benita A. *Escape into a Labyrinth: F. Scott Fitzgerald, Catholic Sensibility, and the American Way*. New York: Garland, 1988.

Moreland, Kim. "Gerald Murphy, F. Scott Fitzgerald, and Dick

Diver: The Artist's Vocation." *Journal of Modern Literature* 23.2 (1999–2000): 357–63.

———. *The Medievalist Impulse in American Literature: Twain, Adams, Fitzgerald, and Hemingway*. Charlottesville: University Press of Virginia, 1996.

Moseley, Edwin M. *F. Scott Fitzgerald: A Critical Essay*. Grand Rapids, Mich.: Eerdmans, 1967.

Moses, Edwin. "F. Scott Fitzgerald and the Quest to the Ice Palace." *CEA Critic* 36 (Jan. 1974): 11–14.

———. "Tragic Inevitability in *The Great Gatsby*." *College Language Association Journal* 21 (Sept. 1977): 51–57.

Moyer, Kermit W. "Fitzgerald's Two Unfinished Novels: The Count and the Tycoon in Spenglerian Perspective." *Contemporary Literature* 15 (Spring 1974): 238–56.

———. "*The Great Gatsby*: Fitzgerald's Meditation on American History." *Fitzgerald/Hemingway Annual* 4 (1972): 43–57.

Murphy, George D. "The Unconscious Dimension of *Tender Is the Night*." *Studies in the Novel* 5 (Fall 1973): 314–23.

Murphy, Patrick D. "Illumination and Affectation in the Parallel Plots of 'The Rich Boy' and 'The Beast in the Jungle.'" *Papers on Language and Literature* 22 (Fall 1986): 406–16.

Nattermann, Udo. "Nicole Diver's Monologue: A Close Examination of a Key Segment." *Massachusetts Studies in English* 10 (Fall 1986): 213–28.

Nettles, Elsa. "Howell's 'A Circle in the Water' and Fitzgerald's 'Babylon Revisited.'" *Studies in Short Fiction* 19 (Summer 1982): 261–67.

Nowlin, Michael. "F. Scott Fitzgerald's Elite Syncopations: The Racial Make-up of the Entertainer in the Early Fiction." *English Studies in Canada* 26.4 (2000): 409–443.

———. "The World's Rarest Work: Modernism and Masculinity in Fitzgerald's *Tender Is the Night*." *College Literature* 25 (Spring 1998): 58–77.

O'Meara, Lauraleigh. *Lost City: Fitzgerald's New York*. New York: Routledge, 2002.

———. "Medium of Exchange: The Blue Coupé Dialogue in *The Great Gatsby*." *Papers on Language and Literature* 30 (Winter 1994): 73–87.

Ornstein, Robert. "Scott Fitzgerald's Fable of East and West." *College English* 18 (Dec. 1956): 139–43.

Owen, Guy. "Imagery and Meaning in *The Great Gatsby.*" In *Essays in Modern American Literature*. Ed. Richard E. Langford. DeLand, Fla.: Stetson University Press, 1963. 46–54.

Pelzer, Linda Claycomb. *Student Companion to F. Scott Fitzgerald.* Westport, Conn.: Greenwood, 2000.

Pendelton, Thomas. *I'm Sorry about the Clock: Chronology, Composition, and Narrative Technique in "The Great Gatsby."* Selinsgrove, Pa.: Susquehanna University Press, 1993.

Perlis, Alan. "The Narrative Is All: A Study of F. Scott Fitzgerald's 'May Day.'" *Western Humanities Review* 33 (Winter 1979): 65–72.

Perlmutter, Ruth. "Malcolm Lowry's Unpublished Filmscripts of *Tender Is the Night.*" *American Quarterly* 28 (Winter 1976): 561–74.

Perosa, Sergio. *The Art of F. Scott Fitzgerald*. Trans. Charles Matz and the author. Ann Arbor: University of Michigan Press, 1965.

Person, Leland S., Jr. "Fitzgerald's 'O Russet Witch!' Dangerous Women, Dangerous Art." *Studies in Short Fiction* 23 (Fall 1986): 443–48.

———. "'Herstory' and Daisy Buchanan." *American Literature* 50 (May 1978): 250–57.

Peterman, Michael A. "A Neglected Source for *The Great Gatsby*: The Influence of Edith Wharton's *The Spark.*" *Canadian Review of American Studies* 8 (Spring 1977): 26–35.

Petry, Alice Hall. *Fitzgerald's Craft of Short Fiction: The Collected Stories, 1920–1935*. Tuscaloosa: University of Alabama Press, 1989.

———. "F. Scott Fitzgerald's 'A Change of Class' and Frank Norris." *Markham Review* 12 (Spring 1983): 49–52.

———. "Love Story: Mock Courtship in F. Scott Fitzgerald's 'The Jelly-Bean.'" *Arizona Quarterly* 39 (Autumn 1983): 251–60.

Phelps, Henry C. "Literary History/Unsolved Mystery: *The Great Gatsby* and the Hall-Mills Murder Case." *ANQ* 14.3 (2001): 33–39.

Phillips, Gene D., *Fiction, Film, and F. Scott Fitzgerald*. Chicago, Ill.: Loyola University Press, 1986.

Pike, Gerald. "Four Voices in 'Winter Dreams.'" *Studies in Short Fiction* 23 (Summer 1986): 315–20.

Piper, Henry Dan. *F. Scott Fitzgerald: A Critical Portrait*. New York: Holt, Rinehart and Winston, 1965.

Podis, Leonard A. "*The Beautiful and Damned*: Fitzgerald's Test of Youth." *Fitzgerald/Hemingway Annual* 5 (1973): 141–47.

———. "Fitzgerald's 'The Diamond as Big as the Ritz' and Hawthorne's 'Rappaccini's Daughter.'" *Studies in Short Fiction* 21 (Summer 1984): 243–50.

———. "'The Unreality of Reality': Metaphor in *The Great Gatsby*." *Style* 11 (Winter 1977): 56–72.

Potts, Stephen W. *The Price of Paradise: The Magazine Career of F. Scott Fitzgerald*. San Bernardino, Calif.: Borgo, 1993.

Prigozy, Ruth. "From Griffith's Girls to *Daddy's Girl*: The Masks of Innocence in *Tender Is the Night*." *Twentieth-Century Literature* 26 (Summer 1980): 189–221.

———. "'A Matter of Measurement': The Tangled Relationship between Fitzgerald and Hemingway." *Commonweal* 95 (Oct. 29, 1971): 103–6, 108–9.

———. "'Poor Butterfly': F. Scott Fitzgerald and Popular Music." *Prospects* 2 (1976): 41–67.

Qualls, Barry V. "Physician in the Counting House: The Religious Motif in *Tender Is the Night*." *Essays in Literature* 2 (Fall 1975): 192–208.

Quick, Jonathan. "F. Scott Fitzgerald's New World: Transfiguring America." In *Modern Fiction and the Art of Subversion*. New York: Lang, 1999. 67–96.

Quirk, Tom. "Fitzgerald and Cather: *The Great Gatsby*." *American Literature* 54 (Dec. 1982): 576–91.

Raleigh, John Henry. "Fitzgerald's *The Great Gatsby*." *University of Kansas City Review* 13 (June 1957): 283–91.

———. "F. Scott Fitzgerald's *The Great Gatsby*: Legendary Bases and Allegorical Significances." *University of Kansas City Review* 4 (Oct. 1957): 55–58.

Rand, William E. "The Structure of the Outsider in the Short Fiction of Richard Wright and F. Scott Fitzgerald." *College Language Association Journal* 40 (Dec. 1996): 230–45.

Rhodes, Robert E. "F. Scott Fitzgerald: 'All My Fathers.'" In *Irish-American Fiction*. Ed. Robert E. Rhodes and Daniel J. Casey. New York: AMS Press, 1979. 29–51.

Riddel, Joseph N. "F. Scott Fitzgerald, the Jamesian Inheritance, and the Morality of Fiction." *Modern Fiction Studies* 11 (Winter 1965–1966): 331–50.

Riggio, Thomas P. "Dreiser, Fitzgerald, and the Question of Influence." In *Theodore Dreiser and American Culture: New Readings.* Ed. Yoshinobu Hakutani. Newark: University of Delaware Press, 2000. 234–47.

Roberts, Ruth E. "Nonverbal Communication in *The Great Gatsby.*" *Language and Literature* 7.1–3 (1982): 107–29.

Robeson, Vincent. "The Psychosocial Conflict and the Distortion of Time: A Study of Diver's Disintegration in *Tender Is the Night.*" *Language and Literature* 1 (Winter 1972): 55–64.

Ross, Alan. "Rumble among the Drums: F. Scott Fitzgerald (1896–1940) and the Jazz Age." *Horizon* 18 (Dec. 1948): 420–35.

Roulston, Robert. "*The Beautiful and Damned*: The Alcoholic's Revenge." *Literature and Psychology* 27.3 (1977): 156–63.

———. "Dick Diver's Plunge into the Roman Void: The Setting of *Tender Is the Night.*" *South Atlantic Quarterly* 77 (Winter 1978): 85–97.

———. "Fitzgerald's 'May Day': The Uses of Irresponsibility." *Modern Fiction Studies* 34 (Summer 1988): 207–15.

———. "Rummaging through F. Scott Fitzgerald's 'Trash': Early Stories in the *Saturday Evening Post.*" *Journal of Popular Culture* 21 (Spring 1988): 151–63.

———. "Slumbering with the Just: A Maryland Lens for *Tender Is the Night.*" *Southern Quarterly* 16 (Jan. 1978): 125–37.

———. "*This Side of Paradise*: The Ghost of Rupert Brooke." *Fitzgerald/Hemingway Annual* 7 (1975): 117–30.

———. "Tom Buchanan: Patrician in Motley." *Arizona Quarterly* 34 (Summer 1978): 101–11.

———. "Traces of *Tono-Bungay* in *The Great Gatsby.*" *Journal of Narrative Technique* 10 (Winter 1980): 68–76.

———. "Whistling 'Dixie' in Encino: *The Last Tycoon* and F. Scott Fitzgerald's Two Souths." *South Atlantic Quarterly* 79 (Autumn 1980): 355–63.

Roulston, Robert, and Helen H. Roulston. *The Winding Road to West Egg: The Artistic Development of F. Scott Fitzgerald.* Lewisburg, Pa.: Bucknell University Press, 1995.

Sander, Barbara Gerber. "Structural Imagery in *The Great Gatsby*:

Metaphor and Matrix." *Linguistics in Literature* 1 (Fall 1975): 53–75.

Saposnik, Irving S. "The Passion and the Life: Technology as Pattern in *The Great Gatsby*." *Fitzgerald/Hemingway Annual* 11 (1979): 181–88.

Scharnhorst, Gary. "Scribbling Upward: Fitzgerald's Debt to Horatio Alger, Jr." *Fitzgerald/Hemingway Annual* 10 (1978): 161–69.

Schiff, Jonathan B. *Ashes to Ashes: Mourning and Social Difference in F. Scott Fitzgerald's Fiction*. Cranbury, N.J.: Susquehanna University Press, 2001.

Schlacks, Deborah Davis. *American Dream Visions: Chaucer's Surprising Influence on F. Scott Fitzgerald*. New York: Lang, 1994.

Schneider, Daniel J. "Color-Symbolism in *The Great Gatsby*." *University Review* 31 (Oct. 1964): 13–17.

Schoenwald, Richard L. "F. Scott Fitzgerald as John Keats." *Boston University Studies in English* 3 (Spring 1957): 12–21.

Scribner, Charles, III. "Celestial Eyes: From Metamorphosis to Masterpiece." *Princeton University Library Chronicle* 53 (Winter 1992): 140–55.

Scrimgeour, Gary J. "Against *The Great Gatsby*." *Criticism* 8 (Winter 1966): 75–86.

Sealts, Merton M., Jr. "Scott Fitzgerald and *The Great Gatsby:* A Reappraisal." *Colorado Quarterly* 25 (Fall–Winter 1998): 137–52.

Seguin, Robert. "*Ressentiment* and the Social Poetics of *The Great Gatsby*: Fitzgerald Reads Cather." *Modern Fiction Studies* 46.4 (2000): 917–40.

Seiters, Dan. *Image Patterns in the Novels of F. Scott Fitzgerald*. Ann Arbor, Mich.: UMI Research Press, 1986.

Settle, Glenn. "Fitzgerald's Daisy: The Siren Voice." *American Literature* 57 (Mar. 1985): 115–24.

Shain, Charles E. *F. Scott Fitzgerald*. Minneapolis: University of Minnesota Press, 1961.

Siloh, Robert. "*Tender Is the Night* or the Rape of the Child." *Literature and Psychology* 40.4 (1994): 40–63.

Sipiora, Phillip. "Vampires in the Heart: Gender Trouble in *The Great Gatsby*." In *The Aching Hearth: Family Violence in Life and Literature*. Ed. Sara Munson Deats and Lagretta Tallent Lenker. New York: Plenum, 1991. 199–220.

Skinner, John. "The Oral and the Written: Kurtz and Gatsby Revisited." *Journal of Narrative Technique* 17 (Winter 1987): 131–40.

Sklar, Robert. *F. Scott Fitzgerald: The Last Laocoön*. New York: Oxford University Press, 1967.

Speer, Roderick S. "*The Great Gatsby*'s 'Romance of Motoring' and 'The Cruise of the Rolling Junk.'" *Modern Fiction Studies* 20 (Winter 1974–1975): 540–43.

Stallman, Robert Wooster. "Conrad and *The Great Gatsby*." *Twentieth-Century Literature* 1 (Apr. 1955): 5–12.

Stark, Bruce R. "The Intricate Pattern in *The Great Gatsby*." *Fitzgerald/Hemingway Annual* 6 (1974): 51–61.

Stark, John. "The Style of *Tender Is the Night*." *Fitzgerald/Hemingway Annual* 4 (1972): 89–95.

Stavola, Thomas J. *Scott Fitzgerald: Crisis in an American Identity*. New York: Barnes and Noble, 1979.

Steinbrink, Jeffrey. "'Boats against the Current': Mortality and the Myth of Renewal in *The Great Gatsby*." *Twentieth-Century Literature* 26 (Summer 1980): 157–70.

Stern, Milton R. *The Golden Moment: The Novels of F. Scott Fitzgerald*. Urbana: University of Illinois Press, 1970.

———. *Tender Is the Night: The Broken Universe*. New York: Twayne, 1994.

Stevens, A. Wilber. "Fitzgerald's *Tender Is the Night*: The Idea as Morality." *Brigham Young University Studies* 3 (Spring–Summer 1961): 95–104.

Stewart, Lawrence D. "'Absolution' and *The Great Gatsby*." *Fitzgerald/Hemingway Annual* 5 (1973): 181–87.

Stouck, David. "White Sheep on Fifth Avenue: *The Great Gatsby* as Pastoral." *Genre* 4 (Dec. 1971): 335–47.

Tanner, Tony. "'The Story of the Moon That Never Rose': F. Scott Fitzgerald's *The Great Gatsby*." In *The American Mystery: American Literature from Emerson to DeLillo*. Cambridge: Cambridge University Press, 2000. 166–200.

Tate, Mary Jo. *F. Scott Fitzgerald A to Z: The Essential Reference to His Life and Work*. New York: Facts on File, 1998.

Taviner-Courbin, Jacqueline. "Sensuality as Key to Characterization in *Tender Is the Night*." *English Studies in Canada* 9 (Dec. 1983): 452–67.

Thorton, Lawrence. "Ford Madox Ford and *The Great Gatsby.*" *Fitzgerald/Hemingway Annual* 7 (1975): 57–74.

Toles, George. "The Metaphysics of Style in *Tender Is the Night.*" *American Literature* 62 (Sept. 1999): 423–44.

Tolmatchoff, V. M. "The Metaphor of History in the Work of F. Scott Fitzgerald." In *Russian Eyes on American Literature.* Ed. Sergei Chakovsky and M. Thomas Inge. Jackson: University Press of Mississippi, 1992. 126–41.

Toor, David. "Guilt and Retribution in 'Babylon Revisited.'" *Fitzgerald/Hemingway Annual* 5 (1973): 155–64.

Trachtenberg, Alan. "The Journey Back: Myth and History in *Tender Is the Night.*" In *Experience in the Novel: Selected Papers from the English Institute.* Ed. Roy Harvey Pearce. New York: Columbia University Press, 1968. 133–62.

Tredell, Nicholas. Ed. *F. Scott Fitzgerald: "The Great Gatsby."* New York: Columbia University Press, 1997.

Trouard, Dawn. "Fitzgerald's Missed Moments: Surrealistic Style in His Major Novels." *Fitzgerald/Hemingway Annual* 11 (1979): 189–205.

Tsimpouki, Theodora. *F. Scott Fitzgerald's Aestheticism: His Unacknowledged Debt to Walter Pater.* Athens, Greece: Parousia, 1992.

Tuttleton, James W. "F. Scott Fitzgerald and the Magical Glory." *New Criterion* 13 (Nov. 13, 1994): 24–31.

Twitchell, James B. "'Babylon Revisited': Chronology and Character." *Fitzgerald/Hemingway Annual* 10 (1978): 155–60.

Varet-Ali, Elizabeth M. "The Unfortunate Fate of Seventeen Fitzgerald 'Originals': Toward a Reading of *The Pat Hobby Stories* 'on Their Own Merits Completely.'" *Journal of the Short Story in English* 14 (Spring 1990): 87–110.

Wagner, Joseph B. "*Gatsby* and John Keats: Another Version." *Fitzgerald/Hemingway Annual* 11 (1979): 91–98.

Wasiolek, Edward. "The Sexual Drama of Nick and Gatsby." *International Fiction Review* 19.1 (1992): 14–22.

Way, Brian. *F. Scott Fitzgerald and the Art of Social Fiction.* London: Arnold, 1980. New York: St. Martin's, 1980.

———. "Scott Fitzgerald." *New Left Review* No. 21 (Oct. 1963): 36–51.

West, James L. W., III. "Annotating Mr. Fitzgerald." *American Scholar* 69 (Spring 2000): 83–91.

———. "Did F. Scott Fitzgerald Have the Right Publisher?" *Sewanee Review* 100 (Fall 1992): 644–56.

———. "Jay Gatsby's Background." *Times Literary Supplement* (London) 5090 (Oct. 20, 2000): 17.

———. "Notes on the Text of F. Scott Fitzgerald's 'Early Success.'" *Resources for American Literary Study* 3 (Spring 1973): 73–99.

———. "Prospects for the Study of F. Scott Fitzgerald." *Resources for American Literary Study* 23.2 (1997): 147–58.

West, James L. W., III, and J. Barclay Inge. "F. Scott Fitzgerald's Revision of 'The Rich Boy.'" *Proof* 5 (1977): 127–46.

West, Suzanne. "Nicole's Gardens." *Fitzgerald/Hemingway Annual* 10 (1978): 85–95.

Westbrook, Wayne W. "Portrait of a Dandy I *The Beautiful and Damned*." *Fitzgerald/Hemingway Annual* 11 (1979): 147–49.

Weston, Elizabeth A. *The International Theme in F. Scott Fitzgerald's Literature*. New York: Lang, 1995.

White, Eugene. "The 'Intricate Destiny' of Dick Diver." *Modern Fiction Studies* 7 (Spring 1961): 55–62.

Whitley, John S. *F. Scott Fitzgerald: "The Great Gatsby."* London: Arnold, 1976.

Wilson, B. W. "The Theatrical Motif in *The Great Gatsby*." *Fitzgerald/Hemingway Annual* 7 (1975): 107–13.

Wilson, Edmund. "The Delegate from Great Neck." In *The Shores of Light*. New York: Farrar, Straus and Young, 1952. 141–55.

Wilson, Raymond J. "Henry James and F. Scott Fitzgerald: Americans Abroad." *Research Studies* 45 (June 1977): 82–91.

Wilt, Judith. "The Spinning Story: Gothic Motifs in *Tender Is the Night*." *Fitzgerald/Hemingway Annual* 8 (1976): 79–95.

Winters, Keith. "Artistic Tension: The Enigma of F. Scott Fitzgerald." *Research Studies* 37 (Dec. 1969): 285–97.

Woodward, Jeffrey Harris. *F. Scott Fitzgerald: The Artist as Public Figure, 1920–1940*. Ann Arbor, Mich.: University Microfilms, 1973.

Young, Philip. "Scott Fitzgerald's Waste Land." *Kansas Magazine* 23 (1956): 73–77.

Zhang, Aiping. *Enchanted Places: The Use of Setting in F. Scott Fitzgerald's Fiction*. Westport, Conn.: Greenwood, 1997.

Selected Studies on Zelda Sayre Fitzgerald

Anderson, W[illiam] R[ichard, Jr.] "Rivalry and Partnership: The Short Fiction of Zelda Sayre Fitzgerald." *Fitzgerald/Hemingway Annual* 9 (1977): 19–42.

Cary, Meredith. "*Save Me the Waltz* as a Novel." *Fitzgerald/Hemingway Annual* 8 (1976): 65–78.

Clemens, Anna Valdine. "Zelda Fitzgerald: An Unromantic Revision." *Dalhousie Review* 62.2 (Summer 1982): 196–211.

Courbin-Tavernier, Jacqueline. "Art as Women's Response and Search: Zelda Fitzgerald's *Save Me the Waltz.*" *Southern Liberty Journal* 11.2 (Spring 1979): 22–42.

Davis, Simone Weil. " 'The Burden of Reflecting': Effort and Desire in Zelda Fitzgerald's *Save Me the Waltz.*" *Modern Language Quarterly* 56 (Sept. 1995): 327–61.

Going, William T. "Two Alabama Writers: Zelda Sayre Fitzgerald and Sara Haardt Mencken." *Alabama Review* 23 (Jan. 1970): 3–29.

Harnett, Koula Svokos. *Zelda Fitzgerald and the Failure of the American Dream for Women*. New York: Lang, 1991.

Hudgins, Andrew. "Zelda Sayre in Montgomery." *Southern Review* 20 (1984): 882–84.

Luce, William. *Zelda*. Off-Broadway one-woman show. New York, Nov. 1984.

Nanney, Lisa. "Zelda Fitzgerald's *Save Me the Waltz* as Southern Novel and *Kunstlerroman.*" In *The Female Tradition in Southern Literature*. Ed. Carol S. Manning. Urbana: University of Illinois Press, 1993. 220–32.

Payne, Michelle. "5'4" x 2": Zelda Fitzgerald, Anorexia Nervosa, and *Save Me the Waltz.*" *Bucknell Review* 39.1 (1995): 39–46.

Pattillo, Edward. *Zelda: Zelda Sayre Fitzgerald Retrospective*. Montgomery, Ala.: Montgomery Museum of Fine Arts, 1974.

Petry, Alice Hall. "Women's Work: The Case of Zelda Fitzgerald." *LIT* 1 (Dec. 1989): 69–83.

Wagner, Linda W. "*Save Me the Waltz*: An Assessment in Craft." *Journal of Narrative Technique* 12 (Fall 1982): 201–9.

Wood, Mary E. "A Wizard Cultivator: Zelda Fitzgerald's *Save Me the Waltz* as Asylum Autobiography." *Tulsa Studies in Women's Literature* 11 (Fall 1992): 247–64.

Yorke, Lane. "Zelda: A Worksheet." *Paris Review* (Fall 1983): 210–63.

Selected Collections of Critical Essays

Bloom, Harold. Ed. *F. Scott Fitzgerald*. New York: Chelsea House, 1985.

———. *F. Scott Fitzgerald*. New York: Chelsea House, 1999.

———. *F. Scott Fitzgerald's "The Great Gatsby."* New Haven, Conn.: Chelsea House, 1986.

———. *F. Scott Fitzgerald's "The Great Gatsby."* New York: Chelsea House, 1996.

———. *F. Scott Fitzgerald's "The Great Gatsby."* Philadelphia, Penn.: Chelsea House, 2004.

———. *Major Literary Characters: Gatsby*. New York: Chelsea House, 1991.

Bruccoli, Matthew J. Ed. *F. Scott Fitzgerald's "The Great Gatsby": A Literary Reference*. Detroit, Mich.: Gale Group, 2000. New York: Carroll and Graf, 2002.

———. *Profile of F. Scott Fitzgerald*. Columbus, Ohio: Merrill, 1971.

———. *New Essays on "The Great Gatsby."* Cambridge: Cambridge University Press, 1985.

Bryer, Jackson R. Ed. *F. Scott Fitzgerald: The Critical Reception*. New York: Franklin, 1978.

———. *New Essays on F. Scott Fitzgerald's Neglected Stories*. Columbia: University of Missouri Press, 1996.

———. *The Short Stories of F. Scott Fitzgerald*: New Approaches in Criticism. Madison: University of Wisconsin Press, 1982.

Bryer, Jackson R., Alan Margolies, and Ruth Prigozy. Eds. *F. Scott Fitzgerald: New Perspectives*. Athens: University of Georgia Press, 2000.

Bryer, Jackson R., Ruth Prigozy, and Milton R. Stern. Eds. *F. Scott Fitzgerald in the Twenty-First Century*. Tuscaloosa: University of Alabama Press, 2003.

Claridge, Henry. Ed. *F. Scott Fitzgerald: Critical Assessments*. 4 vols. Robertsbridge, England: Helm, 1992.

Cowley, Malcolm, and Robert Cowley. Eds. *Fitzgerald and the Jazz Age*. New York: Scribner's, 1966.

de Koster, Katie. Ed. *Readings on F. Scott Fitzgerald*. San Diego, Calif.: Greenhaven, 1998.

———. *Readings on "The Great Gatsby."* San Diego, Calif.: Greenhaven, 1998.

Donaldson, Scott. Ed. *Critical Essays on F. Scott Fitzgerald's "The Great Gatsby."* Boston: Hall, 1984.

Eble, Kenneth. Ed. *F. Scott Fitzgerald: A Collection of Criticism*. New York: McGraw Hill, 1973.

F. Scott Fitzgerald at 100: Centenary Tributes by American Writers. Rockville, Md.: Quill and Brush, 1996.

Kazin, Alfred. Ed. *F. Scott Fitzgerald: The Man and His Work*. Cleveland, Ohio: World, 1951.

Kennedy, J. Gerald, and Jackson R. Bryer. Eds. *French Connections: Hemingway and Fitzgerald Abroad*. New York: St. Martin's, 1998.

LaHood, Marvin J. Ed. *"Tender Is the Night": Essays in Criticism*. Bloomington: Indiana University Press, 1969.

Lee, A. Robert. Ed. *Scott Fitzgerald: The Promises of Life*. London: Vision, 1989. New York: St. Martin's, 1989.

Lockridge, Ernest [H.] Ed. *Twentieth-Century Interpretations of "The Great Gatsby": A Collection of Critical Essays*. Englewood Cliffs, N.J.: Prentice-Hall, 1968.

Mandal, Somdatta. Ed. *F. Scott Fitzgerald: A Centennial Tribute*. 2 vols. New Delhi, India: Prestige, 1997.

Mizener, Arthur. Ed. *F. Scott Fitzgerald: A Collection of Critical Essays*. Englewood Cliffs, N.J.: Prentice-Hall, 1963.

Piper, Henry Dan. Ed. *Fitzgerald's "The Great Gatsby": The Novel, the Critics, the Background*. New York: Scribner's, 1970.

Prigozy, Ruth. Ed. *The Cambridge Companion to F. Scott Fitzgerald*. Cambridge: Cambridge University Press, 2002.

Ramanan, Mohan. Ed. *F. Scott Fitzgerald: Centenary Essays from India*. New Delhi, India: Prestige, 1998.

Stern, Milton R. Ed. *Critical Essays on F. Scott Fitzgerald's "Tender Is the Night."* Boston: Hall, 1986.

Tredell, Nicolas. Ed. *F. Scott Fitzgerald: "The Great Gatsby."* New York: Columbia University Press, 1997.

Bibliographies, Concordances, Catalogs

American Literary Scholarship: An Annual, 1963–. Durham, N.C.: Duke University Press, 1965–.

Bruccoli, Matthew J. *F. Scott Fitzgerald: A Descriptive Bibliography.* Rev. ed. Pittsburgh, Pa.: University of Pittsburgh Press, 1987. Primary.

Bruccoli, Matthew J., and C. E. F[razer] C[lark, Jr.] Eds. *F. Scott Fitzgerald and Ernest M. Hemingway in Paris: An Exhibition at the Bibliothèque Benjamin Franklin.* Bloomfield Hills, Mich. and Columbia, S.C.: Bruccoli Clark, 1972.

Bryer, Jackson R. *The Critical Reputation of F. Scott Fitzgerald: A Bibliographical Study.* Hamden, Conn.: Archon, 1967. Secondary. Annotated bibliography.

———. *The Critical Reputation of F. Scott Fitzgerald: A Bibliographical Study.* Supplement 1 *Through 1981*. Hamden, Conn.: Archon, 1984. Secondary. Annotated bibliography.

Bucker, Park. Ed. *Catalogue of the Matthew J. and Arlyn Bruccoli F. Scott Fitzgerald Collection at the Thomas Cooper Library, the University of South Carolina.* Columbia: University of South Carolina Press, 1997.

Crossland, Andrew T. *A Concordance to F. Scott Fitzgerald's "The Great Gatsby."* Detroit, Mich.: Gale/Bruccoli Clark, 1975.

F. Scott Fitzgerald Centenary Exhibition. Columbia: University of South Carolina for the Thomas Cooper Library, 1996.

The F. Scott Fitzgerald Collection Notes. Columbia: Thomas Cooper Library, University of South Carolina 1995+.

In Their Time/1920–1940: Fiestas, Moveable Feasts, and "Many Fetes": An Exhibition at the University of Virginia Library, December 1977–March 1978. Bloomfield Hills, Mich and Columbia, S.C.: Bruccoli Clark, 1977.

Stanley, Linda C. *The Foreign Critical Reputation of F. Scott Fitzgerald.* Westport, Conn.: Greenwood, 1980.

Journals

Fitzgerald/Hemingway Annual (1969–1979). Washington, D.C.: NCR Microcard Editions, 1969–1973. Englewood Colo.: Information Handling Services, 1974–1976. Detroit, Mich.: Gale Research, 1977–1979.

Fitzgerald Newsletter (quarterly, 1958–1968). Reprinted, Washington, D.C.: NCR Microcard Editions, 1969.

F. Scott Fitzgerald Collection Notes. Columbia: Thomas Cooper Library, University of South Carolina, 1995–.

F. Scott Fitzgerald Society Newsletter. Hempstead, N.Y.: Hofstra University, 1991–.

F. Scott Fitzgerald Review. Hampstead, N.Y.: Hofstra University, 2003.

Selected Websites

"The F. Scott Fitzgerald Society Homepage." http://www.fitzgerald-society.org/.

"Lesson Plans: *The Great Gatsby.*" http://school.discovery.com/lessonplans/programs/greatbooks-greatgatsby/.

"USC: F. Scott Fitzgerald Centenary Homepage." University of South Carolina. http://www.sc.edu./fitzgerald/index.html.

Contributors

RONALD BERMAN received his B.A. from Harvard and his Ph.D. from Yale. Now professor of literature at the University of California, San Diego, he has served as chair of the National Endowment for the Humanities. He is the author of *"The Great Gatsby" and Modern Times* (1994), *"The Great Gatsby" and Fitzgerald's World of Ideas* (1997), *Fitzgerald, Hemingway, and the Twenties* (2001), and *Fitzgerald-Wilson-Hemingway: Language and Idea* (2003).

JACKSON R. BRYER is professor of English at the University of Maryland, College Park. He is the author of *The Critical Reputation of F. Scott Fitzgerald* (1967, 1984) and editor of *New Essays on F. Scott Fitzgerald's Neglected Stories* (1996), *The Short Stories of F. Scott Fitzgerald: New Approaches in Criticism* (1982), and *F. Scott Fitzgerald: The Critical Reception* (1978). He is coeditor of *The Basil and Josephine Stories* (1973), *F. Scott Fitzgerald in His Own Time* (1971), *Dear Scott/Dear Max: The Fitzgerald-Perkins Correspondence* (1971), the *F. Scott Fitzgerald Newsletter* (annually), *F. Scott Fitzgerald: New Perspectives* (2000), and *F. Scott Fitzgerald in the Twenty-First Century* (2003). He is cofounder and President of the F. Scott Fitzgerald Society.

KIRK CURNUTT is professor of English at Troy State University in Montgomery, Alabama, where he serves as department chair. In addition to sitting on the board of the F. Scott Fitzgerald Society, he organizes educational and fundraising events for the Scott and Zelda Fitzgerald Museum, located in the Montgomery home in which the Fitzgeralds resided in 1931–1932. Among his published works are essays on Fitzgerald, Hemingway, Gertrude Stein, the contemporary coming-of-age novel, and youth culture. He is the author of *Wise Economies: Brevity and Storytelling in the American Short Story* (1997), *The Critical Response to Gertrude Stein* (2000), *Ernest Hemingway and the Expatriate Modernist Movement* (2000), *Alienated-Youth Fiction* (2001), as well as a collection of short stories, *Baby, Let's Make a Baby* (2003).

ALBERT J. DEFAZIO III lectures at George Mason University and teaches at George Mason High School in Virginia. Author of *Literary Masterpieces: "The Sun Also Rises"* (2000), he is bibliographer for the *Hemingway Review* and the *F. Scott Fitzgerald Review* and a long-time contributor to *American Literary Scholarship: An Annual.* He is currently editing the *Dictionary of Literary Biography* volume on *The Sun Also Rises*, and his article on teaching that novel at the secondary level appears in *Teaching Hemingway's "The Sun Also Rises"* (2003).

JAMES H. MEREDITH is a lieutenant colonel and professor of English at the U.S. Air Force Academy in Colorado Springs, Colorado, where he works as an associate editor of *War, Literature and the Arts: An International Journal of the Humanities*. Meredith serves on the board of the F. Scott Fitzgerald Society, for which among other duties, he has helped organize several international conferences, including Nice (2000), St. Paul (2002), and Vevey (2004). Additionally, he serves as board secretary for the Ernest Hemingway Foundation and Society. The author of *Understanding the Literature of World War* II (1999), he has published on various topics and authors, including—in addition to Fitzgerald and Hemingway—Theodore Roosevelt, Henry Adams, Stephen Crane, Andre Dubus, Paul West, Joseph Heller, the American Civil War, and World Wars I and II.

RUTH PRIGOZY is professor of English and former chair of the English Department at Hofstra University, where she also teaches film studies. She is author of *F. Scott Fitzgerald* (2001 in the Overlook Illustrated Lives Series), and editor of *The Cambridge Companion to F. Scott Fitzgerald* (2002), *This Side of Paradise* (1995), and *The Great Gatsby* (1998). She is coeditor of *F. Scott Fitzgerald: New Perspectives* (2000) and *F. Scott Fitzgerald in the Twenty-First Century* (2003). She is coeditor of the *F. Scott Fitzgerald Review* and the *F. Scott Fitzgerald Newsletter* and is a cofounder of the F. Scott Fitzgerald Society. She has published many essays on Fitzgerald and on American popular culture.

JAMES L. W. WEST III is Sparks Professor of English at Pennsylvania State University, where he directs the Penn State Conference Center for the History of the Book. He has published books on Fitzgerald's *This Side of Paradise* and on professional authorship in America during the twentieth century. Most recently, he has published a biography of the novelist William Styron. West has edited scholarly editions of Dreiser's *Sister Carrie* and *Jennie Gerhardt*; he is also general editor of the Cambridge Editions of the Works of F. Scott Fitzgerald.

Index